# Palgrave Studies in Disability and International Development

We are pleased to announce the new book series, the Palgrave Studies in Disability and International Development. With this series, we open space for innovative research, debate and critical writings aimed at pushing forward the frontiers of discourse, theory and practice. We are seeking strong new monographs reporting on empirical work, edited books, as well as shorter theoretical writings, and are especially interested in interdisciplinary offerings. In the spirit of openness, we welcome unsolicited book proposals. We accept completed manuscripts, but would also be happy to hear on current research or on writing projects still in-process.

The series is intended to span a range of areas and we would welcome proposals on any topic related to international development and disability, including, though not exclusively:

- Inclusive education
- Employment and livelihoods
- Social protection Disability and poverty
- Human rights and disability rights
- Health and health care
- Discrimination and exclusion
- Religion and spirituality
- Disability definition and measurement – (Data and Disability)
- Rehabilitation and community based rehabilitation
- Enabling and disabling environments
- International development programs and their impacts on disabled people
- Disability cultures and identities
- Histories of disability
- Postcolonial issues
- Indigenous concerns
- Inclusive research and decolonizing approaches

More information about this series at
https://link.springer.com/bookseries/14633

Franziska Felder · Laura Davy ·
Rosemary Kayess
Editors

# Disability Law and Human Rights

## Theory and Policy

palgrave
macmillan

*Editors*
Franziska Felder
University of Vienna
Vienna, Austria

Laura Davy
Australian National University
Canberra, Australia

Rosemary Kayess
University of New South Wales
Sydney
Sydney, Australia

Palgrave Studies in Disability and International Development
ISBN 978-3-030-86544-3 ISBN 978-3-030-86545-0 (eBook)
https://doi.org/10.1007/978-3-030-86545-0



This Palgrave Macmillan imprint is published by the registered company Springer Nature Switzerland AG
The registered company address is: Gewerbestrasse 11, 6330 Cham, Switzerland

# Contents

# Notes on Contributors

**Scott Avery, Ph.D.** is a Senior Lecturer in Indigenous Disability at Western Sydney University and the research partner of First Peoples Disability Network (Australia). He is descendant from the Worimi people and is profoundly deaf. His research focuses on the intersection of Indigeneity and disability in rights and social policy. He has authored the research monograph *Culture is Inclusion: A narrative of Aboriginal and Torres Strait Islander People with disability*, and was the lead investigator in the 'Living our ways' research program that established a community-based disability research agenda from Australia's Indigenous people.

**Laura Davy** is a Research Fellow at the Australia and New Zealand School of Government and the Crawford School of Public Policy at the Australian National University. She is a political theorist and sociologist with a long-standing interest in disability studies and the philosophy of human rights.

**Gauthier de Beco** (JD, University of Leuven; LLM, University of Nottingham; Ph.D. in Law, University of Louvain) is Reader in Law at the University of Huddersfield, and previously taught at the KU Leuven, University College London and the University of Leeds. His expertise lies in the topic of human rights and disability. He has just written a new monograph on Disability in International Human Rights Law with Oxford University Press. He has also been involved in a number of research projects related to disability and provides advice to civil society organisations.

**María Gómez-Carrillo de Castro** is a Marie Skłodowska-Curie fellow currently writing her Ph.D. on participatory research methods at the Institute of Social and Political Sciences, University of Lisbon (Portugal). She is a Spanish lawyer interested in public law, disability studies, access to justice and participation.

**Theresia Degener** is Professor of Law and Disability Studies at the Protestant University of Applied Sciences in Bochum, Germany and Visiting Professor at the Faculty of Law, University of Maastricht, The Netherlands. She is the director of the Bochum Centre for Disability Studies BODYS and former Chair of the United Nations Committee on the Rights of Persons with Disabilities. Her research fields are anti-discrimination law, human rights, disability studies and gender studies.

**Helen Dickinson** is Professor of Public Service Research and Director of the Public Service Research Group at the School of Business, University of New South Wales, Canberra. Her expertise is in public services, particularly in relation to topics such as governance, policy implementation and stewardship of fourth industrial revolution technologies. She has published more than 18 books and eighty peer reviewed journals on these topics. Helen is a Victorian Fellow of the Institute of Public Administration Australia and a Fellow of the Academy of Social Sciences.

**Franziska Felder** is Professor of Inclusive Education and Disability Research at the University of Vienna (Austria). Her work concentrates on justice in education, with a special focus on inclusive education and disability. She is, together with Jerome E. Bickenbach and Barbara Schmitz, the editor of the Cambridge University Press's volume *Disability and the Good Human Life* (2014).

**Leslie P. Francis** is Distinguished Professor of Philosophy and Distinguished Alfred C. Emery Professor of Law at the University of Utah, where she also directs the Center for Law and Biomedical Sciences. She is widely published in disability law and ethics, philosophy of law, and issues of justice in health care. From 2015–2016, she served as President of the Pacific Division of the American Philosophical Association.

**Shaun Grech** is director of The Critical Institute Malta and Affiliate Associate Professor at the Department of International Relations, University of Malta. He is also Editor in Chief of the international journal *Disability and the Global South*. He has published extensively in the field of disability, poverty and international development.

**Celia Green** is a Research Fellow at the Centre for Research Excellence in Disability and Health (CRE-DH) and the Centre for Social Impact (CSI) at the University of New South Wales. Her research interests include public administration and large scale social policy reforms. She is currently examining the implementation of the Australian National Disability Insurance Scheme with a particular focus on issues of market stewardship and equity for participants.

**Anne Kavanagh** is a Professor in Disability and Health at the University of Melbourne. She has a medical degree from Flinders University and a Ph.D. from the Australian National University and is a Fellow of the Australian Faculty of Public Health Medicine and the Academy of Social Sciences of Australia. She is Academic Director of the Melbourne Disability Institute at University of Melbourne and Co-Director of the NHMRC Centre of Research Excellence in Disability and Health. Her research focusses on inequalities in health with a specific interest in the health and wellbeing of people with disabilities.

**Rosemary Kayess** is Chair of the United Nations Committee on the Rights of Persons with Disabilities (CRPD) and a Senior Lecturer in the Faculty of Law at the University of New South Wales. She is also a Senior Research Fellow with the Social Policy Research Centre. Rosemary was a designated expert on the Australian Government delegation to the United Nations negotiations for the CRPD and has held ministerial advisory roles with the Australian Government on a range of issues.

**Gwynyyth Llewellyn** is Professor of Family and Disability Studies, Faculty of Medicine and Health, University of Sydney. She has an undergraduate degree in Arts and a Masters of Education from the University of New England, and an undergraduate degree in Occupational Therapy and Ph.D. from the University of Sydney. She is Head, WHO Collaborating Centre for Strengthening Rehabilitation Capacity in Health Systems and Co-Director of the NHMRC Centre of Research Excellence in Disability and Health. Her work addresses disability and inequity across the lifespan in the context of family and parenting, health and well-being, discrimination and personal safety.

**Michaelis Michael** is an Associate Professor at the University of New South Wales in Sydney. He studied zoology and philosophy at Monash University in Melbourne before doing a Ph.D. in philosophy at Princeton University. He works across a broad range of topics in philosophy, from human rights to formal logic. A recent focus has been on the way Big Data has changed the way we do science and the possible costs of those changes. He has recently published a book on the conceptual and empirical aspects of the theory of natural selection.

**Maria Pisani** is Senior Lecturer with the Department of Youth and Community Studies, University of Malta and a Youth Worker by profession. Her research interests include forced migration with a special focus on gender, 'race' and colonialism, youth, national identity, citizenship and intersectionality.

**Kjersti Skarstad** holds a Ph.D. in political science from the University of Oslo and is an Associate Professor at Bjørknes University College Oslo. She conducts research on the human rights of persons with disabilities, consults with civil society organizations and government agencies in Norway on the topic, is a human rights lecturer, and has also written about the relation between human rights and peace.

**Karen Soldatic** is an Associate Professor at the Institute for Culture and Society at Western Sydney University. She was awarded a Fogarty Foundation Excellence in Education Fellowship for 2006–2009, a British Academy International Fellowship in 2012, a fellowship at The Centre for Human Rights Education at Curtin University (2011–2012), and an Australian Research Council DECRA Fellowship (2016–2019). Her research on global welfare regimes builds on her 20 years of experience as an international, national and state-based senior policy analyst, researcher and practitioner.

**Kay Wilson** is a lawyer, writer and scholar with an interest in mental health, disability and human rights law and a background in psychology. She has recently completed her Ph.D. entitled 'Mental Health Law: Abolish or Reform?' at Melbourne Law School, University of Melbourne, which has recently been published by Oxford University Press. She has also published a number of papers in the field.

CHAPTER 1

# Introduction

*Laura Davy, Franziska Felder, Rosemary Kayess, and Celia Green*

## Introduction

What is the United Nations Convention on the Rights of Persons with Disabilities, and how has it transformed disability theory, policy and law? These questions animate and underpin this collection.

L. Davy (✉)
Australian National University, Canberra, Australia
e-mail: l.davy@unsw.edu.au

F. Felder
University of Vienna, Vienna, Austria
e-mail: franziska.felder@univie.ac.at

R. Kayess · C. Green
University of New South Wales, Sydney, NSW, Australia
e-mail: r.kayess@unsw.edu.au

C. Green
e-mail: celia.green@unsw.edu.au



F. Felder et al. (eds.), *Disability Law and Human Rights*, Palgrave Studies in Disability and International Development, https://doi.org/10.1007/978-3-030-86545-0_1

The United Nations Convention on the Rights of Persons with Disabilities (CRPD) was formally opened for signature and ratification in March 2007. On the day of its opening, over eighty UN member states signed the CRPD, a record number for the first day of signature of any UN Convention so far. Reflecting a paradigm shift that positions people with disabilities as "subjects" of human rights rather than "objects" of pity and charity, it was the culmination of a long and successful campaign by the international disability movement and was celebrated as a catalyst for change on human rights and disability throughout the world.

In many ways, this is a uniquely exciting time for people with disabilities and their allies. The equal rights and personhood of people with disability were affirmed in international law for the first time in the CRPD, which also has the potential to mainstream disability issues in public policy world-wide by shining a spotlight on what reforms are needed to uphold these rights. But systemic change has been slower than many of those who celebrated its entry into force anticipated.

People with disability represent the largest definable disadvantaged group on the planet. The World Health Organisation estimates that over a billion people, or 15% of the world's population, have some form of disability (WHO 2018). Despite these numbers, less than 50 countries have adopted disability discrimination laws or other disability-specific legislation. The countries that do have disability-focused legislation in place have often not matched these innovations with a legal support system that enables people with disability to effectively have access to the law. People with disability are more likely to experience poverty and have limited access to basic services such as housing, education and healthcare than their non-disabled counterparts. They are also more likely to face violence and abuse than others in society, particularly when living in institutional settings. While signatories to the CRPD now have an obligation to address these challenges through legislation and policy, and disability groups have an additional advocacy tool in the CRPD to call for systemic change, disability remains largely at the margins of mainstream policy concern.

These challenges for rights-informed public policy also reveal many underlying philosophical issues. In the decade since the CRPD was developed a rich body of theoretical literature has emerged, exploring the deep ethical and political questions confronting contemporary societies in relation to the rights of people with disability. How does disability challenge conventional notions of "the human" in human rights law? How is the disability rights movement challenging conventional theories of justice, equality and recognition? How does disability relate to human vulnerability? How can we reduce, with the help of public policy, the social vulnerabilities people with disability experience, such as discrimination, marginalization and violence? How do other aspects of the human experience, such as gender, ethnicity and citizenship status, relate to and shape the personal and social experience of disability?

In the first sections of this introduction, we provide a general overview of the development and implementation of the CRPD. We then describe the structure and content of the volume, first by introducing the individual contributions of each author, and secondly by drawing together a number of important and cross-cutting themes that tie these contributions together. We conclude with something a bit different, by spotlighting the reflections and contributions of one of the editors of the book, Rosemary Kayess. Rosemary is an internationally recognised human rights lawyer and an important and well-known figure within the Australian disability rights movement. At the time of writing, she is Chair of the United Nations Committee on the Rights of Persons with Disabilities, the body of independent experts that monitors implementation of the CRPD. Rosemary provides a unique, first-hand perspective on the challenges and promises of implementing the CRPD.

## The Development of the CRPD

The United Nations adopted the Convention on the Rights of Persons with Disabilities (CRPD) on the 13th December 2006. The first human rights treaty to be adopted in the twenty-first century, it has been hailed as a key instrument towards reframing the concerns and needs of people with disability in human rights terms. The CRPD was negotiated in four years, considered "lightning quick" in United Nations terms (Degener and Begg 2017). However, it took decades for disability to be recognised as a human rights issue within the UN architecture, and it required significant and sustained work, particularly from civil society organisations, to prepare the legal and political context that enabled the CRPD to be considered on the international stage.

Prior to the CRPD, when the law did consider people with disability, it traditionally considered them as objects of care rather than as legal subjects entitled to respect and the full gamut of human rights (Hendriks 2007). The development of the CRPD was achieved after decades of activism that challenged the prevailing perception of people with disability as dependent subjects of charity who require society to provide them with support to compensate for their incapacity (Harpur 2012; Hendriks 2007; Kayess and French 2008). Legal responses to disability and impairment demonstrated a "mix of charity, paternalism and social policy rather than human rights" approaches (Quinlivan 2012, p. 73) and drew primarily on the medical model of disability in viewing disability as a personal medical "problem" that adheres to the individual. A key benefit of the CRPD is that it provides an international human rights instrument that directly challenges these assumptions about people with disability (Quinlivan 2012). The CRPD is explicitly underpinned by the social model of disability, which understands disability in the context of the environmental and social conditions and structures that disadvantage people with impairments (Emerson et al. 2011), and embraces a rights-based approach to inclusion (Quinlivan 2012).

Degener and Begg (2017) outline four distinct phases leading to the eventual recognition of disability as a human rights issue by the UN. In the first phase, from the establishment of the UN to about 1970, people with disability were largely invisible within the UN treaty system. The UN Charter of 1945 and the Universal Declaration of Human Rights (UDHR) of 1948 made no mention of people with disability at all. Within the UDHR, disability is referred to only as a condition or an event similar to unemployment or illness, requiring the application of social welfare to affected persons to ensure an acceptable living standard.

The second phase, occurring broadly in the decade between 1970 and 1980, saw a shift towards a recognition of people with disability as subjects deserving of rehabilitation and some recognition of rights (Degener and Begg 2017). This began with two non-binding but important UN declarations; the Declaration on the Rights of Mentally Retarded Persons (1971) and the Declaration of the Rights of Disabled Persons (1975). The title and preamble of the 1971 Declaration suggested it was a rights-based document. However, commentators have argued that it was firmly entrenched within the medical model of disability, with people with cognitive impairments guaranteed the same rights as other persons only "to the maximum degree of feasibility" and impairments still primarily viewed as barriers to being able to hold and exercise rights (Degener and Begg 2017). Similarly, while the 1975 Declaration demanded the same human rights for people with disability as for those who were non-disabled, these were subject to caveats, such as equality rights being restricted for people with intellectual disability as per the 1971 Declaration. However, the 1975 Declaration does mark one of the first instances in which the UN recognised the importance of consulting with organisations representing people with disability (Degener and Begg 2017).

The third phase, beginning in the late 1970s and encompassing the following decades to the turn of the millennium, heralded a much more active period towards the achievement of full human rights for people with disability. Driven by disability activists and academics, principally in the United Kingdom and the United States, the late 70s and early 80s saw disability begin to be conceptualised in political and sociological terms (Barnes 1991; Durell 2014). The social model of disability rose in prominence as "a backlash and as an ideological juxtaposition to the medical model of disability" (Lang 2009, p. 268). The start of the 1980s marked the beginnings of a more organised international disability rights movement and a permanent shift towards a civil rights paradigm (Hendriks 2007). There was a growing consensus within this movement that existing international human rights law was failing to address the inequality, discrimination and segregation experienced by people with disability.

During this period a number of awareness-raising measures, formal statements and other mechanisms for promoting the rights of people with disability were introduced at the international level. The UN proclaimed 1981 as the International Year of Disabled Persons and 1982–1992 was proclaimed as the Decade of Persons with Disabilities. A comprehensive UN action plan—the World Programme of Action Concerning Disabled Persons—was adopted in 1982 and aimed to improve rehabilitation and social and economic opportunities for people with disability. A Special Rapporteur for Human Rights and Disability, Leandro Despouy, was appointed in 1984. This period also marked the beginning of the ongoing relationship between the UN and civil society institutions concerned with disability (Lang 2009). For example, Disabled People's International (DPI) was founded in 1981 and granted consultative status at the UN soon after.

During the 1990s, collaboration between the UN and disability civil society organisations was further developed and reinforced. In 1993 the UN General Assembly adopted what would prove to be a pivotal document leading to the development of the CRPD, the UN Standard Rules on the Equalization of Opportunities for Persons with Disabilities. The

Standard Rules stipulated that a Special Rapporteur for Disability be engaged to monitor their implementation, and in 1994 an active member of DPI, Bengt Lindqvist, was appointed as the first Special Rapporteur. This role continues to be a crucial component of the monitoring and oversight architecture of the CRPD. This period also saw increasing recognition that the social model of disability should form the ideological basis of any future international disability policy and that this needed to be systematised in an internationally recognised document sitting under the umbrella of the UN (Lang 2009). The end of the 1990s thus saw growing impetus for the drafting of a legally binding international treaty that would hold signatory States to account for protecting and upholding the human rights of people with disability.

The start of the new millennium can be seen as marking the beginning of the fourth phase towards UN recognition of human rights for people with disability (Degener and Begg 2017). A growing number of Disabled People's Organisations (DPOs)—organisations of and for people with disability—with increasing capacity for transnational cooperation and coordination, actively championed the necessity of a UN treaty to specifically address the human rights of people with disability (Lang 2009). In 2001, following a proposal from Mexico, an Ad Hoc Committee was created by the UN General Assembly to study proposals for a convention on the rights of people with disability. Between 2002 and 2006 eight sessions of the Ad Hoc Committee were held, during which the CRPD text was drafted, negotiated and later finalised by state delegations, with the participation of civil society organisations (Table 1.1).

The development and subsequent implementation of the CRPD has contributed to an evolving and exciting new disability rights paradigm (Harpur 2012). Within just over a decade the Convention has gained 163 signatories and has been ratified by 181 countries. No other treaty has been ratified so fast and by such a large number of nation states (Degener 2017). The CRPD has the potential to transform the lives of over a billion people (Mittler 2015) and its passage into international law has rightly been heralded as a cause for celebration, representing a "high water mark not only in the area of disability rights, but also in the development of international human rights laws and concepts and implementation measures more generally" (Kayess and French 2008, p. 33).

Harpur (2012) argues that the potential for significant change the CRPD offers for people with disability stems from two key factors. Firstly,

**Table 1.1** Key milestones in the development of the CRPD

| | |
|---|---|
| December 20, 1971 | The Declaration on the Rights of Mentally Retarded Persons is proclaimed by the United Nations General Assembly |
| December 9, 1975 | The Declaration of the Rights of Disabled Persons is proclaimed by the United Nations General Assembly |
| 1981 | The United Nations proclaims the International Year of Disabled Persons. Disabled People's International (DPI) is founded |
| 1982 | The United Nations proclaims the Decade of Persons with Disabilities. The World Programme of Action Concerning Disabled Persons is adopted by the United Nations General Assembly |
| 1984 | A Special Rapporteur for Human Rights and Disability is appointed |
| December 20, 1993 | The UN Standard Rules on the Equalisation of Opportunities for Persons with Disabilities is adopted by the United Nations General Assembly |
| 1994 | A Special Rapporteur for Disability is appointed to monitor implementation of the Standard Rules |
| 2001 | An Ad Hoc Committee is established by the UN General Assembly to study proposals for a convention to promote the rights and dignity of persons with disabilities |
| 2002–2006 | The Ad Hoc Committee holds eight sessions in New York, during which the need for a Convention addressing the rights of people with disability is established and the CRPD text is then drafted, negotiated and finalised |
| December 13, 2006 | The CRPD is adopted by the United Nations General Assembly |
| March 30, 2007 | The CRPD is opened for signature by state parties and other bodies |
| April 3, 2008 | The CRPD receives its 20th ratification, triggering its entry into force 30 days later |
| May 3, 2008 | The CRPD and Optional Protocol enter into force |

the CRPD was not designed to create new rights—instead it has restated existing human rights and then constructed incidental rights to ensure existing rights are attained. This process has provided greater clarity to existing rights, thus providing advocates with a stronger tool to hold states accountable. Secondly, the CRPD codified the importance of people with disability being appropriately and adequately represented in rights processes, and its development modelled this through the formal involvement of people with disability and their representative organisation during the process of drafting and negotiating. By officially requiring the UN and individual states to provide people with disability a meaningful voice, the CRPD embraces the "nothing about us without us" politics of inclusion.

## The Implementation of the CRPD

Within its first ten years, the CPRD has achieved some significant impacts, especially in relation to the development of other treaties. For example, the UN Millennium Development Goals set in 2000 made no mention of disability, however, when they were replaced in 2016 by the Sustainable Development Goals (SDGs), people with disability were referenced in all main areas of focus. Other human rights treaty bodies have included disability in their agendas and undertaken specific actions in response to the jurisprudence of the Committee on the Rights of Persons with Disabilities (Degener 2017). Regional human rights bodies such as the European Court of Human Rights have made significant decisions that reflect the Committee's legal philosophy. Charter-based bodies like the Human Rights Council have established task forces to ensure equitable access to all processes and documents. Degener (2017) argues that these steps show how the CRPD has made disability visible as a key human rights theme.

The CRPD has spurred many countries into greater action on disability policy and law to bring domestic legislation in line with international norms. The CRPD requires States Parties to take positive action, such as through law reform, to implement the rights recognised within its text. In many countries, new domestic laws are being drawn up or amended to enable compliance with the CRPD (Kanter 2019). Even in nations with already established disability legislation, the CRPD provides an opportunity for a complete re-evaluation of disability policy and legislation, to assess what is working well and to remove what is not working (Umeasiegbu et al. 2012). Many nations are reviewing the impact on people with disability of their existing laws. As Kanter (2019) explains in her analysis of why human rights treaties matter, even if a law currently prohibits discrimination on the basis of disability, people with disability may still face discrimination when other domestic laws are applied. For example, family laws may prevent people with disability from being parents, education laws may deny them the right to the same educational standards and settings as their peers, and mental health laws may prevent them from making decisions about medical treatment and permit involuntary confinement. Many nation states, including India, Ireland,

Australia, Hungary, Bulgaria, Croatia, Israel, Peru and Colombia have or are currently reviewing existing guardianship laws to examine how they can be brought into further alignment with the CRPD.

As well as being a catalyst for domestic law reform, the CRPD has also been a shaping influence on high-level government disability strategies and policies across the world. For example, the European Disability Strategy 2010–2020 was significantly informed by the CRPD. Moving forward past 2020, Lawson (2017) suggests that a strengthened European Union (EU) disability strategy will build on the increasing number of CRPD related collaborations between different EU institutions and enable more weight to be placed on certain implementation priorities than in the 2010–2020 strategy because this architecture is now in place. Australia, which ratified the CRPD in 2008, is an example of a country which has seen a dramatic shift in its disability policy landscape in recent years, with the CRPD acting as a "philosophical and moral statement and framework guiding integrated and strategic policy across the nation" (Madden et al. 2011, p. 1). Two key policy responses developed in acknowledgement of the inequities faced by Australians with disability have been the National Disability Strategy, a 10-year plan with the vision of developing "an inclusive Australian society that enables people with disability to fulfil their potential as equal citizens" (Commonwealth of Australia 2011), and the introduction of the National Disability Insurance Scheme, Australia's most expansive disability policy reform to date (Malbon et al. 2019). New Zealand, South Africa and Slovenia are also examples of nation states that are incorporating CRPD principles in the development of their domestic disability strategies.

Three areas have been highlighted as particularly critical to the successful implementation of disability policy by a variety of researchers (Flynn 2011; Fougeyrollas and Grenier 2018; Laufey et al. 2018; Mahomed et al. 2019) and the Committee on the Rights of Persons with Disabilities[1]:

- Grassroots consultation from the outset of policy design,
- Participation of people with disability in implementation processes and

[1] General comment No. 7 (2018) on the participation of persons with disabilities, including children with disabilities, through their representative organisations, in the implementation and monitoring of the Convention.

- Independent monitoring and reporting on progress.

Speaking generally of CRPD-aligned domestic disability policy, Flynn (2011) argues that aligning national disability strategies with other domestic, regional and international initiatives is critical to maintaining the momentum for reform. This includes looking outside the more narrow frame of disability policy to ensure alignment with other strategies, for example those relating to the rights and status of women, children and groups experiencing ethnic or racial discrimination.

In addition to recognition of the positive changes the CRPD is enabling, there have also been words of caution on its ability to facilitate the momentous changes needed for the full gamut of human rights to be recognised and acted upon for people with disability. Umeasiegbu et al. (2013, p. 62) argue that history has demonstrated that the existence of constitutional recognition and formal international human rights conventions do not necessarily lead to implementation, and thus, "the direct impact and significant potential of the UN CRPD may be oversold". There are myriad historic and systemic factors which must be overcome for the full intent of the CRPD to be realised and fully implemented on a global scale. Even in nations which have a history of upholding human rights, people with disability still experience significant discrimination, social exclusion and inequitable treatment (Milner et al. 2019). They have lower income levels and lower education levels, are more likely to be unemployed, live in more precarious housing and have poorer health outcomes than people without disability (United Nations Department of Economic and Social Affairs 2019; Frier et al. 2018). Socio-cultural norms that perpetuate negative perceptions of and exclusion of people with disability will need to change if the CRPD's goal of full human rights for people with disability is to be realised. Within this context, there are numerous areas where more work still needs to be done for nation states to realise its full transformative potential.

More than a decade has passed since the CPRD entered into force on May 3, 2008. This volume is a timely contribution to the literature on human rights and disability and reflects on the lessons learned and challenges encountered in the intervening ten years. Work towards transforming domestic legal frameworks and global public policy has only just begun, and new implications and new interpretations of the UNCRPD continue to emerge as countries progress with the ratification process, scholars from new fields engage with disability and human rights and new voices within the disability movement are amplified and heard.

## Structure and Content of This Book

The aim of this book is to explore the intersections between disability theory and philosophy and the concrete policy issues impacting on the lives of people with disability on a day-to-day basis. It brings together an interdisciplinary group of researchers in the areas of philosophy of disability, disability law and disability policy. The authors are international, drawn primarily from countries in Europe, North America and Australia, and their contributions address pressing questions about the philosophical foundations of the CRPD, as well as complex contemporary policy debates. The book makes the case that human rights instruments, and particularly the ground-breaking CRPD, which represents a far-reaching intervention into thinking and practice concerning disability, have vital implications in the philosophical and policy domains as well as in the field of law. Disability theory and disability rights policy and practice have always been closely intertwined, and a theme of cross-fertilisation and mutual transformation between these two strands reoccurs throughout many of the chapters of this book.

The volume begins with a chapter by Theresia Degener and María Gómez-Carrillo de Castro titled "Towards Inclusive Equality: Ten Years of the Human Rights Model of Disability in the Work of the UN Committee on the Rights of Persons with Disabilities". The authors describe how, with the United Nations' adoption of the CRPD in 2006, a new era of human rights began, one in which people with disability were firmly established as subjects of international human rights law for the first time. Degener and Gómez-Carrillo de Castro trace the emergence of a new model of disability in the CRPD—the human rights model—that presents a rich alternative to both the medical and social models of disability. Through a close reading of the CRPD Committee's General Comments, guidelines and country reports, they argue that a new concept of equality has also evolved and been introduced to international anti-discrimination law over the first ten years of the CRPD's monitoring. This concept, which the authors describe as "inclusive equality", extends well beyond existing conceptions of formal and substantive equality. Building on important work in feminist scholarship and disability studies, it incorporates dimensions of (1) redistribution, (2) recognition,

(3) participation and (4) accommodation, in order to fully address the systemic and relational conditions of equality of opportunity for persons with disabilities.

In "What does the CRPD tell us about being human?", Franziska Felder stresses the need to develop an inclusive justification for human rights that encompasses not only the putatively rational and autonomous subject in the community of rights subjects, but all human beings, including those living with severe cognitive and multiple disabilities. She draws on the work of American developmental psychologist and primatologist Michael Tomasello in suggesting that we should view a capability entitled "We-capability" as the "essential" or foundational human capability. The "We-capability" is the ability to formulate a collective intentionality by thinking as, with and for a conception of "we". It involves a form of affiliation with a human community which is the precursor for caring for and identifying with others. Felder argues that this uniquely human capability can adequately account for the problems of speciesism and metaphysical foundationalism, creating a genuinely inclusive vision of the "right to have rights", and that the CRPD is a powerful example of the "We-capability" in action.

In "Rights, Justice and Flourishing: The Uses and Limitations of Human Rights", Michaelis Michael and Karen Soldatic provide us with an important reminder of the potential limits of the human rights project. They describe the primary role of human rights frameworks "as a safety net rather than as a guarantee of the good life", originally and principally formulated to protect individuals from the coercive power of the state. But disability is a highly complex socio-political phenomenon, and for many people with disability, legal articulations of human rights offer only a prescribed set of minimum requirements that are insufficient for addressing the poorer life outcomes and past and continuing injustices faced by persons with disability. Given the complexity and diversity of disabled people's lifeworlds across the lived experience of disability, Michael and Soldatic ask whether rights are really enough for the realisation of a self-determined life of flourishing.

Kjersti Skarstad explores the difference debate in "Disability and the Dilemma of Difference", demonstrating that the concept of substantial equality expressed in the CRPD moves beyond the way the terms of this debate are conventionally configured in philosophy. In the context of disability rights, the dilemma of difference can be reinterpreted as the question of how to perceive of human beings as different, yet equal in their human rights. Skarstad argues that applying different approaches to different groups is a necessity for the universal application of human rights, rather than representing a negative form of discrimination. Achieving equality is not a choice between integrated or targeted approaches, she claims; rather, the rights of persons with disabilities (and others) should be taken fully into account in general policies as well as having targeted policies or measures combating specific human rights challenges.

Leslie P. Francis surveys the difference between human rights, civil rights accounts and welfarist accounts of disability rights in "Forms of Equality, Faces of Discrimination: CRPD Article 5, Article 12, and the Disability's Difference Debate". She argues that a civil rights interpretation of Articles 5 and 12 of the CRPD (the articles that deal with equality and non-discrimination and equality before the law) is preferable as a ground for disability justice. According to Francis, a civil rights frame is focused on achieving increased inclusion of human difference and sidesteps the philosophical debate around whether disability represents "mere" difference or "bad" difference (difference that necessarily diminishes welfare). It also avoids grounding human rights in a special characteristic of human beings that some humans may not share. She concludes the chapter by exploring some of the implications of the civil rights approach to equality before the law in the context of healthcare decision-making.

Laura Davy and Celia Green explore the tension between recent transnational developments in disability service provision and the human rights paradigm in "The right to autonomy and the conditions that secure it: the relationship between the CRPD and market-based policy reform". They use the development and implementation of Australia's National Disability Insurance Scheme as an example of the contested understandings of autonomy in disability policy. Davy and Green argue that the conception of personal autonomy that underpins the Convention represents a valuable alternative vision of human flourishing, particularly when contrasted with the conception of autonomy that underpins the individualisation and marketisation of disability policy and services that is occurring in many nation states. The CRPD provides a basis for claiming the basic material and social conditions of autonomy such as housing, medical attention, safety, and inclusive education, health, and transport systems, factors that can be lost in the more neoliberal discourse of choice and consumer empowerment that underpins individualisation.

In "At the Intersection of Childhood and Disability: Improving Human Rights Protection for Disabled Children", Gauthier de Beco addresses issues of intersectionality, exploring the compounded prejudice and disadvantage that can result from the intersection of childhood and disability. His chapter critically examines the strengths and weaknesses of the CRPD and the Convention on the Rights of the Child (CRC). While both treaties give consideration to children with disability, they view these children predominantly from the perspective of a single identity, that is, as children first or as disabled people first. De Beco proposes that it is only through reading and applying the two treaties together that the rights of children with disability are adequately safeguarded. He illustrates this point through analysis of the right to education, arguing that it is only through implementing the CRC and the CRPD together that strategies to promote the right to education for children with disability will be sufficiently robust.

Kay Wilson explores how the implementation of the CRPD into mental health law has been fraught with tensions between State Parties, the CRPD Committee, human rights scholars, clinicians, disability advocates, and people with psychosocial disability. In her chapter, "The CRPD and Mental Health: the Conflict About Abolition, Practical Dilemmas of Implementation and Untapped Potential" she describes the conflict as centring on whether the CRPD requires the abolition of mental health law (the repeal of the power of the state to detain and give psychiatric treatment to persons with mental impairment in certain circumstances without their consent). Wilson advocates for holistic interpretation of the CRPD which balances rights to liberty and legal capacity with the rights to life, health and maximising participation in the community. In a careful and nuanced discussion, she argues that such an interpretation of the CRPD does not require the abolition of mental health law, but it will require significant legal and systemic reform and increased recognition and respect for the subjective will and preferences of the individual.

In "Disability and Forced Migration: Critical Connections and the Global South Debate", Shaun Grech and Maria Pisani advocate for greater cross-disciplinary engagement between disability studies and forced migration studies. They argue that disability is poorly understood and under-prioritised in humanitarian and migration theory and practice and that similarly, disability studies and policy has tended to neglect the situation of people with disability who are experiencing displacement. When disabled refugees are addressed within these fields, it is too often through a vulnerability lens that disempowers and denies their agency. In this chapter, Grech and Pisani address the rich and often neglected discursive and practice intersections of disability and forced migration, exploring the need for inclusive and interdisciplinary data collection, responsive and accessible services, and a transnational approach to disability and care research that challenges Eurocentric and citizenship-focused biases.

In "Intersections in Human Rights and Public Policy for Indigenous People with Disability", Scott Avery argues that Australia's Indigenous people with disability experience significantly greater social inequality than other groups in society, including Indigenous people without disability and people with disability who are not Indigenous. He explores how, as a group intersecting two marginalised populations, human rights frameworks and social policy that are designed to address only one aspect of their rights have proven woefully inadequate in securing their composite rights as an Indigenous person and as a person with disability. By sketching out an Indigenous interpretation of cultural rights within the CRPD, Avery offers readers a powerful frame for analysing and addressing systemic intersectional disadvantage, and a glimpse of "an Indigenous culture of inclusion" that is both generous and emancipatory.

In the final chapter of the volume, "Examining Australia's Performance in Realising CRPD Obligations in Health Through the Lens of COVID-19", Helen Dickinson, Gwynyyth Llewellyn and Anne Kavanagh provide a timely analysis of the way in which the coronavirus pandemic has shone a spotlight on the existing health inequities experienced by people with disability. The CPRD sets out a number of obligations with respect to ensuring people with disability have the right to the enjoyment of the highest attainable standard of health without discrimination on the basis of disability. This chapter explores the Australian experience of reform to disability services and the degree to which these CRPD obligations in the health domain have been implemented. The authors identify a number of implementation gaps and argue that better attention to these may have mitigated some of the worse impacts of the pandemic. They argue that the only way for nation states to systemically address the existing health inequities experienced by people with disability—and mitigate the negative impacts of possible future health emergencies—is to more effectively implement the CRPD and in particular its health provisions.

As can be seen from the overview of the chapters above, the contributors to this volume have addressed some of the most fundamental questions that the CRPD raises for the way we think about human rights, law and disability, and how we operationalise rights in the legal and policy domains. Several cross-cutting themes, central to disability law and human rights, feature across the book.

The first of these is the issue of personhood. In a number of chapters, the CRPD is understood as a major milestone in the disability movement's fight for recognition of the legal personhood of people with disability. Felder reminds us that competing conceptions of the person have often been tightly bound with arguments around the foundation or justification of human rights. The cognitivist and individualistic approaches to defining personhood emerging from liberal philosophy have often linked entitlement to rights ("the right to have rights") to individual capacities of rationality, autonomy or self-awareness. In her chapter Felder offers an inclusive account of the person, one that can be seen as complementary to the inclusive accounts of equality (Degener and Gómez–Carrillo de Castro) and autonomy (Davy and Green) explored in other chapters.

This theme is closely related to a second: the link between autonomy, capacity and flourishing. Davy and Green describe how autonomy, the capacity to pursue one's own conception of the good and therefore to be an agent over one's own life, is seen to be central to human personhood. Rights are seen as a key mechanism for safeguarding the individual's capacity for autonomy within the liberal tradition, but the CRPD draws attention to the relational, material and structural conditions of enabling the autonomy of people with disability in practice. Michael and Soldatic argue that the notion of flourishing provides a critical part of the moral picture that a focus solely on human rights may miss. Personal flourishing requires an individual to develop (or discover) a conception of their own lives he or she wholeheartedly endorses. The chapters by Francis and Wilson explore some of the potential contradictions and practical dilemmas involved in claims about individual autonomy, self-determination and legal capacity in their discussions of supported and substitute decision-making. Wilson argues that a widespread focus on the abolition of mental health law may obscure other critical reforms that would greatly benefit people with mental impairments, particularly when the goal is understood to be promoting personal flourishing and wellbeing as well as legal capacity. Francis discusses the need to respect difference as well as autonomy when providing decision-making support for the exercise of legal capacity.

Another key theme addressed in this book is how to understand the relation between equality, difference and discrimination in disability rights law. Degener and Gómez-Carrillo de Castro's chapter argues that the understanding of equality inherent in the new human rights model of disability differs both from existing notions of formal and substantive equality by taking heterogeneity among people with disability seriously. There are similarities between their account of equality and the view elaborated in Skarstad's chapter. For Skarstad, differential treatment can be equal treatment, if the treatment is a legitimate measure to secure equal rights in practice. With a specific focus on Articles 5 and 12 of the Convention, the chapter by Francis examines how this principle of "different but equal" can be interpreted through a civil rights frame.

The chapters by Shaun Grech and Maria Pisani, Scott Avery and Gauthier de Beco explore issues of intersectionality. For Grech and Pisani, the liminal position of disabled refugees has resulted in their invisibility within much contemporary theory and practice. The intersection of disability and forced migration must be better understood and prioritised. Avery explores the compounded disadvantage experienced by Indigenous Australians with disability as a result of the enduring effects of colonisation, while de Beco analyses the concept of intersectionality in reference to the often disempowered position of children with disability. Both Avery and de Beco advocate for human rights treaties to be jointly read and interpreted, in order to avoid an unidimensional view that fails to capture the composite rights of people with disability who face multiple forms of inequality and discrimination.

Two of the chapters deal with the critical theme of maintaining focus on human rights during states of emergency and exception. In times of crisis—such as armed conflict, natural disasters or health emergencies—the human rights of people with disability are liable to be neglected. Grech and Pisani explore this idea in relation to the invisibility of refugees with disability, while Dickinson, Llewellyn and Kavanagh examine the way people with disability were initially largely forgotten in government responses to the public health emergency represented by the COVID-19 pandemic.

This, in turn, relates to a final key theme: the limitations of the human rights project. Michael and Soldatic explore the boundaries of the rights approach and the need to draw on other political and moral resources to secure justice for persons with disability. Grech and Pisani also reflect on the limitations of rights approaches, including their boundedness to citizenship and their embeddedness in liberal theories originating in the Global North. Other chapters explore the difficulties inherent to the translation of human principles into concrete policy and practice, particularly those by Francis, Wilson, and Davy and Green. All are important reminders that despite the powerful symbolic and practical victories heralded by the CRPD so far, much work remains to be done.

## View from the Committee: In Conversation with Rosemary Kayess

The unifying theme that animates this book is the rich, complex and occasionally troubled relationship between theory, policy and practice in the field of disability rights. We conclude this introduction on a more conversational note, by highlighting the reflections of someone who has made important contributions within each of these domains, Rosemary Kayess. Rosemary was a key contributor to the development of the CRPD, as a designated expert on the Australian Government delegation and as the facilitator of the drafting of Article 24 on the right to education. She has a background in human rights law and policy studies as well as personal lived experience of disability.

When she was nineteen, Rosemary was in a serious car accident that resulted in a spinal injury. The experience profoundly changed the trajectory of her life. She was thrust into an awareness of disability policy and politics that she had never had before, and her pre-existing prejudices and stereotypes about people with disability were challenged. After her accident, she lived in a group home for some time, experiencing first-hand the lack of choice and control that can "institutionalise" people living in congregate care, even those who enjoy access to a good education and a close and loving family.

Rosemary graduated from the University of New South Wales with a Bachelor of Social Science (Honours) in 1993 and a Bachelor of Laws in 2002. She obtained her degrees in a time before electronic books were common in university libraries, personal computers were still new and accessibility options were limited. Since then, her career has spanned the advocacy, legal and research fields. Among other roles, she was Chairperson of the Australian Centre for Disability Law and has held a number of advisory positions to government including being a member of the Department of Foreign Affairs and Trade Disability Reference Group.

Between 2004 and 2006, Rosemary was a part of the Australian Government delegation to the CRPD negotiations. The Australian delegation was approached to facilitate the negotiations to develop the text of Article 24 on Education in 2004, and Rosemary led this process. Since Australia's ratification of the CRPD in 2008, she has worked closely with Australian DPOs in monitoring and advocating for its full implementation. In 2018 she was elected to the United Nations Committee on the Rights of Persons with Disabilities, and the following year was appointed to the role of Vice-Chair of the Committee. She was awarded the Australian Human Rights Commission's Human Rights Medal in 2019 in recognition of her work in international human rights law for people with disability. She researches and teaches in the areas of human rights, law and policy as a Senior Lecturer at the Faculty of Law, UNSW and a Senior Research Fellow at the Social Policy Research Centre, UNSW.

This volume was primarily written during 2020, a year of uncertainty and tragedy for many people across the world. It was often a particularly terrifying year for people with disability, their families and allies. Rosemary experienced first-hand the anxiety that characterised this period for many people with disability. Her impairment means she is at more risk of experiencing serious complications from COVID-19, and she remained in her home for much of 2020. She has spoken out in various public fora about how a lack of accessible information and access to essential protective equipment has disproportionately impacted people with disability, and criticised the ableist policies and triage protocols developed in some jurisdictions to guide medical decision-making.[2] In a statement available on the Office of the High Commissioner for Human Rights (OHCHR) website,[3] Rosemary commented that:

> The exclusion of people with disabilities from the pandemic response is the result of pre-existing inequality and discrimination based on ableism, the view that disability is 'abnormal' and able-bodied is 'normal'. This devaluing of people with disabilities is embedded in law, policy and practice, prejudicing the decisions about who is deserving of critical health care and life saving measures. [...] Looking beyond the pandemic, it is critical that CPRD is the standard for disability inclusive planning and recovery measures.

[2] See for example the Statement of Concern issued by independent Australian experts in disability and human rights, available at https://dpoa.org.au/statement-of-concern-covid-19-human-rights-disability-and-ethical-decision-making/.

[3] https://www.ohchr.org/EN/NewsEvents/Pages/CRPD-COVID-19.aspx.

For Rosemary, the human rights project, and especially the CRPD, is transformative because it reframes the way we approach the position of people with disability in society. The CRPD is premised on the concept of diversity, and views impairment as a normal part of the human condition. It displaces the assumption that people with disability need "exceptional" care in parallel, segregated systems, stressing that what they need, first and foremost, is for their human rights to be upheld across all domains of life. For these reasons, she views the right to education as a cornerstone right of the CRPD. Educating young people together sets up a trajectory in which they expect an inclusive society.

The following conversation between Rosemary and Laura was recorded and transcribed in late 2020. In it we traverse a number of subjects, including the way in which the coronavirus pandemic has highlighted the importance of rights-based approaches to disability policy, the theory and praxis nexus that animates so much disability studies scholarship and the importance of inclusive education, a topic of great importance to Rosemary.

*Laura*: It has been over a decade since the CRPD entered into force. What do you think have been the greatest achievements in disability law and human rights over this period?

*Rosemary*: It's the beginning of a slow, incremental process. Like all policy, it's going to operate incrementally. The thing about it is that now there's the Convention, there are standards that people can debate and people can use to hold their governments to account. I'd say the CRPD has got maybe a fifty year trajectory. Twenty to see some solid change, but fifty before you can truly... [laughs] maybe I'm being a bit negative though. Considering what has been done in twelve years... There's definitely been shifts in the ideas around supported decision making and around changing the default assumption that people with disability lack legal capacity. And there's been some significant work done in terms of unfit to plea provisions and justice diversion mechanisms. There have been some significant legislative reviews, and people are starting to grapple with the issues. There's also been shifts in terms of the recognition of disability discrimination. You still tend to find that the new framework around reasonable accommodation is not picked up in areas other than employment. I think it's starting to broaden out in some places but it's not universal yet.

The Committee is doing some good work. But what concerns me is the limited resources that the UN has, and that's just going to get worse post-COVID-19 and after the US election. Only three per cent of the

UN budget is spent on human rights. It's one of the four pillars, you'd think it would be twenty-five per cent... It's a very difficult situation.

I don't think the CRPD is the panacea. But I definitely think it's a good foundation, as a catalyst for change.

*Laura*: The topics addressed in this volume range from how the CRPD has introduced new concepts or new versions of existing concepts to international human rights law, to future trends in inclusive education and health policy. In other words, they span issues in both theory and policy. How important is it to question and think deeply about what we mean by concepts like inclusion and equality?

*Rosemary*: It's incredibly important. You know, the funny thing about the disability rights movement is that, in many senses – and I know the social model isn't a full social theory, but in a loose sort of way – the disability rights movement started with a theory, a very challenging theory. There was this dominant idea, this dominant paradigm around disability, and that needed to be challenged. And so, I think if we as academics or theorists don't continually challenge the theory, then we're letting the same thing happen.

The social model can be reduced to a really social constructionist model but it's much more complex than that. And the CRPD fleshes a lot of that out, because we're basically saying to people, 'Diagnosis is irrelevant. It's not about the diagnosis. The focus is on the disadvantage which may be experienced in similar ways by people across a variety of diagnostic groups. And it says, 'We're not talking about what are we doing for blind people, what are we doing for people in wheelchairs, ra ra -- we're talking about inclusion. What is inclusion, how are people with disability included, how do they belong?'

So yeah, critical theory analysis is incredibly important. And the same with applying an intersectional or a life course approach. It's about recognising people as not defined by their impairment but as human beings. So it's about recognising those multiple layers and stages of life.

*Laura*: And it may not be a social theory as such, but the social model has been – like the CRPD—such a huge catalyst for change.

Back to concrete policy, what do you think should be on the agenda for the next 10 years? What human rights policy areas that impact people with disability do you think national governments should prioritise over the next decade?

*Rosemary*: I'd really like to see some consolidation and traction in the areas that have started. Supported decision making, justice diversion, breaking the nexus between health and disability, challenging the psychiatric system… Segregation is also a big one. Segregation and autonomy are the two big ones. I think education is critical. And getting people living in the community is critical as well.

*Laura*: The COVID-19 pandemic has impacted on everyone over the past year in often devastating ways. But evidence is amassing about the pandemic's disproportionate impact on people with disability. How has the pandemic highlighted the inequities that people with disability face on a day to day basis?

*Rosemary*: It exposed inherent inequality and discrimination that people with disability experience. They were an afterthought. They weren't factored in from the beginning. And then everything was focused around disability services, so the view was, 'if you've got care, everything is sorted.' The assumption was that people's lives are defined by disability services. But where were the vulnerabilities? The vulnerabilities were people living in congregate care - aged care homes, residential facilities, group homes... So it just exposed all those.

And then that triage stuff (crisis triage protocols in healthcare settings) was really really damning. It highlighted that disability wasn't really understood, and that people with disability just weren't valued. We were dispensable, absolutely dispensable. It was the arbitrary nature of just naming impairment types without there being any commensurate clinical analysis on an individual level. They were doing it with older persons as well in some places... It was horrendous, it was absolutely horrendous.

*Laura*: A volume like this one aims at contributing to the discussion about the future of disability law and human rights from a variety of disciplinary perspectives. How do we encourage and sustain more conversations like this one, and how can we make sure they're inclusive ones?

*Rosemary*: I think it's about getting people with disability into academia. This is the whole point around segregation. If you don't have people with disability participating in life domains, then you're never going to get change in those domains. Mainly because people aren't going to see the need, and there will be nobody on the inside saying 'this has got to change'. If we can also build research capacity and research capability and get researchers with disability into not just applied disability research but into all disciplines, then it will be done more inclusively across the board because people will think of it.

*Laura*: And I think that means supporting them once they're in as well. Because we know that all marginalised groups with less access to the academy face a huge amount of barriers just to be there that other people don't have to get through.

*Rosemary*: And it's not just the academy though, it's all facets of life. It's public life, it's business and industry. People with disability participating in employment. People with disability getting access to good education so they can become economists and doctors and [laughs] if they seriously must, lawyers—whatever they want to do.

*Laura*: And is there a role for governments in pressing the levers that would enable that to happen?

*Rosemary*: Absolutely. Keeping the conversation going is about good advice. If we don't have good inclusion then we need a strong voice from people with disability. One of the things I said in my submission to the Commission (Australian Royal Commission into Violence, Abuse, Neglect and Exploitation of People with Disability) around COVID-19 was that they need a strong effective national voice for people with disability to parliament. There's got to be an effective mechanism that can talk across all portfolios. Because otherwise all those stereotypes will just continue to be held. That's why I think education is so important. Because if kids go to school together they recognise diversity and they expect diversity, so it's not foreign to them, it's part of their everyday existence.

*Laura*: Was that a vision that was shared in the process of negotiating the CRPD article on education?

*Rosemary*: Yes it was shared, in abstract, but when it comes down to it—and I've got to tread carefully here—there were a whole bunch of people who were educated in the 60s in special schools because mainstream education provided no support for them who participated in these negotiations. These are quite privileged people who have achieved a lot, and see that as a result of their special education. But what they don't see is the fact that it just reinforces segregation in other aspects of people's lives.

*Laura*: I find the debate really interesting, because I think in some ways it's a matter of people—and society—catching up to your perspective.

*Rosemary*: If you've got the supports, it can be done. Where do we start to drive this change? Is it in the education of the educators? That's one of the biggest blocks. Inclusive education is still an elective, and it's only done for one semester, when it should frame the whole damn curriculum. And then, if educators and the pedagogy are more inclusive, then there's not such a need for intensive disability support for people to be able to learn in those settings because we might move beyond traditional classroom set ups and beyond traditional educating modes and styles.

*Laura*: I wonder if it was difficult in the UN environment to shepherd people into thinking about education in this future oriented way.

Because your vision here seems to be an idealistic one about how things can be, and perhaps people were a bit limited by their own experiences and trajectories.

*Rosemary*: I don't know why everyone thinks the Convention is about drawing a line in the sand and doing everything tomorrow. It's not. I don't expect to see fruition of the Convention in my lifetime. Now I know that would be a bolder statement if I were I younger woman, but even when I was forty I didn't expect to see much movement in terms of the Convention in my lifetime. It's a big transformative project. But it's got to happen. It's about changing the way we think and what we do in regards to impairment. And COVID has really demonstrated that. You've got a whole group of people that is devalued, and not included, and are living a miserable existence for the most part.

*Laura*: And the CRPD was meant to be an antidote to that. It's meant to be principled, to be visionary.

*Rosemary*: Exactly. And that's why I see education as a real cornerstone right, because educating kids together sets their trajectory up to expect an inclusive society. Keeping kids segregated reinforces that difference and so when they get to segregated workplaces, that makes sense to them, because they're not expecting diversity. If you go to school and sit in a classroom with a whole bunch of kids that really do reflect the broad spectrum of the human condition, then you just expect that to be a normal representation in life.

*Laura*: So in a sense, if we do the right things now, then 10 or 20 years down the track…

*Rosemary*: …The new generation should look very different.

## References


Barnes, C. 1991. *Disabled People in Britain and Discrimination: A Case for Anti-discrimination Legislation*. C. Hurst & Company.

Beco, G. de. 2016. Transition to Inclusive Education Systems According to the Convention on the Rights of Persons with Disabilities. *Nordic Journal of Human Rights*, *34*(1), 40–59.

Commonwealth of Australia. 2011. *National Disability Strategy 2010–2020: An Initiative of the Council of Australian Governments*. Council of Australian Governments, Canberra.

Degener, T. 2017. 10 Years of Convention on the Rights of Persons with Disabilities. *Netherlands Quarterly of Human Rights*, *35*(3), 152–157.

Degener, T., & Begg, A. 2017. From Invisible Citizens to Agents of Change: A Shoty History from the Struggle for the Recognition of the Rights of Persons with Disabilities at the United Nations. In V. Della Fina, R. Cera, & G. Palmisano (Eds.), *The United Nations Convention on the Rights of Persons with Disabilities* (pp. 1–39). Springer.

Durell, S. 2014, December 10. How the Social Model of Disability Evolved. *Nursing Times: NT; London, 110*(50), 20–22.

Emerson, E., Madden, R., Graham, H., Llewellyn, G., Hatton, C., & Robertson, J. 2011. The Health of Disabled People and the Social Determinants of Health. *Public Health, 125*(3), 145–147.

Flynn, E. 2011. *From Rhetoric to Action: Implementing the UN Convention on the Rights of Persons with Disabilities*. Cambridge University Press.

Fougeyrollas, P., & Grenier, Y. 2018. Monitoring Disability Policies and Legislation towards Effective Exercise of Rights to Equality and Inclusive Access for Persons with Disabilities: The Case of the Quebec Model. *Societies, 8*(2), 41.

Frier, A., Barnett, F., Devine, S., & Barker, R. 2018. Understanding Disability and the 'Social Determinants of Health': How Does Disability Affect Peoples' Social Determinants of Health? *Disability and Rehabilitation, 40*(5), 538–547.

Harpur, P. 2012. Embracing the New Disability Rights Paradigm: The Importance of the Convention on the Rights of Persons with Disabilities. *Disability & Society, 27*(1), 1–14.

Hendriks, A. 2007. UN Convention on the Rights of Persons with Disabilities. *European Journal of Health Law, 14*(3), 273–280.

Kanter, A. S. 2019. Do Human Rights Treaties Matter? The Case for the United Nations Convention on the Rights of People with Disabilities. *Vanderbilt Journal of Transnational Law, 52*(3), 577–610.

Kayess, R., & French, P. 2008. Out of Darkness into Light? Introducing the Convention on the Rights of Persons with Disabilities. *Human Rights Law Review, 8*(1), 1–34.

Lang, R. 2009. The United Nations Convention on the Right and Dignities for Persons with Disability: A Panacea for Ending Disability Discrimination? *Alter, 3*(3), 266–285.

Lawson, A. 2017. The European Union and the Convention on the Rights of Persons with Disabilities: Complexities, Challenges and Opportunities. In V. Della Fina, R. Cera, & G. Palmisano (Eds.), *The United Nations Convention on the Rights of Persons with Disabilities: A Commentary* (pp. 61–76). Springer.

Laufey, L., Traustadóttir, R., & Rice, J. G. 2018. Achieving Disability Equality: Empowering Disabled People to Take the Lead. *Social Inclusion, 6*(1), 1–8.

Madden, R., Glozier, N., Mpofu, E., & Llewellyn, G. 2011. Eligibility, the ICF and the UN Convention: Australian perspectives. *BMC Public Health, 11*(4), S6.

Mahomed, F., Lord, J. E., & Stein, M. A. 2019. Transposing the Convention on the Rights of Persons with Disabilities in Africa: The Role of Disabled Peoples' Organisations. *African Journal of International and Comparative Law, 27*(3), 335–358.

Malbon, E., Alexander, D., Carey, G., Reeders, D., Green, C., Dickinson, H., & Kavanagh, A. 2019. Adapting to a Marketised System: Network Analysis of a Personalisation Scheme in Early Implementation. *Health & Social Care in the Community, 27*(1), 191–198.

Milner, A., Shields, M., King, T. L., Aitken, Z., LaMontagne, A. D., & Kavanagh, A. M. 2019. Disabling Working Environments and Mental Health: A commentary. *Disability and Health Journal, 12*(4), 537–541. https://doi.org/10.1016/j.dhjo.2019.06.002.

Mittler, P. 2015. The UN Convention on the Rights of Persons with Disabilities: Implementing a Paradigm Shift. *Journal of Policy and Practice in Intellectual Disabilities, 12*(2), 79–89.

Quinlivan, S. 2012. The United Nations Convention on the Rights of Persons with Disabilities: An introduction. *ERA Forum, 13*(1), 71–85.

Umeasiegbu, V. I., Bishop, M., & Mpofu, E. 2013. The Conventional and Unconventional About Disability Conventions: A Reflective Analysis of United Nations Convention on the Rights of Persons With Disabilities. *Rehabilitation Research, Policy, and Education; Athens, 27*(1), 58–72.

Umeasiegbu, V. I., Mpofu, E., & Johnson, E. 2012. Disability and Rehabilitation in the International Context. In P. J. Toriello, M. L. Bishop, & P. D. Rumrill (Eds.), *New Directions in Rehabilitation Counseling: Creative Responses to Professional, Clinical, and Educational Challenges*. (Sage CA: Los Angeles, CA). Aspen Professional Services.

United Nations Department of Economic and Social Affairs. 2019. *Disability and Development Report: Realizing the Sustainable Development Goals by, for and with Persons with Disabilities*. New York. https://www.un.org/development/desa/disabilities/wp-content/uploads/sites/15/2019/07/disability-report-chapter2.pdf.

WHO. 2018. *Disability and Health*. World Health Organisation, https://www.who.int/news-room/fact-sheets/detail/disability-and-health.

CHAPTER 2

# Toward Inclusive Equality: Ten Years of the Human Rights Model of Disability in the Work of the UN Committee on the Rights of Persons with Disabilities

*Theresia Degener and María Gómez-Carrillo de Castro*

"The purpose of the present Convention is to promote, protect and ensure the full and equal enjoyment of all human rights and fundamental freedoms by all persons with disabilities, and to promote respect for their inherent dignity."

Article 1 of the UN Convention on the Rights of Persons with Disabilities

T. Degener (✉)
Protestant University of Applied Sciences, Bochum, Germany
e-mail: degener@evh-bochum.de

M. G.-C. de Castro
Institute of Social and Political Sciences, University of Lisbon, Lisbon, Portugal
e-mail: mariagomez-carrillo@edu.ulisboa.pt



F. Felder et al. (eds.), *Disability Law and Human Rights*, Palgrave Studies in Disability and International Development, https://doi.org/10.1007/978-3-030-86545-0_2

## Introduction

Equality underlines dignity and is a principle of the UN Convention on the Rights of Persons with Disabilities (CRPD) that informs all other rights. Discrimination not only undermines the enjoyment of civil and political rights, but also the enjoyment of economic, social and cultural rights. The CRPD crystalizes the indivisibility, interrelatedness and interdependency of human rights, overcoming the traditional division of civil and political rights and cultural, social and economic rights, and recognizes people with disabilities as full subjects of rights and right holders.

The Committee on the Rights of Persons with Disabilities (the Committee or CRPD Committee), through its General Comments, guidelines, country reports and individual complaints, has contributed to the evolution of the interpretation of legal meaning of equality. General Comment No. 6 specifically covers non-discrimination and exemplifies the breadth of the principle and rule of non-discrimination and equality.

This chapter will outline the work of the CRPD Committee on equality, with special attention to the human rights model of disability as basis of the work of the CRPD Committee and introduce the concept of inclusive equality.

## The Convention on the Rights of Persons with Disabilities as Hallmark

The CRPD is champion among United Nations' human rights treaties with its speedy record of ratifications. As of 2020, 181 countries have ratified it. No other treaty has been ratified by such a large number of states in such a short time. The involvement of civil society and persons with disabilities during the negotiations was extraordinary and an improved practice from previous experiences at the United Nations (UN) (art. 44 CRPD). No other human rights treaty has a comparable emphasis on participation, notably of organizations of persons with disabilities. The CRPD is the first human rights treaty to include a duty to involve civil society in the implementation and monitoring of the treaty (art. 4[3]; 33[3] CRPD), to legally recognize the concept of multiple discrimination (art. 6 CRPD) and to enshrine an accessibility norm (Broderick 2020, 393). Additionally, the CRPD extends the definition of discrimination in international law by including "denial of reasonable accommodation" as a form of discrimination (art. 2 CRPD).

Disability organizations around the world spread words on the new inclusive freedom and inclusive equality agenda that the CRPD brought to the table of human rights and disability policy. The motto of the drafting of the convention "Nothing about us without us" became the guiding principle of future implementation (Paré 2019, 209; Lord and Stein 2017, 732). At national and at international level, significant efforts are made to include persons with disabilities as experts and their representative organizations in the implementation and monitoring process. States parties reports are drafted in consultation with disabled persons' organizations, and the two international bodies of the treaty, the CRPD Committee and the annual States parties Conference, include a high number of experts with disabilities. The States parties Conference on the CRPD does not only elect the independent experts of the treaty body, but always has a three days agenda full of substantial issues related to law and policy of the treaty, such as accessibility, legal capacity, gender discrimination or inclusive development.

## The Committee on the Rights of Persons with Disabilities

The CRPD Committee, which was initially established in 2009 with 12 independent experts, was enlarged to 18 experts in 2011 after the 80th ratification of the Convention. Since the beginning, the vast majority of its experts have been disabled persons. This composition of treaty body experts brought new challenges to UN administration, who had never paid much attention to accessibility. Ramps and lifts for wheelchairs had to be installed at UN headquarter buildings in Geneva and New York, websites had to be made accessible for blind and visually impaired persons, sign language interpreters and captioning had to be provided.

Travel rules had to be changed to allow independent experts travel with personal assistants. The CRPD Committee also contributed to green policy innovations by being the first treaty body to adopt a green bureau strategy, meaning that all documents were produced electronically and printing paper was abolished.

The Committee started with two meetings for 5 days each in 2009. Because of its high number of ratifications and the comparably short meeting time, the backlog of States parties reports review very soon reached seven years in 2012, which was called the highest among all treaty bodies. The meeting time was thus extended to currently 10 weeks in 2018 as a result of the treaty body strengthening process.

When the 20th session closed in September 2018, the Committee had reviewed about 70 initial States parties reports. While it is commonly understood that disability only triggers economic, social and cultural rights, the constructive dialogues with States parties focused on both sets of human rights. The freedom and equality agenda is as important as the values of solidarity, inclusion and social protection.

## Disability and Human Rights

It has been repeatedly emphasized that the CRPD did not create new human rights but tailored the existing catalogue of international human rights to the context of disability (Paré 2019). The right to freedom of expression and opinion as enshrined in article 21 is a good example of this tailoring. It copies the text of article 19 Universal Declaration of Human Rights on freedom of expression and opinion and adds to it disability-specific aspects, such as the right to accessible information, the right to use sign language, Braille and other modes and forms of communication.

Tailoring the existing catalogue of international human rights to the context of disability additionally led to more interdependence and interrelatedness of both categories of human rights (Paré 2019). Article 19 CRPD on living independently and being included in the community enshrines both, social and cultural rights as well as civil rights. The dialogues with States parties reflect this modern understanding of human rights. Dialogues on initial States parties reports cover all rights enshrined in the treaty. From these dialogues, some issues are identified as particularly challenging for States parties in the implementation of the CRPD. Most of them are the same issues which had been major conflicts during the treaty negotiation. Among these are denial of legal capacity, institutionalization, segregation in education and employment and, above all, the human rights model of disability. The latter reflects a new understanding of disability as an issue of human rights rather than being merely an issue of medical rehabilitation and social welfare. The human rights model of disability negates the assumption that persons with disabilities need to be institutionalized or segregated from the rest of society because of their impairments. It further condemns the idea that impairment might limit a disabled person's right to legal capacity and assumes that all disabled persons are rights holders and that human rights cannot be conditioned upon physical, mental or health status. The human rights model of disability has far-reaching implications for states parties, and thus, they struggle with a number of articles in the treaty, e.g., article 12 on the right to be equal standing before the law, article 14 on the right to liberty and security, article 19 on independent living and article 24 on inclusive education. Article 12 requires States parties to abolish traditional guardianship and mental-health laws which are based on a system of substituted decision-making and forced treatment. In all its concluding observations, the Committee has emphasized that substituted decision-making needs to be replaced by supported decision-making based on the preferences and will of the disabled person. Article 14 prohibits impairment-based detention such as forced hospitalization. It further outlaws other forms of disability-specific forms of deprivation of liberty, such as denial of freedom of movement due to legal guardianship. Again, many countries have legislation that legitimizes this practice which is commonly applied in mental-health settings and in the context of services for intellectually disabled persons. Article 19 provides that each and every disabled person, irrespective of his or her impairment, has the right to choose where and with whom to live in the community. It denounces institutional settings as a barrier to independent living and as a form of discrimination. The right to inclusive education as enshrined in article 24 is a particular challenge to those countries which have a dense system of special education schools which are incompatible with the right to inclusive education.

## General Comments

The CRPD Committee has adopted a number of general comments in order to address these issues. All of them pivot around the idea of equality and non-discrimination, focusing on specific aspects of these principles. General Comment No. 1 (2012) interprets article 12 as not allowing any form of guardianship or interdiction or other forms of substituted decision-making. In combination with the guidelines on the right to liberty and security (art. 14 CRPD) (CRPD Committee 2017c), it becomes clear that forced medical treatment and forced institutionalization are a violation of the CRPD.

General Comment No. 2 focuses on accessibility (art. 9 CRPD), which is key to guaranteeing equality (Broderick 2020). According to some experts in the field is the heart of the convention together with its non-discrimination clause of article 5 (ibid.; Ferri 2010). In the context of disability, access to the built environment, to public transportation and to information and communication is a precondition and essential for the realization of all human rights. While most states parties have accepted the importance of this provision, implementation rarely covers all three areas adequately.

General Comment No. 3 addresses human rights of disabled women and girls (art. 6 CRPD) and four additional General Comments cover inclusive education (art. 24 CRPD), independent living within the community (art. 19 CRPD), equality and non-discrimination (art. 5 CRPD) and meaningful participation (art. 4[3] and 33[3] CRPD) (CRPD Committee 2016, 2017b, 2018a, b).

## The Disability Model of the CRPD

The CRPD reflects the shift of understanding of disability from medical and charity models of disability that focus on personal impairments as the cause of social exclusion and persons with disabilities as objects to be "protected", to the human rights model of disability. The preamble[1] and the definition of persons with disabilities in article 1[2] reflect this new understanding according to which disability is a social construct and that it is the barriers *within* society, rather than personal impairments, that cause exclusion.

The CRPD Committee endorsed and stressed the importance of this new understanding. In its first statement, the Committee highlighted the importance of immediate transition from the medical model to the human rights model of disability (General Assembly 2011, Annex IX para. 3). At several occasions, the Committee noted that the failure to understand and implement the human rights model of disability is the major cause of exclusion of persons with disabilities in society. For instance, this is

[1] The preamble (e) recognizes that disability is an evolving concept and that disability "*results from the interaction between persons with impairments and attitudinal and environmental barriers that hinders their full and effective participation in society on an equal basis with others*".

[2] In article 1 persons with disabilities are defined as "*those who have long-term physical, mental, intellectual or sensory impairments which in interaction with various barriers may hinder their full and effective participation in society on an equal basis with others*".

reflected in the difficulties States parties have to ensure access to inclusive education for persons with disabilities (CRPD Committee 2016, para. 4[a]). In General Comment No. 4 (2016) on the right to inclusive education (ibid.), the Committee stressed that States parties should adopt the human rights model of disability (ibid., para. 44), implement legislation based on the human rights model of disability (ibid., para. 62), and organize trainings based on the human rights model of disability (ibid., para. 36).

Over time the Committee brought specific clarification on how States parties must understand and implement the human rights model of disability. General Comment No. 5 on living independently and being included in the community highlighted that the human rights model of disability "*does not allow the exclusion of persons with disabilities* [from society] *for any reason, including the kind and amount of support services required*" (CRPD Committee 2017b, para. 60). In General Comment No. 6 on equality and non-discrimination, the Committee reiterates its position from its 2014 views on communication *S.C. v. Brazil* (CRPD 2014) according to which the human rights-based model of disability requires taking into account the diversity of persons with disabilities as "*disability is one of several layers of identity*" (CRPD 2018a, para. 9).

The human rights model of disability is consistently mentioned in the concluding observations of the Committee under articles 1–4 of the Convention, and more infrequently under article 8 on awareness raising, article 14 on liberty and security (in particular in relation to deinstitutionalization), article 25 on health and article 28 on adequate standard of living and social protection.[3]

## The Human Rights Model

The human rights model emerged from the CRPD Committee's responses to the States parties' difficulties in grasping equality of persons with disabilities and preparatory work (Quinn and Degener 2002). Many of the States parties reports reflect this difficulty and an understanding based on the traditional medical model of disability. During the discussions of the CRPD, the social model served as philosophical basis to the

[3] Other articles under which the Committee mentioned the human rights model of disability in one or a couple of concluding observations are articles 7, 12, 15, 19, 24, 27, 31 and 32.

treaty negotiations (Lawson and Beckett 2020). There was a clear rejection of the medical model (Trömel 2009). The CRPD, however, goes further and, from the outset of equality and non-discrimination, codifies the human rights model of disability and sets out an agenda for change (Degener 2017).

The social model of disability was coined by Mike Oliver, and differentiates between impairment and disability, which is described as a social construct, that results from the interaction between the person and the environment and society's response to the impairment. The social model constitutes an expression of disabled people's activism, born within the Union of the Physically Impaired Against Segregation (UPIAS) in UK (Terzi 2004). The social model focuses on the barriers and exclusion created by society. It speaks in terms of oppression, political identity and differentiating impairment from disability. The model has been described as open and flexible to respond to different contexts (Lawson and Beckett 2020). It has also been criticized for unilaterally defining disability as socially caused, for downplaying the role of other dimensions in disability, e.g., cultural processes, by focusing heavily on the economic or materialist aspect of exclusion or minimizing the effects of impairment. Following this critique, it is taken that disablement will not affect people with different impairments in the same way. Postmodernist authors have also contested the social model and argued that the concept of impairment too is socially constructed (Carlson 2016, 541). Feminist philosophers found it problematic to view disability solely as a social construction, as it denies the experiences of both people living with pain and of those living with cognitive impairments (ibid.; O'Donnovan 2013; Kittay 1999). There is also a feminist proposal of an account for relational autonomy, recognizing the existence of vulnerability, dependency and *inter*dependency (Carlson 2016). Various feminist scholars (Morris 1991; Wendell 1996; Thomas 1999, 14 cit. in Terzi 2004) have also reconsidered impairment by accepting and building on the social model in various degrees (Terzi 2004).

The human rights model has been used by the CRPD Committee to guide States parties through dialogue and recommendations. At the heart of this model is the recognition of human inherent dignity, guaranteeing equality for persons with disabilities in the full enjoyment of human rights (Degener 2017). It sets out values for disability policy, while the social model proposes an analysis of the systemic exclusion and discrimination of persons with disabilities, without providing for a roadmap to guarantee full enjoyment of human rights for persons with disabilities (ibid.). Under the human rights model, impairment is recognized and valued as part of human diversity and human dignity (ibid.). Equality is firstly and foremost a recognition of dignity, humanity and personhood, and the human rights model includes first and second generation of human rights (ibid.). It does not explain disability; instead, it provides a framework to conceptualize agency, rights and the content of rights. The human rights model builds on the social model, which exposes structural discrimination, but recognizes different experiences of impairment and disability. It is this recognition of diversity in humankind that allows the human rights model of disability to house different epistemic and political claims from people with disabilities. While the social model looks beyond the individual and to the social dimension of impairment and disability, the human rights model takes into account the social dimension, but also looks at the individual and recognizes it as full subject of rights.

## CRPD as an Equality Treaty

The CRPD has been drawn from existing treaties (Degener 2016), which embody different classifications of human rights. The International Covenant on Civil and Political Rights (ICCPR) and the International Covenant on Economic, Social and Cultural Rights (ICESCR) are considered the core group of human rights,[4] while the second group[5] are considered group focused with a different legal character, as stronger anti-discrimination instruments or, in the case of the Convention on the Rights of the Child (CRC), as a more holistic treaty (ibid.). From the early negotiations, the CRPD was conceived as a hybrid of these two categories.

Equality and anti-discrimination are at the heart of the CRPD. Equality constitutes a right in itself and an overarching principle and is understood as equality of opportunity (Paré 2019). Throughout the text, every single substantive article includes an equality or anti-discrimination reference

[4] Together with the Universal Declaration of Human Rights of 1948.

[5] The second group includes: the Convention on the Elimination of all Form of Racial Discrimination (CERD), the Convention Against All Forms of Discrimination Against Women (CEDAW), and the Convention on the Rights of the Child (CRC).

(Degener 2016). Similar to the International Convention on the Elimination of All Forms of Racial Discrimination (ICERD), the CRPD takes the concept of equality further (Paré 2019). States parties are required to take positive measures in public and private life (Degener 2016), indirectly requiring private actors to take action too (Broderick 2020).

During the negotiations, there was consensus that the CRPD should not create new human rights or special rights for disabled persons and that the goal was to provide human rights for disabled persons on an equal basis with the general population.[6] The social model had a strong influence during the negotiations, which translated into non-discrimination and equality as a way of superseding the medical model. Disability is recognized as a social construct—disablement—which effects people with an impairment. This definition in turn places the duties for action on society. The CRPD, however, expanded the meanings of equality and non-discrimination within international human rights law to ensure that people with disabilities have equal standing within human rights (Degener 2016).

## General Comment No. 6 on Equality and Non-Discrimination

General Comment No. 6 introduces the inclusive equality model as an innovation to international human rights law. During its drafting, the CRPD Committee received more than 70 submissions and the Day of General Discussion was held in Geneva in August 2017. Based on the debates within the Committee, the submissions received and the Day of General Discussion the General Comment No. 6 was adopted in March 2018 at the 19th Session of the Committee. The 19-page document contains 8 sections with three main parts. The introductory part gives an overview of the development of international disability equality law, the models of disability and equality and the legal character of non-discrimination and equality. The main part elaborates on the normative content of all four subparagraphs of article 5 and deriving obligations of States parties, on the relation between article 5 and other CRPD articles. The final part gives guidelines for implementing article 5 at a national level.

[6] Note that this is still disputed (e.g. Broderick 2020).

## Inclusive Equality as a New Equality Concept

Inclusive equality is introduced as a new term in General Comment No. 6 which goes beyond formal and substantive equality models. International law is constantly evolving, and so can the legal meanings of rights (Paré 2019). For instance, the interpretation by the CESCR Committee to the right to an adequate standard of living now includes a right to independent living for disabled persons (art. 11 ICESCR; Degener 2017). The term "inclusive equality" can be found in earlier literature (Sheppard 2004). Sally Witcher has coined the term "inclusive equality" with regard to social policy theory (Witcher 2013) and Colleen Sheppard has elaborated on inclusive equality in the context of education rights (Sheppard 2004). General Comment No. 6 describes the concept inclusive equality as

> a new model of equality developed throughout the Convention. It embraces a substantive model of equality and extends and elaborates on the content of equality in: (a) a fair redistributive dimension to address socioeconomic disadvantages; (b) a recognition dimension to combat stigma, stereotyping, prejudice and violence and to recognize the dignity of human beings and their intersectionality; (c) a participative dimension to reaffirm the social nature of people as members of social groups and the full recognition of humanity through inclusion in society; and (d) an accommodating dimension to make space for difference as a matter of human dignity. The Convention is based on inclusive equality. (CRPD Committee 2018a, para. 11)

These four dimensions are almost identical with the components of the transformative model of equality developed by Sandra Fredman and her research team (Fredman et al., n.d.). The Committee was significantly inspired by this submission. The term "transformative equality" was not chosen because it was felt that it could be misunderstood by States parties. The term "transformation" does not direct the way in which society has to be transformed. Transformation means structural change relating to the systems of our societies. However, structural changes may lead to an extension of rights or to a limitation of rights. This was a lesson learned from "the structural adjustment programs" which were the central component of development policy introduced by the UN financial institutions in the 1980s and is now used most prominently by the European Union as a response to the 2008 financial crisis. As

Rodwan Abouharb and David Cingranelli have shown in their landmark publication "Human Rights and Structural Adjustment", these policies undermined economic, social and cultural rights in developing countries, led to more civil conflicts and more repression of human rights (Abouharb and Cingranelli 2007). The Committee felt that the term "transformative equality" could be misunderstood as allowing "structural change" in terms of legitimizing social cutbacks.

During the inquiry procedure undertaken by the Committee with regard to welfare reforms in the UK, the Committee found the reform had a disproportionate impact on disabled people. The reforms were justified in the context of austerity measures to achieve fiscal and budgetary policy consolidation. The report on the inquiry found there was reliable evidence that the threshold of grave or systematic violations of the rights of persons with disabilities had been met (CRPD Committee 2017d). These results were discussed during the dialogue with the UK Government before the initial State party report in 2017. In its Concluding Observations, the Committee expressed concern about the impact of austerity measures and anti-poverty initiatives introduced as a consequence of the financial crisis in 2008/2009, the negative impact on the standard of living for persons with disabilities of, among others, the reductions in social support, unemployment allowance, the insufficient social protection and support (CRPD 2017a). After this inquiry and State party review with major focus on austerity measures, the Committee felt that the term "transformative equality" might be misunderstood. Note that Fredman never wrote about transformative equality as a concept which could be misinterpreted as legitimizing structural adjustment measures of this sort. However, the Committee had ample opportunity to realize how often terms of the Convention are misunderstood. During its first decade, it reviewed more than 70 States parties reports and the dialogues revealed how often the term "reasonable accommodation" was misunderstood as a demand on housing policy. Therefore, the Committee opted for "inclusive equality" as a more appropriate term. This means that inclusive equality differs from other equality models and Fredman's four dimensions. The difference between inclusive and other equality measures is addressed in paragraph 10:

> Equalization of opportunities, as a general principle of the Convention under article 3, marks a significant development from a formal model of equality to a substantive model of equality. Formal equality seeks to combat

> direct discrimination by treating persons in a similar situation similarly. It may help to combat negative stereotyping and prejudices, but it cannot offer solutions for the 'dilemma of difference', as it does not consider and embrace differences among human beings. Substantive equality, by contrast, also seeks to address structural and indirect discrimination and takes into account power relations. It acknowledges that the 'dilemma of difference' entails both ignoring and acknowledging differences among human beings in order to achieve equality. (CRPD 2018a, para. 10)

Thus, inclusive equality is to be distinguished from formal and substantive equality. The latter has been developed by scholars of feminist legal theory as a critique of formal equality (MacKinnon 2012, 1). Inclusive equality builds on legal feminist and disability studies and encompasses both procedural and substantive dimensions of equality rights (Sheppard 2004). It is conceived as a necessarily systemic and relational concept (ibid.).

Inclusive equality goes beyond substantive equality in that it encapsulates the four dimensions mentioned earlier. The first is the fair redistributive dimension to address socioeconomic disadvantages. The General Comment addresses this in relation to poverty and in relation to specific measures under article 5(4). As regards article 28 on adequate standard of living and social protection the General Comment No. 6 reads:

> poverty is both a compounding factor and the result of multiple discrimination. Failure to implement the right of persons with disabilities to an adequate standard of living for themselves and their families is contrary to the objectives of the Convention. This failure is particularly worrying with regard to persons with disabilities living in extreme poverty or destitution. To reach an adequate standard of living comparable to others, persons with disabilities typically have additional expenses. This represents a particular disadvantage for children or older women with disabilities who live in extreme poverty and destitution. States parties should take effective measures to enable persons with disabilities to cover the additional expenses linked to disability. States parties are required to take immediate steps to provide persons with disabilities living in extreme poverty and destitution with a core minimum in terms of adequate food, clothing and housing. (CRPD 2018a, para. 68)

In article 5(4) the Convention refers to specific measures as "necessary to accelerate or achieve de facto equality of persons with disabilities", which shall not be considered discrimination under the terms of the Convention.

General Comment No. 6 describes these measures as positive or affirmative measures similar to special measures mentioned in article 4 CEDAW or article 1(4) CERD, e.g., adopting or maintaining certain advantages in favor of an underrepresented or marginalized group. They are usually temporary measures in nature, although in some instances permanent specific measures are required, depending on context and circumstances, including by virtue of a particular impairment or the structural barriers of society. Specific measures include *"outreach and support programs, allocation and/or reallocation of resources, targeted recruitment, hiring and promotion, quota systems, advancement and empowerment measures, as well as respite care and technological aids"* (CRPD 2018a, para. 28).

The second dimension combats stigma, stereotyping, prejudice and violence and recognizes the dignity of human beings and their intersectionality, which is covered by at least nine paragraphs in General Comment No. 6 (CRPD 2018a, paras. 6, 29, 19, 39, 45, 56, 73, 52, 55). It reminds readers that the term "dignity" appears in the CPRD more often than in any other UN human rights convention (ibid., para. 6). Two articles in the CRPD relate most obviously to this second dimension: article 8 on awareness raising and article 16 on freedom from violence, exploitation and abuse. With regard to awareness raising, General Comment No. 6 reminds States parties, that:

> *Discrimination cannot be combated without awareness-raising among all sectors of government and society. Thus, any non-discrimination and equality measure must be accompanied by adequate awareness-raising measures and measures to change or abolish compounded pejorative disability stereotypes and negative attitudes. In addition, violence, harmful practices and prejudices must be tackled by awareness-raising campaigns. States parties should undertake measures to encourage, inter alia, the media to portray persons with disabilities in a manner consistent with the purpose of the Convention and to modify harmful views of persons with disabilities, such as those that portray them unrealistically as being dangerous to themselves and others, or sufferers and dependent objects of care without autonomy who are unproductive economic and social burdens to society.* (ibid., para. 39)

In relation to article 16 and other provisions, the General Comment outlines disability-specific forms of violence, such as restraint or corrective disability treatment (ibid., para. 56) and intersectional violence, such as sexual violence, abuse and exploitation (ibid., para. 45). Harassment and other forms of violence, such as hate crimes, are included in the definition of discrimination (ibid., para. 19). Intersectional discrimination is defined and addressed in several places of the General Comment (ibid., paras. 19, 22, 32). The CRPD is the first international human rights convention specifically recognizing multiple discrimination in relation to disabled women (art. 6 CRPD) and the Committee has provided guidance on this article in General Comment No. 3 and General Comment No. 6. Both define intersectionality and emphasize the importance on training and awareness raising on this complex appearance of discrimination.

Specific measures undertaken with the best intent to help disabled people are well-known practices of de facto discrimination. This is why General Comment No. 6 emphasizes that

> *specific measures adopted by States parties under article 5 (4) of the Convention must be consistent with all its principles and provisions. In particular, they must not result in perpetuation of isolation, segregation, stereotyping, stigmatization or otherwise discrimination against persons with disabilities. Thus, States parties must consult closely with and actively involve representative organizations of persons with disabilities when they adopt specific measures.* (CRPD 2018a, para. 29)

Turning to the third dimension, the participative dimension, General Comment No. 6 reaffirms the social nature of disabled people as members of social groups and the full recognition of humanity through inclusion in society in various parts of the document. Participation of disabled persons via individuals or representative organizations is demanded in relation to research on disability discrimination and equality rights (ibid., para. 35) as well as with respect to access to justice (ibid., para. 52). In addition to these explicit references to collective participation of disabled persons, the CRPD's equality concept has a clear group reference in two of its provisions and in its legal concepts of accessibility and reasonable accommodation. The most prominent provisions are articles 4(3) and 33(3) CRPD, which demand the meaningful involvement of disabled people and their representative organizations in the implementation and the monitoring of the Convention. These provisions are the codification of the slogan "Nothing about us without us". During the first decade, the Committee has seen that most States parties take note of these participation obligations, but that they often misunderstand their dimension and scope. Therefore, the Committee has adopted General Comment

No. 7 on the participation of persons with disabilities, including children with disabilities, through their representative organizations, in the implementation and monitoring of the Convention.

The participative dimension of the inclusive equality concept is further comprised in the legal concepts of accessibility (art. 9 CRPD) and reasonable accommodation (art. 5[3] CRPD). Accessibility and reasonable accommodation are both requisites and basic elements of equality rights. Accessibility is conceived by some as "*a gateway to all other human rights*" (Broderick 2020) or as a human right per se (Lawson 2014, 380). Removing barriers in the built environment, in communication and information systems, in public transportation and other services is of paramount importance for combating disability-based exclusion. Adapting the environment by providing reasonable accommodation is part of anti-discrimination duties under the Convention. While both duties may result in the same measures, their legal character is quite different. The Committee has repeatedly explained both legal concepts in General Comment No. 2 on article 9 and in General Comment No. 6. Whereas accessibility obligations are group-oriented and impose *ex ante* duties, reasonable accommodation duties are individual-oriented and constitute "an *ex nunc* duty", which means that the right is enforceable from the moment a person needs it in a specific situation (Broderick 2020). Accessibility duties need to be laid down in general regulations which must be negotiated with representative disabled people's organizations. Obligations in relation to reasonable accommodation are negotiated with the disabled individual, taking into account the context of the situation to establish the content and limit. The group-oriented legal character of accessibility acknowledges that disabled persons are members of social groups and these groups need to participate in negotiating inclusive equality. The social group may be determined by the kind of impairment or by other factors, such as age, gender or sexual orientation and identity. It is not enough to only acknowledge disabled persons as members of social groups. Full recognition of disabled persons as part of humanity demands to respect their individual human dignity. In the context of impairment respect for autonomy of choice in relation to how to cope with this impairment is significant. One blind person may choose to use a guide dog, the other may want to rely on a white cane. One person with mobility impairment may choose to use a wheelchair, the other may want to use crutches and braces. No representative organization has the mandate to take away these personal decisions. As a result, accessibility standards may help to negotiate reasonable accommodation duties; however, they must not narrowly prescribe them.

This would conflict with the fourth inclusive equality dimension, the accommodating dimension to make space for difference as a matter of human dignity. General Comment No. 6 distinguishes the obligation to provide reasonable accommodation from the concept of disproportionate or undue burden, from specific measures and individual support as well as from procedural accommodations and accessibility (CRPD 2018a, paras. 24, 25). It further elaborates precisely on the steps which have to be taken in the process of negotiating reasonable accommodation (ibid., para. 26).

## Inclusive Equality and Models of Disability

Inclusive equality goes beyond substantive and formal equality models, which corresponds to the human rights model of disability. General Comment No. 6 describes this new model of disability as follows:

> *The human rights model of disability recognizes that disability is a social construct and impairments must not be taken as a legitimate ground for the denial or restriction of human rights. It acknowledges that disability is one of several layers of identity. Hence, disability laws and policies must take the diversity of persons with disabilities into account. It also recognizes that human rights are interdependent, interrelated and indivisible.* (CRPD 2018a, para. 9)

The "human rights model" of disability is a term which initially the Committee used interchangeably with "social model of disability". More recently, however, the Committee has replaced the social model with the human rights model of disability. The three models of equality discussed here correspond with three models of disability. Inclusive equality parallels the human rights model of disability, substantive equality matches the social model of disability and formal equality is consistent with the medical model of disability. Inclusive equality relates to the human rights model because both models are holistic models which address structural and power-related disadvantages and oppression, recognize social and individual identities and take into account different dimensions of equality and discrimination.

Formal equality and the medical model of disability are reductionist concepts. The medical model of disability reduces disabled persons to their impairments and formal equality may be utilized to legitimize discrimination. Impairment is simply taken as a legitimate and objective reason for denying disabled persons the right to inclusive education, or the right to vote, or the right to sign a contract or the right to marry. The medical model of disability makes formal equality look "just".

Substantive equality matches the social model of disability, because both are based on the assumption that equality and disability are social constructs which need to be analyzed from the viewpoint of human variety and human contingency.

## Conclusion

Inclusive equality acknowledges the fundamental moral equality of persons and allows for a more adequate response from a human rights perspective on a social and an individual level. It values human diversity and recognizes disability as a layer within the multiple identities a person may have. The human rights model of disability lays out a roadmap for change, including both categories of rights (social, cultural, economic and civil and political rights). Further, it recognizes the inherent value of the person and equality in access to full enjoyment of rights, regardless of existing impairments. Inclusive equality raises the equality standards, with far-reaching implications on all other rights. It epitomizes the interrelatedness, interdependency and indivisibility of human rights and searches for the flourishment of each human being, calling on States parties and inviting private actors to embrace human diversity and mutually recognize each other.

## References

Abouharb M. Rodwan, and David Cingranelli. 2007. *Human Rights and Structural Adjustment*. Cambridge: Cambridge University Press.

Broderick, Andrea. 2020. "Of Rights and Obligations: The Birth of Accessibility." *The International Journal of Human Rights* 24 (4): 393–413.

Carlson, Licia. 2016. "Feminist Approaches to Cognitive Disability." *Philosophy Compass* 11 (10): 541–53.

Committee on the Rights of Persons with Disabilities. 2014. *Communication No. 10/2013*. CRPD/C/12/D/10/2013.

Committee on the Rights of Persons with Disabilities. 2016. *General Comment No. 4 (2016) on the Right to Inclusive Education*. CRPD/C/GC/4.

Committee on the Rights of Persons with Disabilities. 2017a. *Concluding Observations on the Initial Report of the United Kingdom of Great Britain and Northern Ireland*. CRPD/C/GBR/CO 1.

Committee on the Rights of Persons with Disabilities. 2017b. *General Comment No. 5 (2017) on Living Independently and Being Included in the Community*. CRPD/C/GC/5.

Committee on the Rights of Persons with Disabilities. 2017c. "Guidelines on the Right to Liberty and Security of Persons with Disabilities." In *Report of the Committee on the Rights of Persons with Disabilities. Thirteenth Session (25 March–17 April 2015), Fourteenth Session (17 August–4 September 2015), Fifteenth Session (29 March–21 April 2016), Sixteenth Session (15 August–2 September 2016)*, edited by General Assembly, Annex 16–21. A/72/55. New York: United Nations.

Committee on the Rights of Persons with Disabilities. 2017d. *Inquiry Concerning the United Kingdom of Great Britain and Northern Ireland Carried Out by the Committee Under Article 6 of the Optional Protocol to the Convention. Report of the Committee*. CRPD/C/15/R.2/Rev.2 (2016).

Committee on the Rights of Persons with Disabilities. 2018a. *General Comment No. 6 (2018) on Equality and Non-Discrimination*. CRPD/C/GC/6.

Committee on the Rights of Persons with Disabilities. 2018b. *General Comment No. 7 (2018) on the Participation of Persons with Disabilities, Including Children with Disabilities, Through Their Representative Organizations, in the Implementation and Monitoring of the Convention*. CRPD/C/GC/7.

Degener, Theresia. 2016. "Disability in a Human Rights Context." *Laws* 5 (35): 1–24. https://doi.org/10.3390/laws5030035.

Degener, Theresia. 2017. "A Human Rights Model of Disability." In *Routledge Handbook of Disability Law and Human Rights*, edited by Peter Blanck and Eilionóir Flynn, 31–50. Routledge.

Ferri, Delia. 2010. "The Conclusion of the UN Convention on the Rights of Persons with Disabilities by the EU/EC: A Constitutional Perspective." In *European Yearbook of Disability Law 2*, edited by Lisa Waddington and Gerard Quinn, 47–72. Antwerp: Intersentia.

Fredman, Sandra, Meghan Campbell, Shreya Atrey, Jason Brickhill, Nomfundo Ramalekana, and Sanya Samtani. n.d. *Achieving Transformative Equality for Persons with Disabilities: Submission to the CRPD Committee for General Comment No. 6 on Article 5 of the UN Convention on the Rights of Persons with Disabilities*. http://ohrh.law.ox.ac.uk/wordpress/wp-content/uploads/2017/12/CPRD-Submission-1.pdf.

General Assembly. 2011. *Report of the Committee on the Rights of Persons with Disabilities. First Session (23–27 February 2009), Second Session (19–23 October 2009), Third Session (22–26 February 2010), Fourth Session (4–8 October 2010)*. A/66/55. New York: United Nations.

Kittay, Eva. 1999. *Love's Labor: Essays on Women, Equality, and Dependency*. New York: Routledge.
Lawson, Anna. 2014. "Accessibility Obligations in the UN Convention on the Rights of Persons with Disabilities: Nyusti & Takacs V Hungary." *South African Journal on Human Rights* 30 (2): 380–92.
Lawson, Anna, and Angharad E. Beckett. 2020. "The Social and Human Rights Models of Disability: Towards a Complementarity Thesis." *The International Journal of Human Rights*. https://doi.org/10.1080/13642987.2020.1783533.
Lord, Janet, and Michael Stein. 2017. "Charting the Development of Human Rights Law Through the CRPD." In *The United Nations Convention on the Rights of Persons with Disabilities: A Commentary*, edited by Valentina Della Fina, Rachele Cera, and Giuseppe Palmisano, 731–48. Cham: Springer.
MacKinnon, Catharine A. 2012. "Substantive Equality: A Perspective." *Minnesota Law Review* 96 (1): 1–27.
Morris, Jenny. 1991. *Pride Against Prejudice: Transforming Attitudes to Disability*. London: Women Press.
O'Donnovan, Maeve. 2013. "Feminism, Disability and Evolutionary Psychology: What's Missing?" *Disability Studies Quarterly* 33 (4), retrieved from: https://dsq-sds.org/article/view/3872/3403.
Paré, Mona. 2019. "The Convention on the Rights of Persons with Disabilities: Its Contribution to the Development of International Human Rights Law." *Revista ESMAT* 11 (17): 209–30.
Quinn, Gerard, and Theresia Degener. 2002. *Human Rights and Disability*. New York and Geneva: United Nations.
Sheppard, Colleen. 2004. "Inclusive Equality and New Forms of Social Governance." *Supreme Court Law Review* 24: 45–76.
Terzi, Lorella. 2004. "The Social Model of Disability: A Philosophical Critique." *Journal of Applied Philosophy* 21 (2): 141–57.
Thomas, Carol. 1999. *Female Forms: Experiencing and Understanding Disability*. Buckingham: Open University Press.
Trömel, Stefan. 2009. "A Personal Perspective on the Drafting History of the United Nations Convention on the Rights of Persons with Disabilities." In *European Yearbook of Disability Law 1*, edited by Gerard Quinn and Lisa Waddington, 115–38. Antwerp and Portland: Intersentia.
Wendell, Susan. 1996. *The Rejected Body: Feminist Philosophical Reflections on Disability*. London: Routledge.
Witcher, Sally. 2013. *Inclusive Equality: A Vision for Social Justice*. Bristol: Policy Press.

CHAPTER 3

# What Does the CRPD Tell Us About Being Human?

*Franziska Felder*

## Introduction

The UN Convention on the Rights of Persons with Disabilities (hereinafter the CRPD), which was adopted by the United Nations General Assembly in New York in 2006, and entered into force in 2008, has proved a great success in many respects. The Convention has far-reaching international implications for the establishment of new policies and the treatment of people with disabilities in general. Over 80% of nations worldwide have ratified the CRPD, which is unprecedented in the history of UN conventions and in itself bears witness to an important political shift. It is an expression of a change in the perception of previously excluded groups and their status as legal subjects.

But the Convention also calls for constant active political engagement, which should in turn also shape a new ethos of justice (Fredman 2008).

F. Felder (✉)
University of Vienna, Vienna, Austria
e-mail: franziska.felder@univie.ac.at



F. Felder et al. (eds.), *Disability Law and Human Rights*, Palgrave Studies in Disability and International Development,
https://doi.org/10.1007/978-3-030-86545-0_3

However, without doubt, any new ethos that is established by means of the Convention cannot exist in isolation from prevailing notions of justice. We cannot specify the concept or content of human rights if we consider worldviews and values to be predetermined, fixed and given entities, on the basis of which we seek points of de facto agreement. Rather, we must bring new concepts of justice into play that bridge the utopian, idealistic aspects of human rights with current social realities (Cohen 2004, 213). In this respect, Jürgen Habermas writes that "[H]uman rights form a realistic utopia in that they no longer masquerade as social-utopian images of collective happiness, but anchor the ideal aim of a just society in the institutions of constitutional states themselves" (2010, 354). If these realistic ideals are then enshrined in the institutions of acceding states, views about people and their ways of life are not simply assumed as a given. Instead, a vision is developed, with the implication that the mutual obligations of people, on grounds of justice and other reasons, can and should be expanded.

However, it is precisely in the tension between realism and utopianism that we encounter the difficulty, in a sense, of promoting the full legal and social implementation of human rights such as those proposed by the CRPD. The tension especially occurs where the social majority opinions are conservative and the CRPD is visionary, extensive and new compared to existing law. At these points, the establishment of rights for all people without exception is particularly important. On the one hand, it could be argued that those parties (both people and institutions) who have internalized human rights thinking or have operationalized it in policy and concrete measures—i.e., the values of substantive equality, human dignity and freedom, to name but three—would not actually need any conventions or legal directives. This is because they have already integrated the values and visions that underpin the CRPD into their mindset, and act accordingly on a voluntary basis, that is, without the pressure of any legal obligation. On the other hand, there are those (the critics, the skeptics, the conservatives, however you call them) who do not consider human rights superfluous in practice, but are skeptical of their theoretical justification and also criticize the fact that they apply to all human beings, but not, for example, animals, irrespective of their cognitive capabilities. Prominent philosophers like Peter Singer or Jeff McMahan, for instance, while recognizing the importance of human rights, doubt that some people with severe cognitive and multiple disabilities (McMahan 2009, 9; Singer 2009, 220) are subjects of full human rights. And their voices are accompanied by part of the civilian population who have no contact with people with disabilities and who perceive them primarily as others and not as equals (Minow 1990).

In order to develop a theoretically sound basis of human rights that is most inclusive, it is important not only to address the first group, but also the skeptics of a truly inclusive vision of human rights, that embraces all human beings, including people with severe cognitive and multiple disabilities (Becker 2005, 9; Waldron 2017, 220),[1] the group of people subject to the greatest real and potential risk of exclusion (Mietola et al. 2017).

In the following, I aim to build a justification for such an inclusive morality that encompasses all human beings irrespective of their intrinsic potential and their cognitive abilities—and not just in an affirmative and rhetorical way.[2] More concretely, I will show that we need to reformulate our very understanding of equality in order to develop a truly inclusive morality and an all-embracing understanding of human rights. The equality I have in mind is socially and relationally conditioned in a fundamental sense. From such an understanding of equality follows the implication that the exercise of human rights should not be viewed in an individualistic manner, detached from a social environment, but must itself be socially expressed and comprehended.

The justification that I propose for a fully inclusive understanding of human rights is useful for two reasons: First, unlike most approaches to human rights, it does not sidestep the tough question of the value and

[1] There is no clear terminological definition that provides a consistent, non-controversial use of severe cognitive and multiple disability. When, in the following, I speak of "people with severe cognitive and multiple disabilities", I am referring to a small group of disabled people who live a life characterized by major cognitive impairment, no, little or no intelligible speech, great dependence on the care and support of others, and medical diagnoses that are often serious or life-threatening (World Health Organization 1992, 230).

[2] In my view, well-intentioned rhetorical inclusion in particular is dangerous unless its meaning is explained in precise and substantive terms. For example, Michael A. Stein writes: "A more inclusive approach is the disability human rights paradigm, which maintains as a moral imperative that every person is entitled to the means necessary to develop and express his or her own individual talent" (Stein 2007, 77). However, talent would seem to be a questionable concept in the case of a person with severe cognitive and multiple disabilities, or there is a risk that this concept itself could be taken *ad absurdum*, such that people who do not have talent (at least according to the usual understanding) might be included on a rhetorical basis only, but ultimately excluded in practice.

significance of the human capacity to act.[3] And second, the justification presented here is inclusive because it takes into account a capability that has been shown to be specific to human beings alone, which we can refer to as a "we" capability. It thus provides an answer to critics like Peter Singer or Jeff McMahan, who assume that certain more sophisticated animals have more "human" abilities than human beings with severe cognitive and multiple disabilities (McMahan 2009; Singer 2009), and who use the issue of disability primarily to improve the status of non-human animals, an undoubtedly important concern that however tends to lead to the misuse of disability for other purposes.

I structure my discussion as follows: First, I identify the specific challenges to such an inclusive understanding of human rights. Two problems in justifying human rights emerge, especially in the case of severe cognitive and multiple disabilities: speciesism and the metaphysical assumptions in the justification of human rights that are not shared by all persons or in all societies today. I aim to address these two challenges by presenting empirically sound and morally coherent arguments as to why human rights apply to all humans, but not to animals. This is followed by an examination of the moral implications of these arguments for the needs of people with severe cognitive and multiple disabilities. In the final section, I propose a perhaps surprising reorientation or interpretation of the previous discussion. For I argue that the existence of the CRPD itself can exert inclusive power and have status-changing implications for people with severe cognitive and multiple disabilities, precisely *because* human rights (and individual capabilities as the basis for personhood) can be socially interpreted. The CRPD is designed in a way that is able to bridge the gap between reality and utopia, and encourage developments which may, over time, lead to real, lasting improvement in the lives of people with severe cognitive and multiple disabilities.

[3] This is to some extent the case, for example, in an article by Arstein-Kerslake and Flynn (2017, 25), where the authors define legal agency as "an action or an inaction that the individual intended and which has legal consequences or creates, modifies or extinguishes a legal relationship". This definition is problematic because a personal capacity for action is equated with the action itself.

## Severe Cognitive and Multiple Disabilities and the Challenge They Present for Human Rights

The exclusion of people with severe cognitive and multiple disabilities is a particularly serious problem, which occurs both in practice and in theory. Members of this group are subject to fundamental theoretical exclusion to the extent that even their personhood status (and thus their entitlement to rights) is called into question (Vehmas 2010). Their needs for closeness, belonging, but also cognitive stimulation, education and support are often ignored. Their lifeworld exclusion is often so fundamental that the coverage of fundamental human needs is not guaranteed.

Inclusive theories of justice such as those underpinning the CRPD are intended to combat such exclusion. However, inclusive approaches of this kind face three serious criticisms: they are described as being unhistorical, speciesist and, thirdly, dependent on theological or metaphysical assumptions that are no longer shared by all persons and in all societies today (Lohmann 2007, 77).

The first criticism, that of being unhistorical, is not unique to the CRPD. This objection is actually raised against all human rights conventions, specifically with regard to their premise that human rights apply to *all* people at *all* times and in *all* places. There is no doubt that a claim or statement of this kind is factually inaccurate in several respects: human rights are still systematically disregarded in many places in the world, and this was even more the case in earlier times. This is also the reality faced, to a special degree, by people with disabilities. In ancient times, for example, people who had a visible disability at birth were often killed directly, for example by being thrown off a cliff or abandoned in the forest, and the Nazis in the Third Reich also practiced active euthanasia, i.e., the systematic killing of disabled people, on an industrial scale (Stiker 1999). The critics of inclusive approaches argue that these very examples show that human rights have *not* applied to all people, at all times and in all places. However, I think that this argument confuses description with prescription. Although the statement that human rights apply at all times and in all places is written in descriptive language, it does not represent a description, but a vision associated with a prescription: human rights *should* apply to all people at all times and in all places (and, one might add, precisely *because* there are so many bad forms of exclusion).

In my view, therefore, this criticism is not worthy of further consideration and can be safely set aside. It does, however, draw attention to the other two challenges by implicitly raising the highly charged question: *should* human rights apply to *all* people without exception (and why *only* to people and not to animals)?[4] I think it is worth for a while to focus on these two other challenges and not immediately dismiss the questions that arise here as morally indecent.

## The Charge of Speciesism and the Question of Application of Human Rights to *All* Human Beings

In my discussion, I address the two remaining criticisms together, but I begin with the charge of speciesism, offering empirically based reasons why we should proceed from an assumption that all human beings are equal, in both a vertical and a horizontal sense, and then demand equal treatment for them on this basis. Specifically, my reasoning leads me to show, first of all, that we have reasons to assume, from a horizontal perspective, that all people are substantially equal in at least one essential respect. Such de facto equality also leads to a call for moral—or "continuous"—equality. This further implies the principle that all people deserve to receive the same amount of social care and consideration. Second, we have reasons to conclude that humans differ in a crucial way (vertically) from animals. This in turn leads to a demand for "distinctive equality", and thus to the assumption that humans, unlike animals, have *specific* rights to care (Waldron 2017, 49).

To understand the debate about speciesism, we must first consider the orthodox assumption that human rights apply to *all* people, and *only* to people, *by virtue of their humanness*.[5] The speciesist perspective can be interpreted in two ways. First, it might be assumed that all members of the human species share morally relevant capabilities that are specific only

[4] This is a point that not only applies to the inclusion of people with disabilities, but also to historical debates about the inclusion of slaves, of women, children, black or indigenous people (Coates 2004; Horton and Horton 2006; Medina 2013; Soldatic and Johnson 2017; Young 2001).

[5] This assumption is undoubtedly not only an important aspect in the thinking of all world religions, but also a supporting pillar of democracies that protect all of their citizens equally.

to them. Second, it might be interpreted as implying that the fact of being a member of the human species is in itself a morally relevant reason for being granted human rights.

Both interpretations have been severely criticized in the philosophical literature, including by the proponents of various currents of utilitarianism (McMahan 1996; Singer 1993).

We have to recognize that the problem of entitlement is not a trivial one (nor one that is specific to utilitarianism), because the recognition granted to a subject of rights forms the very basis of entitlement to rights in our society, and therefore has far-reaching practical consequences. These consequences become transparent if one turns to the question of what constitutes rights or what distinguishes legal ethics from voluntary morality, but also from pure ethics of duty (for example the Ten Commandments or the obligation to wear a belt in the car).

The difference to voluntary action based on e.g., benevolence is obvious: the bearers of duties are obliged to act in a certain way, so they are no longer free to act as they were in a benevolent, but voluntary position. Strictly speaking, however, if this would be the only focus of human rights, it could also be regulated via an ethics of duty. Because of certain duties to act toward people with disabilities, people would need to justify their behavior and also expect sanctions if they fail to fulfill their obligations.

Yet even an ethics of duty—or a "one-sided" duty that does not correspond to any law or right, such as the obligation to wear seat belts in the car—is far less demanding and far-reaching than a rights ethic. What changes with the transition from a duty ethic to a legal ethic is the direction of interpretation. If there is no reference to rights, e.g., subject A believes she has an obligation to B because there is a certain moral norm (a well-founded commandment, for example); B is therefore only an object of moral obligations. But if A thinks that B has a right to expect X from her, then she knows that she is obliged to comply for two reasons. First, simply because B has a right to certain obligations being fulfilled, and second, because this right is justified with reference to a certain (well-founded) norm. Being not only an object of a moral obligation, but inhabiting a moral subject role as a bearer of rights is a subtle but important difference: B could, for example, waive her rights in a special case and release A from her duty to act. Rights thus trigger a restriction of freedom in the person carrying out the duties and at the same time promote the freedom of the subject, who now has the power to demand a certain action (or the omission of an action) with the threat of sanctions (Feinberg 1970).

The consequence of this structure of rights, however, is often seen as that subjects of rights must have certain abilities that allow them to actually be able to claim rights, that is, to ask legal objects to actually fulfill their obligations toward them. Often skills such as rationality or common sense are addressed, capabilities are often associated with personhood. These capabilities, it is assumed, give rise to special entitlements, including rights. This is the position that is—although not embraced by feminist, post-structural, continental and non-western theoretical approaches—taken by the most dominant liberal paradigm and beyond (ranging from Aristotle, to John Locke and Kant, just to name three), either explicitly, or, as in the case of Nussbaum (2006, 2009) and Rawls (1999), implicitly.[6] It is also reflected in public policy and legal practice, including those in the tradition of human rights with their strong concurrent history with liberalism (Kittay 2001). The problem with this position is its background assumption in liberalism: "Liberalism invokes a notion of political participation in which one makes one's voice heard. It depends on a conception of the person as independent, rational, and capable of self-sufficiency. And it holds to a conception of society as an association of such independent equals. Yet many with severe retardation cannot ever hope to be equal in these terms. Some, at least, may never be able to be independent or capable of participating in rational deliberation" (Kittay 2001, 559).[7]

The utilitarian philosophers Peter Singer (1993, 2009) and Jeff McMahan (1996, 2002) have taken up these concerns and have raised accusations of discrimination against those who deny rights to animals which possess these capabilities in contrast to certain people with severe

[6] John Rawls never claimed that his theory of justice was inclusive. On the contrary, he believed that the problem of disability should be solved at the level of practice, not theory (Rawls 1999, 10). Eva Feder Kittay, for example, is critical of this (1999, 88). Martha Nussbaum, for her part, considers that her capability approach stands out in particular by being maximally inclusive (Nussbaum 2009), but this has been called into question by other philosophers (Davy 2015; Stein 2007).

[7] One of the problem is that the liberal tradition focuses exclusively on the limitations of people with severe cognitive and multiple disabilities and thus set them outside of the liberal definitions of personhood and citizenship with their fixation on intellect, independence, and productivity. This problem will be the focus in the following section.

cognitive and multiple disabilities. Singer defines this form of discrimination, which he calls *speciesism*, as follows: "Racists violate the principle of equality by giving greater weight to the interests of members of their own race when there is a clash between their interests and the interests of those of another race. Sexists violate the principle of equality by favoring the interests of their own sex. Similarly, speciesists allow the interests of their own species to override the greater interests of members of their own species. The pattern is identical in each case" (Singer 2002 [1975], 9).[8] Singer's objections in particular have led to a decades-long debate in legal ethics and disability studies.

Philosopher Richard Arneson has called this linking of cognitive capacities with the moral status of being a subject of rights the "Singer problem". He writes: "What I call the 'Singer Problem' arises if one accepts that the morally significant cognitive capacities that are relevant to the determination of the fundamental moral status of a being vary from individual to individual by degree. The problem is to specify a moral principle determining fundamental moral status that assigns a superior status to humans compared to other animals on the basis of the superior cognitive capacities of humans but also assigns all human persons an equal fundamental moral status regardless of their differing cognitive capacities" (Arneson 1999, 105).

To answer the objections brought up by Singer and others that threaten an inclusive understanding of human rights, I next propose a developmental-psychological and ontogenetic approach that can escape the "Singer problem", while at the same time leading us to recognize as subjects of rights even those people who do *not* in fact possess certain higher functionings. I believe that this approach is capable, on the one hand, of presenting a specifically human ability that even more highly developed animals such as primates do *not* have, without, on the other hand, working in a way that excludes certain people or groups of people. In other words, it offers both a vertically and a horizontally sound argument for a truly inclusive theory of human rights.

[8] It should be noted that these approaches apply the *species neutrality requirement* (Cruft et al. 2015, 9), according to which some humans are excluded, while certain highly developed animals, such as dolphins, dogs and apes, are included.

## "We" Capability as a Genuine Human Capability

The American developmental psychologist and primatologist Michael Tomasello (2000, 2009, 2019) considers a capability he calls the human "we" capability to be *the* crucial ability distinguishing us from our closest relatives. Tomasello's main research question, pursued over decades, is basically this: Why has the human species been able to develop cognitive capabilities that go beyond those of other species (including our closest relatives, the great apes)? And what are those capabilities?

Highly developed animals are not fundamentally different from humans, he shows, and this could even be said of plants. Just like plants and animals, human beings need an environment (a natural and, in the case of animals, a social environment) that allows them to thrive, supplementing their genetic and physical attributes. But the specific quality of human beings, Tomasello demonstrates, is that, unlike non-human primates, they are intentional social beings.[9] Human development is dependent on maturation processes that are lengthy and complex compared to those of plants and animals. People thus are prepared from birth to become functional adults because they have (with few exceptions) the necessary genes and live in a pre-structured cultural world that usually supports their development and active education in certain areas. But unlike many animals, humans are not fully grown organisms at birth. Human growth is full of developmental challenges. And the activities involved, insofar as they go beyond automatically occurring biological processes, are influenced by other people. For these developmental hurdles, the cultural environment of a human individual is therefore vitally important. Humans are predisposed to live in a certain type of social environment, without which their offspring will not develop

[9] Non-human primates may well be intentional and causal beings, but according to Tomasello they do not understand the world in intentional or causal terms. For instance, in their natural environment, non-human primates do not point to external objects, do not hold up objects to present them to others, do not try to lead others somewhere to see a particular object, do not actively engage in showing or demonstrating to others and do not intentionally teach others new behaviors. As an example, when non-human primates see another of their kind go to a watering hole, they can deduce what will happen next (e.g., they will see the other begin to drink) and they can even devise strategies to influence events they foresee, but they lack intentional understanding. Humans, however, understand that another human heading toward the watering hole has a goal in mind (to quench their thirst), and in turn they can seek to influence the cognitive and intentional states of others, not only their behavior.

normal social or cognitive abilities. "Culture" is what we call that special kind of social environment, and it is, according to Tomasello (2008), a species-typical and unique ontogenetic niche for human development.

The fact that humans (and only humans) possess the social abilities necessary for cultural adaptation and appropriation of this kind is made apparent when we compare them with their closest relatives, the great apes. Two-year-old humans, according to Tomasello (2008), do about as well as adult chimpanzees and orangutans on IQ tests when it comes to demonstrating their understanding of space, quantity and causality. But differences become evident in social coexistence. Humans, in contrast to apes, structure their common activities through shared goals and agreement. Tomasello's different studies (ibid.) have shown, for example, that if children wish to interrupt or quit a shared activity, they ask for permission to leave the group. Another key difference can be seen in communication. While apes communicate primarily with the aim of getting others to do what they want, human children also communicate to share information and be helpful to others. They furthermore want to share their beliefs and feelings with others. Experiments for instance have shown that even very young children will point to a bird, look at their mother and cry out joyfully.

Shared activities can also be seen as a prerequisite for human upbringing and education, in the process of adults passing on information that children receive and use in a trusting manner. Finally, it has been shown that only human children, not monkeys, will play games in which they might use a pencil, for example, as if it were a hammer. According to Tomasello (ibid.), this kind of play with objects represents a preliminary stage in learning about specifically human social institutions. Human learning can only be achieved through joint action and (in another contrast to the animal world) it takes place over the course of generations, which means that it can be passed on and built up within the species over a long time horizon. All in all, this results in unique possibilities for the species: it is humans' ability to coordinate their elaborate activities that has enabled them, as a species, to do so many extraordinarily complex things. These are not the achievements of individuals acting alone, e.g., because some of them are particularly intelligent or clever, but collectively, as a group, using their "we" capability (Tomasello 2008).

In Tomasello's view, this is exactly the capability that made the success and development of the human species possible in the first place. All human societies engage in common activities for mutual benefit. And most of these cognitive achievements of mankind—from technology to formal symbol systems such as writing to social institutions such as schools—are only possible because individuals are able and motivated to coordinate their thoughts and actions with others. These collaborative activities for mutual benefit are also the birthplace of unique human sociality and morality. Mutual collaborative activities contain the germs of all the socio-moral motivations and attitudes that most clearly distinguish human sociality from that of other apes. When working with other people—initially adults and later peers—small children, for example, create a new cognitive order in which they refer to "we" instead of just to "them" and "I". Compared to the ape social order, which is mainly based on competition and dominance, this new social order represents a radically new kind of relationship with others—namely based on mutual trust, respect and commitment. Crossing the development path from collaboration on two levels to shared engagement is therefore the basis for virtually all unique human socialities and morals (Tomasello 2019, 217f.).

According to Tomasello (2019, 305), there are two sets of human capabilities—joint intentionality and collective intentionality—of which the latter represents the "we" capability in its truest sense and thus the ability that is truly specific to humans. Joint intentionality comprises the following: the motivation to affiliate socially with and commit to others; to share emotions, goals, attention and knowledge with others; the cognition necessary to create a shared "we"; and the ability to take the perspective of others and interact with them as equals. But the heart of our discussion here concerns only the capability of collective intentionality, which, according to Tomasello, comprises both the motivation "to affiliate with and care for the social group by respecting and conforming to (aligning with) its conventions and norms (that is, under the pressure of obligation)" and the cognitive capacity "to form a group-minded 'we' and so to participate in conventions, norms and institutions, and to view things from 'objective' and normative perspectives" (ibid., 305). The specific human qualities that lead to "we" concerns develop as follows: First, "me" concerns develop ontogenetically, as self-interested concerns that enable an individual to survive and flourish. The second step is development of "you" concerns, which are expressed through sympathy and support for others in the group. The third step sees the emergence of human-specific "equality" concerns, at which stage individuals want themselves and others to be treated equally. Finally, in the fourth step, "we" concerns are formed, comprising both concerns that originate from face-to-face dyadic we-relationships and those that relate to larger social groups, i.e., social norms "among us". These "we" concerns, as the final stage of development, provide humans with the qualities specific to them, according to Tomasello (2019, 285). This "core moral identity" is in turn enclosed by an "interpretative-justificatory protective belt" (ibid., 289), which places limits, in a sense, on what is effectively considered moral (or immoral) behavior in a society. This perspective can also be molded and changed to some extent, as is impressively demonstrated by the existence of the CRPD.

But this "we" capability has not only an ontogenetic, individual meaning, but also a social one. To use "we" in a collective sense basically means to identify oneself and the fellow beings referred to as belonging to some form of *community*. The "we" in question here means "we *collectively*" (Schmid 2007, 7). To include a being in a "we" means to have a certain normative relationship with that being. In the first instance, it is not relevant whether the beings we encounter in such relationships are actually persons (with relevant personhood characteristics) or not. Or so at least it seems when we meet a newborn baby or visit our aunt with last-stage dementia living in a care home. In a sense, we approach such people as people (who they may not yet or no longer are), and we do this differently than we would toward a stone. We can, therefore, include a person who lives with severe cognitive and multiple disability (let's call this person Henry) in this "we", and in fact we do so, at least if this person is close to us.[10]

But we do this because we have normative, not just cognitive, expectations of a person like Henry (Schmid 2007). According to Schmid, our normative expectations are met by beings "we count on", and whom we consider in a fundamental sense to "belong to us". These expectations are counterfactually stabilized, as Niklas Luhmann once pointed out, this means that disappointment does usually not result in changing the attitude toward these objects. Normative expectations are, according to Schmid (ibid.) only brought toward persons, not toward animals or

[10] For a relevant approach that is also very substantive philosophically, see the work of Eva Feder Kittay, whose daughter Sesha falls within the group that is our specific focus here.

non-living entities.[11] Cognitive expectations, on the other hand, are satisfied by entities that we "reckon with", but which belong to the rest of the world. These may be animals or even objects, such as hairbrushes, which we can expect to function reliably. The key point separating normative from cognitive expectations is thus the resistance to disappointment that characterizes normative (but not cognitive) expectations. Thus, even after being disappointed on one or more occasions, people retain their normative expectations, including those they hold toward people like Henry.[12]

This is because the normative expectations we have toward human beings (but not toward animals, plants or objects) are concerned with genuinely human *potential*. This must be understood in three ways. First, the potential is organically innate in human beings (and only in them). This means that the "we" capability (to which I will return in a moment) is unique to the human species, and is inherent as a seed, so to speak, in every human being. Second, an understanding of this capability as a biological predisposition also implies that we have to move away from a static view of potential. We must instead assume that abilities develop from potential as a biological asset over the course of a human life to a varying degree. Third, it is in turn implied that we must regard the human species as inherently fragile: humans are constantly subject to latent threats to their general well-being, but also—specifically—to the development of concrete human capacities such as the capability for social cooperation.

So, we can conclude that these normative expectations we exclusively have toward human beings undoubtedly have two sides. On the one hand, people like Henry constantly fail to meet the expectations that people usually have of other people (for example, regarding their physical or cognitive abilities). And this breach of expectations is part of the social handicap that Henry experiences. On the other hand, the normative expectations we have of other people are also part or an expression of fundamental inclusion in the human community, precisely because we

[11] For instance, we expect from the personnel in a hotel that they tidy up the room during our absence. Most normative expectations we have toward persons are tied to social roles, rights and resources people occupy or have access to.

[12] In a sense, this also points out one major problem for people with severe cognitive and multiple disability as they constantly experience rejection and exclusion because of their inability to fulfil those normative expectations we have toward persons.

only have normative expectations of people, not animals, plants or objects. It is these expectations that are also a reason why we usually choose more and different forms of care and support for our fellow human beings than for entities or other living creatures.

## The Consequences for People with Severe Cognitive and Multiple Disabilities

Tomasello's research has shown that the "we" capability (the capability for social cooperation) can be considered *the* human-specific characteristic that distinguishes us from our closest relatives, the non-human primates. This, in turn, gives us a reason to reject at least part of the accusation of speciesism put forward by Singer and other utilitarians. It can be shown that there is actually an ability that is typically human, but it is neither language ability nor rationality, but the social capability to relate to each other (and to learn from other fellow beings in ways that transcend generations). According to Tomasello, the "we" capability is the *only* capability that is specifically human and cannot be found—like rationality or language, for example—in other highly developed animals. This specific human ability also justifies why people should be treated differently than animals, for example, that they should have more extensive rights than animals.

The existence of the "we" capability also gives us grounds for assuming and demanding continuous equality, i.e., for giving *all* people without exception—regardless of the actual existence of such capabilities in specific individuals—consideration via rights, and seeing them as persons entitled to rights. There are at least two reasons for this.

First, we can assume that the concept of personhood has not only an active but also a passive meaning. This implies that people are also beings worthy of protection, who deserve consideration and care (Ladwig 2007). This includes people with severe cognitive and multiple disabilities, even if they are not able to develop the "we" capability to the same extent as other people. The reason for this is that this ability is always already socially oriented, i.e., it cannot be understood independently of a social counterpart. It may be intrinsic and individual as potential. But it can only be expressed in a social context, and this distinguishes this ability in a fundamental way from abilities such as rationality or reason, which function to a certain extent independently from their social environment. In developing and exercising this ability, the social context is always included.

It is not an individual activity that can be understood independently and in a self-sufficient way. Therefore, in order to develop and successfully use this capability, individuals require a thriving social environment and must necessarily be integrated into what Tomasello calls "culture". This applies all the more when a given individual does not yet possess the "we" capability (as in the case of very young children), does not possess it on a lasting basis (as in the case of some people with severe cognitive and multiple disabilities) or no longer possesses it (as in the case of some people with dementia). The normative expectation that people have the potential to develop "we" capabilities and that they need care and support to develop, survive and thrive applies to all people.

Second, adopting the notion of care proposed by Stephen Darwall (2002), we find that care encompasses not only care for oneself, but also for the well-being of others, and this might include people with severe cognitive and multiple disabilities. The mutual recognition that exists between a subject and an object of recognition applies not only to relationships of full reciprocal recognition (as is usually the case with adults), but also to people who are (perhaps one-sidedly) dependent on our care. The carer and the cared-for cannot be seen completely independently of one another. Rather, the well-being of both is linked to one another.

Given these two reasons, we are able to justify the active and enduring protection of rights for people with severe cognitive and multiple disabilities. Although such people may not possess the "we" capability discussed earlier, they are integrated in the social network of a community (indeed, the entire human community), whose members in most cases do possess that capability. Consequently, they are part of this community, which is itself worth protecting.

And here lies a crucial difference between both strongly cognitivist and individualistic approaches, which link personhood status and thus entitlement to rights to *purely individual* abilities of rationality, autonomy or self-awareness (to name just a few examples), and to approaches that assert a metaphysical basis for human rights (often with the argument that human beings have an innate dignity). To be maximally inclusive, a human rights approach cannot simply claim the existence of human abilities metaphysically or delegate them to a higher power (e.g., God), but must draw moral conclusions from empirically proven facts and at the same time—again with reference to the empirical data—interpret them from a social perspective, not just with respect to individualistic and self-interested concerns. Of course, such an understanding of care does not encompass all relationships in our society, and it does not include strict equality and mutuality. But it does indicate the need for family and friendship relationships to be protected through rights. And these rights cannot be protected if they are only granted unilaterally to the caring persons, but also to those who are dependent on care and help, as in the case of people with severe cognitive and multiple disabilities.

I also think that it is possible to reach another conclusion, which is not without its own problems, but creates a further interesting twist: if we human beings are truly set apart by our "we" capability, ***and*** if we take into account the fact that the CRPD already exists in reality, with its aim of including all people with disabilities, then the very existence of such a convention could give rise to a new ethos of genuinely, comprehensively inclusive human rights, which at present only exists in rudimentary form at the international level. And this new ethos will be formed not least through existing case law and concrete interpretation of the CRPD. An ethos of this kind—in the process of being formed or yet to be formed—will also operate in social circles where people generally possess a "we" capability and skills. However, it can only develop successfully if people with severe cognitive and multiple disabilities are truly visible in their everyday lives, and if their needs and interests are actively communicated to society, including through relatives and friends. Rights can also only be fully guaranteed if it is socially recognized that the legal standing of all human beings is absolutely necessary in order to protect fundamentally important care relationships.

Moreover, if we recognize that people with severe cognitive and multiple disabilities are as integral as any of us to a genuine social community of human beings, this leads us, I believe, to a completely new interpretation of the social, cultural and economic rights contained in the CRPD. First, the rights expressed in the CRPD must be understood in a far more inclusive and social way, so as to encompass people with severe cognitive and multiple disabilities and their environment, not leaving them behind as objects of pity and social care. Second, we clearly need to take a much closer look at communities and societies themselves and the ways in which they enable inclusion and standing as a subject of human rights, or obstruct or even prevent it. The mere existence of relationships (e.g., within families) is not enough, as these relationships can be abusive and discriminatory. The question of whether communities are socially enabling at all, and if so, in what respect and manner, essentially goes far beyond the principles and paragraphs of the CRPD, reaching into the realm of (hopefully realistic) utopia.

As an important milestone in the development and advancement of human rights, the CRPD is charged with the great task and opportunity of truly bringing the present world closer to the (realistic) utopia of a future in which people with severe cognitive and multiple disabilities can be part of our community in a real way, not just in a rhetorical sense. To have an empirically validated argument as a basis for effectively defending a full and inclusive understanding of human rights is to identify at least a small theoretical piece of the puzzle for this agenda.

**Acknowledgements** I would like to thank my co-editor Laura Davy for her very helpful and inspiring comments on an earlier draft of this paper.

## References

Arneson, Richard J. 1999. "What, If Anything, Renders All Humans Morally Equal?" In *Singer and His Critics*, edited by Dale Jamieson, 103–28. Oxford: Blackwell Publishers.

Arstein-Kerslake, Anna, and Eilionoir Flynn. 2017. "The Right to Legal Agency: Domination, Disability and the Protection of Article 12 of the Convention on the Rights of Persons with Disabilities." *International Journal of Law in Context* 13 (1): 22–38.

Becker, Lawrence. 2005. "Reciprocity, Justice, and Disability." *Ethics* 116 (1): 9–39.

Coates, Ken S. 2004. *Global History of Indigenous Peoples: Struggle and Survival*. Basingstoke: Palgrave Macmillan.

Cohen, Joshua. 2004. "Minimalism About Human Rights: The Most We Can Hope For?" *The Journal of Political Philosophy* 12 (2): 190–213.

Cruft, Rowan, Matthew S. Liao, and Massimo Renzo. 2015. "The Philosophical Foundations of Human Rights—An Overview." In *Philosophical Foundations of Human Rights*, edited by Rowan Cruft, Matthew S. Liao, and Massimo Renzo, 1–41. Oxford: Oxford University Press.

Darwall, Stephen. 2002. *Welfare and Rational Care*. Princeton: Princeton University Press.

Davy, Laura. 2015. "Philosophical Inclusive Design: Intellectual Disability and the Limits of Individual Autonomy in Moral and Political Theory." *Hypatia* 30 (1): 132–48.

Feinberg, Joel. 1970. "The Nature and Value of Rights." *Journal of Value Inquiry* 4: 243–57.

Fredman, Sandra. 2008. *Human Rights Transformed: Positive Rights and Positive Duties*. Oxford: Oxford University Press.

Habermas, Jürgen. 2010. "Das Konzept der Menschenwürde und die realistische Utopie der Menschenrechte." *Deutsche Zeitschrift für Philosophie* 58 (3): 343–57.

Horton, James Oliver, and Lois E. Horton, eds. 2006. *Slavery and Public History: The Tough Stuff of American Memory*. New York: The New Press.

Kittay, Eva Feder. 1999. *Love's Labor: Essays in Women, Equality and Dependency*. New York: Routledge.

Kittay, Eva Feder. 2001. "When Caring Is Just and Justice Is Caring: Justice and Mental Retardation." *Public Culture* 13 (3): 557–79.

Ladwig, Bernd. 2007. "Das Recht auf Leben - nicht nur für Personen." *Deutsche Zeitschrift für Philosophie* 55 (1): 17–39.

Lohmann, Georg. 2007. "Menschenrechte zwischen Moral und Recht." In *Philosophie der Menschenrechte*, edited by Stefan Gosepath and Georg Lohmann, 62–95. Frankfurt a. M.: Suhrkamp.

McMahan, Jeff. 1996. "Cognitive Disability, Misfortune, and Justice." *Philosophy and Public Affairs* 25 (1): 3–25.

McMahan, Jeff. 2002. *The Ethics of Killing—Problems at the Margins of Life*. New York: Oxford University Press.

McMahan, Jeff. 2009. "Radical Cognitive Limitation." In *Disability and Disadvantage*, edited by Kimberley Brownlee and Adam Cureton, 240–59. Oxford: Oxford University Press.

Medina, José. 2013. *The Epistemology of Resistance: Gender and Racial Oppression, Epistemic Injustice, and Resistant Imaginations*. New York: Oxford University Press.

Mietola, Reetta, Sonja Miettinen, and Simo Vehmas. 2017. "Voiceless Subjects? Research Ethics and Persons with Profound Intellectual Disabilities." *International Journal of Social Research Methodology* 20 (3): 263–74.

Minow, Martha. 1990. *Making All the Difference—Inclusion, Exclusion, and American Law*. Ithaca: Cornell University Press.

Nussbaum, Martha C. 2006. *Frontiers of Justice: Disability, Nationality, Species Membership*. Cambridge, MA: Harvard University Press.

Nussbaum, Martha. 2009. "The Capabilities of People with Cognitive Disabilities." *Metaphilosophy* 40 (3/4): 331–51.

Rawls, John. 1999. *A Theory of Justice* (Revised ed.). Oxford: Oxford University Press.

Schmid, Hans Bernhard. 2007. "'Person'—Nostrologische Notizen." In *Personalität*, edited by Frank Kannetzky and Henning Tegtmeyer. Leipzig: Leipziger Universitätsverlag.

Singer, Peter. 1993. *Practical Ethics* (Second ed.). Cambridge: Cambridge University Press.

Singer, Peter. 2002 (1975). *Animal Liberation* (Third ed.). New York: Harper Collins.

Singer, Peter. 2009. "Speciesism and Moral Status." *Metaphilosophy* 40 (3–4): 567–81.

Soldatic, Karen, and Kelley Johnson, eds. 2017. *Disability and Rurality: Identity, Gender and Belonging*. London: Routledge.

Stein, Michael Ashley. 2007. "Disability Human Rights." *California Law Review* 95: 75–121.

Stiker, Henri-Jacques. 1999. *A History of Disability*. Ann Arbor: The University of Michigan Press.

Tomasello, Michael. 2000. *The Cultural Origins of Human Cognition*. Cambridge, MA: Harvard University Press.

Tomasello, Michael. 2008. "How Are Humans Unique." *The New York Times*, May 25.

Tomasello, Michael. 2009. *Why We Cooperate*. Cambridge, MA: MIT Press.

Tomasello, Michael. 2019. *Becoming Human: A Theory of Ontogeny*. Cambridge, MA: Harvard University Press.

Vehmas, Simo. 2010. "The Who or What of Steve: Severe Cognitive Impairment and Its Implications." In *Arguments and Analysis in Bioethics*, edited by Matti Häyry, Tuija Takala, Peter Herissone-Kelly, and Gardar Arnason, 263–80. Amsterdam: Rodopi.

Waldron, Jeremy. 2017. *One Another's Equal: The Basis of Human Equality*. Cambridge, MA: The Belknap Press.

World Health Organization. 1992. *The ICD-10 Classification of Mental and Behavioural Disorders*. Geneva: World Health Organization.

Young, Iris Marion. 2001. "Equality of Whom? Social Groups and Judgments of Injustice." *Journal of Political Philosophy* 9 (1): 1–18.

CHAPTER 4

# Rights, Justice and Flourishing: The Uses and Limitations of Human Rights

*Michaelis Michael and Karen Soldatic*

## Introduction

The development of the discourse of human rights, first in the United Nations Charter and then in the Universal Declaration, is rightly identified as a positive step in the legal protection of the vulnerable from the unfettered actions of the powerful. The intent of the UN Charter, as stated in the Preamble, is "to reaffirm faith in fundamental human rights, in the dignity and worth of the human person, in the equal rights of men and women and of nations large and small." This central valuing of the human subject, to be recognized as a human worthy of dignity and respect, has been critical for the disability rights movement and

M. Michael (✉)
The University of New South Wales, Kensington, Australia
e-mail: M.Michael@unsw.edu.au

K. Soldatic
Western Sydney University, Penrith, Australia
e-mail: K.Soldatic@westernsydney.edu.au



F. Felder et al. (eds.), *Disability Law and Human Rights*, Palgrave Studies in Disability and International Development,
https://doi.org/10.1007/978-3-030-86545-0_4

persons with disability (Kayess and French 2008). It is this promise of human rights that has driven disability rights movements to pursue an international convention—the United Nations Convention on the Rights of Persons with Disabilities (2006)—as an instrument to advance their dignity and worth as the largest minority group of the human family (Soldatic and Johnson 2019). The CRPD has received unprecedented acceptance across governments, global institutions and legal institutions. Ratification has been both rapid and extensive, defining national systems of disability governance and inclusion alongside directing international relations of global trade, development and resource exchange.

Yet, as we explore in this chapter, certain questions arise in relation to the promise of legal articulations of disability rights as the dominant precursor for a life of flourishing for persons who live with impairments who identify as having a disability. This is not only in terms of ensuring socio-political recognition as legal persons worthy of respect and dignity, the central tenets of human rights principles, but also recognition of past injustices that may impede a life of flourishing. Disability, unlike other identities, is both part of the human condition and also is often created by deliberate harms and injuries. For example, we know that many women become disabled after experiencing ongoing intimate partner violence (Didi et al. 2016). It is well documented that during armed conflict and war, often ethnic, racial and/or religious minorities are targeted with forms of violence that leave their bodies with a disability, resulting in deep stigmatization long after the armed conflict is over (Berghs 2012). Many gender-diverse people acquire severe disability as a result of random or targeted transphobic and homophobic attacks (Richter 2019). While we do not address each of these groups specifically, these cases illustrate that the category of disability is positioned along spectrums of fluidity and stability, normalization and stigmatization, inclusion and exclusion. Our aim is to recognize this heterogeneity across what is framed as disability within Western human rights socio-legal understandings and, in turn, to identify the necessary conditions which would enable a life of flourishing for all persons living with disability, regardless of whether they identify as a person with disability.

We openly acknowledge that what a life of flourishing entails, what it looks like, is severely contested. We do not propose to suggest what this should be for each person living with disability, nor do we prescribe what the substantive content of a flourishing life should be. Our concern in this chapter is on what is required to realize a flourishing life as one self-determines, with full subjective agency.

## The Struggle for Personhood and the Promise of Human Rights

Since the early 2000s, there has been global recognition that persons living with disability experience some of the highest levels of inequality, poverty and discrimination (World Health Organization and World Bank 2011). Global efforts to address disabled people's poor life outcomes have focused on changing socio-political understandings of disability and pursuing legal recognition of disabled people's personhood. Disabled people argue that formal, legislated recognition of personhood will enable them, their families and communities to pursue structural, institutional and socio-political strategies to redress their significantly reduced life outcomes (Flynn and Arstein-Kerslake 2014). International legal recognition of disabled people's personhood is particularly important in revoking the dominance of medical discourses, practices and interventions in defining all aspects of disabled people's lives (Kayess and French 2008), what is commonly referred to as the medicalization of their bodies, minds and lives (Soldatic and Chapman 2010). With full recognition in international and national law, disability rights movements argue that governments have a set of duties and obligations towards disabled people that must be progressively realized over time (Meyers 2014). For this to be fulfilled at the everyday level for disabled people, there must be a relationship between grassroots movements and legal ratification through parliamentary deliberation (Encalada 2019). Critically, legal recognition of disabled people will provide greater power to repeal existing unjust socio-economic policies, programs and ideologies that are discriminatory and exclusionary.

The aim of legal personhood is transformation—transforming structures, institutions, socio-cultural practices, environments, spaces and places, rather than disabled people. An example often described is the person who uses a wheelchair, who, with the passage of anti-discrimination disability law, is now able to navigate the streetscape, access government buildings and participate in educational programs with full access to education facilities and supports, with the changed built environment such national legislation brings. It is argued that such broader, legally determined structural and institutional transformations would enable disabled people to have greater agency and autonomy over their everyday lives, actively facilitate their mobility and freedom through the removal of physical barriers and promote their self-determining capabilities for agency, autonomy and decision-making, as they now have the environmental and institutional opportunity to access life-affirming journeys on par with their able-bodied counterparts.

## Distributive Justice: State Power and Constraints on the Realization of Rights

Australia ratified the CRPD in July 2008 and since this time the Australian government has implemented significant policy reform to meet its obligations and duties to Australian citizens with disability. In 2010, Australian state governments developed and implemented the National Disability Strategy (NDS) of legislative and policy reform in response to the CRPD with a focus on the advancement of disability rights. The NDS outlines a broad range of policy objectives over a 10-year plan, including: inclusive and accessible communities, economic security, rights protection, justice and legislation, personal and community support, health and well-being, and learning and skills. Australian governments stated that the NDS was "a national approach to supporting people with disability to maximise their potential and participate as equal citizens in Australian society" (Council of Australian Governments 2011).

The translation of international law into the domestic sphere, particularly its articulation via redistributive systems to enable disabled people's participation in longstanding ableist structures, institutions, systems and processes on par with non-disabled citizens, as Teodor Mladenov (2018) argues, is always troublesome. In Australia, this has been the case with the onset of a new national disability support scheme—the National Disability Insurance Scheme—a core component of the NDIS (2020). Central to the socio-legal representations of persons with disability within the scheme are the liberal principles of personhood, agency and autonomy, through the legislative articulation of "choice" and "control". Yet, even with this rights-based premise, it is now well documented that the NDIS covers only a very small portion of persons with disabilities (Soldatic et al. 2020); that its funding is allocated premise upon a functionalized notion of participation drawing on medicalized conceptions of what disability "is" and what disability-specific supports and services "are" (Gilroy 2019); and that the people least likely to receive access to, or achieve equitable distribution of, the resources available carry markers of diversity, such as Indigeneity, race, ethnicity, religion, sexuality, gender and socio-economic inequality, which represent the heterogeneity of persons with disability (Soldatic et al. 2020).

These concerns and the concomitant withholding of rights are largely associated with the suspension or delay of national budgetary allocations for the redistributive measures necessary for the progressive realization of rights. That is, the assertion of state sovereign power and the mandate of states to define, assess and determine the needs of all citizens, conceptualized in political discourse as competing sets of rights and interests across the polity, determine the allocation of resources to different categories of citizen—the aged, children, the unemployed, persons with disability, refugees, new migrants and Indigenous Australians (Ashford 2007). The political struggle for rights, and the distributive claims—individual and collective—for justice to fully realize rights, is a highly contentious sphere within the realm of distributive justice. In the Australian case, access to the individualized support scheme for persons with disabilities as a social right is always determined by states' sovereign right to decide whose, and how, when and if, rights can, or should be, fully realized at any one given time and to what effect (ibid.). Political reframing of rights within distributive discourses establishes competing political claims—whose rights should be realized, at what cost for the nation state, and how should the distributive claims for the realization of these rights be determined?

## Western Individualist Claims vs Social Autonomy and Freedom

Many of these questions are associated with Western assumptions of what it means to be a person living with disability and the principle of autonomous personhood constructed in human rights models that focuses on the individual alone when translated into national political discourses and policies of distribution. Western liberal traditions in the political sphere center individual freedom as determined by the capacity of the individual. That is, for a person to decide freely, this must be an individualized choice, without the facilitative collective support from others—whether that be through redistributive policies, regulatory categories of social citizenship or how one self-defines one's social identity (Soldatic 2019).

German philosopher Regina Kreide (2007) argues that Western framings of human rights often violate commitments to deeper political ideas of social autonomy and our responsibilities towards others. Kreide argues that this responsibility also needs to acknowledge past injustices, harms and injuries to ensure redress in order for the value of rights to be fully realized. This is not only injustices, harms and injuries experienced by individuals, but also often broader communities who have experienced longstanding dispossession, exclusion and inequality, and the ongoing ramifications of these experiences on the person to fully realize their personhood, exercising their right to "control" and "choose" their life path. If we apply Kreide's argument to the case of Australia, the longstanding harms and injuries caused to Indigenous Australians become foregrounded, as do their effects, including significantly higher rates of disability (see Avery in this volume). In Australia, a settler-colonial society, notions of human rights across the structural, institutional and political framing of citizenship are grounded in Western liberal principles of citizenship that were established in constitutional law, where Indigenous Australians were not considered part of the national polity. This raises the question, is affording disability rights to Indigenous Australians enough to address the creation of disability as an outcome of longstanding colonial rule? And what about claims for reparations from the Australian settler-colonial state due to the creation of disability—does this reinforce medicalized notions of disability which rights are supposed to overcome?

## Heterogeneity and Intersectionality

Human rights, as they belong to all humans, are premised upon ideas about what the human subject is and who, therefore, belongs to the human family (Griffin 2008). Human rights philosopher Charles Beitz (2009) has argued that, historically, human rights have been contested, particularly by groups who have long been excluded from dominant elite discourses of human rights. Disability feminist philosopher Shelley Tremain (2002) has shown extensively that disability has long been excluded from the liberal traditions of human rights. As Tremain (2019) has documented in her work, the notion of impairment itself is grounded in particular liberal scientific traditions of the human species. Her work demonstrates that these human rights traditions are grounded in highly westernized masculine notions of the autonomous individual, and she emphasizes the critical importance of identifying the ways the foundational principles of human rights are themselves gendering in their individualist assumptions of autonomy, independence and human capability (ibid., 24).

Extending Tremain's philosophical arguments to the realm of the empirical, we see that this has been acknowledged within the human rights system of international socio-legal governance itself. There has been a flourishing of treaties and conventions to address the diversity of our humanity, with the United Nations Convention on the Rights of Persons with Disabilities being one of the latest articulations. Yet there is a large level of dissatisfaction with this splintering of human rights into highly prescribed rights for highly defined categories, such as women, children, ethnic minorities and races, refugees and asylum seekers, Indigenous peoples and people with disability, to name a few (Smith 2016). Over time, this splintering of human rights into specific categories across the super-diversity of the human species has demanded greater recognition that, to be fully human, our subjective agency emerges from not only our individual agency, but also from the historiography of the communities in which we belong (Brysk and Shafir 2004). Socio-legal scholars from the Global South, such as Boaventura de Sousa Santos (2002), argue that we need a new legal common sense to recognize the complexity of one's lifeworlds. Otherwise, we fall into Western masculine understandings of the human subject, a one-dimensional man, and of what it takes to be human (Marcus 1964).

Moreover, as Spivak (1988) argues, one of the central issues of Western human rights understandings is that often it forces the subaltern, those most marginalized within society, to strategically essentialize a singular characteristic of their identity so that they can make claims for rights. Further, as Crenshaw (1991) has pointed out, the multiplicity of our human identity beyond a single characteristic often results in unique experiences of discrimination, inequality and stigmatization. Indigenous disability scholars, such as Scott Avery (2018), have illustrated empirically in their work that Indigenous disability rights are not only intersectional for an Indigenous person living with disability, but also socio-cultural, where belonging to collective claims for rights is expansionary beyond individual self-determination. Our collective responsibilities, obligations and duties towards others within our defined socio-cultural communities, which encompass numerous kinship commitments, are all intertwined with human identity, our subjective relational understandings of belonging and our individual, intra-subjective experiences of being human (Fitts and Soldatic 2020).

## Reparatory Justice and Structural Transformation: Can Rights Address the Historical Continuity of Past Injustices?

How we understand the struggle for justice is centrally important to understanding the possibility, constraints and limitations of rights in disabled people's lifeworlds and the ways in which rights are often grounded in a political ethical orientation towards the pursuit of justice. The disability movement's struggles for personhood and the realization of disability rights, both globally and within the nation state, have often been framed within the politics of social justice. As the international volume edited by Pamela Block and colleagues illustrates (2016), disability rights may provide a framework of minimum redress, but it does not necessarily progressively realize disabled people's dignity as full human subjects. As outlined earlier in the Australian case, the translation of human rights to disabled people narrows their complex identities to a single area of personhood—disability—and the primary response has been to construct a separate, readily identifiable system of "disability care and support". It has not focused on structural nor institutional transformation to redress the historical normative ableist foundations of these core structures and institutions that are central to our flourishing as full human subjects and our struggle to realize our personhood.

Far more complex engagement with disabled people's social identity, alongside the building of a social solidarity, across the super-diversity of disability experiences of social injustices is required. This engagement must be comprehensive, reparatory (not retributory), and beyond that of mere inclusion. This is most clearly articulated in disability justice campaigns that place emphasis on "nothing about us without us". As Charlton (2000) identified in his seminal work, rights do not guarantee the democratization of disability social justice claims. To be genuinely democratic and just, disabled people would have to be democratically engaged in the deliberative process of deciding what those rights should be and, more significantly, how those rights should be realized in everyday nation-state policy deliberations, legislation and resourcing. Thus, the implementing of disability rights to address issues of justice is not only about the materiality of rights realization in everyday practice, but also about the deliberative political process of determining how those rights should be conceptualized and enacted in nation-state institutions with their transformation in practice.

It is more than the recognition of rights in law, but is grounded in the iterative deliberations of deciding what those rights should be, to both redress past injustices and to determine what they should be at some future time. Processes of iterative deliberations, as Seyla Benhabib (2013) argues, are a necessary social justice strategy to address the limitations and constraints of human rights, with the changing political landscape in each historical moment to intervene and transgress the sovereign power of the nation state. Yet, as Bulgarian disability scholar of the post-socialist age Teodor Mladenov (2018) has identified, liberal democratic practice is limited as a single-pronged approach to the full realization of disabled people's dignity. Drawing on the work of American philosopher Nancy Fraser, Mladenov documents that in this post-socialist age, to both redress past injustices and ensure that substantive institutional change and political trajectories are enabling, disability justice claims for rights, dignity and respect need to encompass deliberative representation and recognition of one's personhood, alongside redistributive transfers to address the materiality of disabled people's lifeworlds. The disability movement's justice claims encompass these three spheres: reparatory strategies of redress; the realization of rights to ensure that disabled peoples are free from state coercion, such as institutional incarceration; and the exercise of one's agency in maintaining bodily self-determination and control over one's social relationships.

## The Critical Limitations of Rights Frameworks

In an important articulation of the goal of the United Nations, and so the place of human rights discourse as a critical tool, the second UN secretary-general, Dag Hammarskjöld, said in 1954, "The UN was not created to take mankind to heaven, but to save humanity from hell" (Hammarskjöld 1954).

This sets the goal of human rights as a safety net rather than as a guarantee of the good life. Safety nets are important and without them (or by ignoring them) we all too readily find ourselves in hellish situations. We have been guided by this goal to see the discourse of human rights as essentially outlining a safeguard; their crucial role is the protection of individuals from powerful players (Michael 2006). In particular, human rights have been formulated as essential to protect individuals from state players. While there are legitimate questions whether, in the situation we find ourselves, there might not be a need to extend these protections to cover the actions of other powerful players, such as corporations, this safeguarding role is hugely important and violations of human rights are desperately problematic. The language of human rights is one type of normative assessment of a situation.

However, on the conception of human rights we argue for, these do not exhaust all the rights possessed by an individual. Not all legal rights ceded to individuals by legal frameworks are human rights. This is so, even though we think it is plausible that extending human rights on two distinct dimensions might be required. First, as witnessed by the rights implicitly and explicitly recognized by the CRPD, some rights might have cultural, social and economic character. That extends the scope of human rights but another dimension of extension which seems required is to go beyond protections against state players to deal with the changing power dynamics associated with very powerful non-state players, such as multinational corporations. Even if such extensions were endorsed, there is in Hammarskjöld's remark an important delimiting of the critical perspective available through human rights discourse. It is vitally important that societies are liable to be normatively criticizable even while they do not violate human rights. A society which avoids hell might yet allow the flourishing of very few and that would provide grounds for normative criticism. In this section, we outline just how the ideal of flourishing plays a role in affording that normative criticism. This is not to be thought of as an alternative to human rights discourse but rather as playing a quite different role. We see that it is limiting to think there is only one form of normative.

While we have argued that the language of human rights has an important normative role in criticizing state (and non-state) players, there are inherent limitations in using rights discourse at all. Rights are shrouded in metaphysical obscurity. That obscurity is displayed in their articulation. On the one hand, we can think of these rights as marching in step with antecedent natural rights. From this perspective legislation merely recognizes what is there already. But then the nature of these antecedent natural rights is left shrouded in mystery, as is the process of discovering them. Such natural rights are often the subject of "discovery" by judges, not the self-conscious expression of the political will of an organized society. In debate, playing the "human rights" card can be seen as the trump card, which brooks no further debate. This has the effect of stymying, not facilitating, debate and understanding. Rights themselves, even when they are conceded to exist, are liable to clash. The claim that all such rights are inalienable is, for this reason, implausible. Debate in this complex situation cannot stay at the level of these conflicting rights but must move to the reason we have been tempted to talk of rights: to wit, the manner in which rights protect the abilities of agents we see as crucial to their being able to realize themselves, to live their life as they think will allow them to flourish. When the requirements for flourishing lives are in tension, talk of rights is inadequate to resolve that tension.

It might be suggested that, since Hammarskjöld's time, the UN has found human rights that round out the bare rights in the Universal Declaration of Human Rights. In particular, the CRPD, with its optional protocol, which was adopted in late 2006, brought into being, or recognized, additional human rights, and recognized persons with disabilities and their autonomy, along with a suite of human rights which were cultural, social and economic. Or, as in the language of the preamble to that Convention, it might be that, having recognized that the "principles proclaimed in the Charter of the United Nations which recognize the inherent dignity and worth and equal and inalienable rights of all members of the human family as the foundation of freedom, justice and peace in the world", that we need to identify the way persons with disabilities, by dint of being persons with disabilities, have particular needs to realize those inalienable rights.

We challenge the idea that a focus on human rights gives all the normative content we need to engage in normative criticism of states and powerful players in relation to economic, social and cultural arrangements and their differential impacts on persons with disabilities. We suggest that the notion of flourishing provides a missing component of the normative concepts we need to deploy to engage in assessment of our moral situation.

Avoiding hell, to use Hammarskjöld's phrase, means living a tolerable life, or, perhaps equivalently, avoiding a miserable life. However, neither living a tolerable life nor avoiding a miserable life guarantees flourishing. Human rights are vitally important since avoiding the intolerable, and so avoiding a miserable life, is vitally important. Yet, by emphasizing flourishing as a normative notion, in addition to human rights, we seek to highlight the aspirational character of flourishing.

## Beyond Rights: Seeking a Flourishing Life

Flourishing is living a life that is fully realized. So what is it to realize a life? Why is it so important that it can have the normative force associated with ethical appraisal? In this brief section, we outline some of the important history of the notion of flourishing as a normative notion. Though it has a history as a naturalized notion in the work of Aristotle, we see a crucial role in the self-development of a notion of flourishing as part of the project of self-constitution, as fundamental an aspect of the self as belief and love.

The safeguards provided by human rights would, if respected, provide a buffer against the sorts of injustice powerful agents can inflict both structurally and by commission on the less powerful. We need the additional normative force of the idea of flourishing. It is wrong for persons with disabilities to be deprived of opportunities to flourish in a manner they themselves fashion as constitutive of their own substantive good. Flourishing is a goal to aim at, and many a life falls short of flourishing by its own standards. That does not make such a life intolerable.

Talk of flourishing is historically associated with Aristotle and his naturalized understanding of natural goals, or ends, of human life. In his *Nicomachean Ethics*, he presents a picture of human development as following natural tendencies. Flourishing is the realizing of the inherent excellences that a human life can achieve. For Aristotle, our development follows natural tendencies in the same way other biological entities develop; we have intrinsic goals. These goals are not chosen, but are natural (Lear 2009; Lobel 2017). This account makes seeking these goals natural and to that extent normative. Insofar as someone fails to develop in the direction of these goals, then to that extent they are contrary to nature and criticizable. It is understandable that this idea of a natural goal for persons is not widely shared today. The idea of intrinsic natural goals associated with human flourishing was criticized from the Enlightenment onwards. That there is a significant role for our choices in shaping what counts as flourishing for us is part and parcel of the idea that our autonomy is to a large extent part of a project of self-making. Our values and beliefs are crucially involved in the fashioning of our own conceptions of our own flourishing. Moreover, different people will fashion quite different conceptions of their own flourishing. These differing conceptions will depend, in different ways, on the material and social conditions prevailing. The preconditions associated with flourishing for a mathematician are quite different from those for a classical musician and again quite different for a horticulturalist or for a political activist. It is also important to recognize that the mere fact that, in this conception of a flourishing life, the agent plays a constitutive role will not guarantee that they achieve the sort of life they seek. A political activist will likely not achieve their goals. A musician will turn out not to have the talent they would like to have. Appraised of these facts, agents can recalibrate their conceptions of flourishing or they can come to regard their lives as falling short of the goals they sought.

As Martha Nussbaum (2001 [1986]) noted, Aristotle's normative conception of human excellence explicitly emphasizes the fragility of that excellence, its dependence on social conditions and the role of sheer luck.

The Enlightenment's repudiation of Aristotle's naturalism of human goals did not lead to a wholesale repudiation of the importance of flourishing as a normative notion. Still, the notion of flourishing gripped thinkers' imagination as a normative ideal. With the recognition that individuals can play a constitutive role in determining their own ends and so what counts as valuable for them, a more nuanced, variegated and contextualized conception of flourishing is possible and this has influenced diverse thinkers such as Immanuel Kant (1996 [1785]), Bernard Williams (1985) and Harry G. Frankfurt (1987).

Flourishing requires an individual to develop (or discover) a conception of their own lives they wholeheartedly endorse (Frankfurt 1987). This is no simple matter but can occur only in certain conditions. Moreover, the conditions under which choices can be made require autonomy, enabling material conditions and a space of possibilities to be available to the person.

Although presented as focussed upon the individual, it is vital to see that both the goals and the structures that facilitate or frustrate the attempt to realize those goals are essentially social. Another important aspect of Aristotle's views is the idea that the human is a *zoön politikon*. This recognition on his part is independent of his naturalism about the *telos* of humans. We are social, and the social conditions of our lives provide the crucial scaffolding of the possibility of their excellence. The conditions that allow us to develop those facets in our lives that reflect what we value will often be social. Like a tail breeze, these social conditions can readily be taken for granted; the goals they facilitate us to achieve can seem to have been achieved entirely on our own. The social conditions, the support of friends and family, the social programs we have participated in, can all seem insignificant. And yet, just as the impact of the tailwind can be best reckoned when we encounter a headwind, the role of these social factors can often be best seen when we lack them. For many of us, these conditions will be a part of being inculcated with values and goals and habits of mind which allow for critical reflection on those very values, goals and habits of mind. However, as with T.S. Eliot's "Little Gidding",

> We shall not cease from exploration
> And the end of all our exploring
> Will be to arrive where we started
> And know the place for the first time.

Our ceaseless questioning often finds the structures of the familiar attractive, but not always, and the space to shape a conception of a life worth chasing needs to be left open.

People with disabilities are often markedly more vulnerable to the structures that facilitate our active choices which would shape our lives. Vision-impaired people can have their autonomy undergirded by technical innovations that were not available a few short years previously. Eminent Australian law professor and totally blind Ron McCallum entitled his autobiography *Born at the Right Time* (2019) since he was able to use text to an audio machine to gain an education and a career as a law professor. He was able to shape his own life in a way he could not have without that machine. The social conditions allowed him to fashion a life which he chose, which he valued and which, though difficult, he wholeheartedly endorsed. People with disabilities are not different in kind here but only in degree. To flourish we need the social setting and resources that facilitate our developing and pursuing of a life we value.

## Conclusion

Human rights discourse provides a powerful critique not of all situations but rather of when the situation is not tolerable and is brought about by the actions of the powerful against the less powerful. The point of the discourse is to provide a way of protecting the vulnerable from the ugly vicissitudes of the powerful. Returning to Hammarskjöld's quote, "The UN was not created to take mankind to heaven, but to save humanity from hell," this is a task for which the whole discourse of human rights is eminently well suited. However, as we have seen, it has its limitations, even when extended in scope and in the range of powerful agents they offer protections against. We have signalled some of these but more significant is the idea that the normative landscape involves the articulation of concepts beyond those of human rights, important though they are.

Human rights discourse works only to set a standard which can "save humanity from hell". This is a very important aim. However, not being in hell is not the same as flourishing. This is even more starkly true when considering those whose vulnerabilities bring with them particular needs. In this way, human rights are vital to protect the less powerful from the powerful and to avoid hell, the intolerable. We argue that human rights legislation is vital to set a standard below which is unacceptable, but that such social instruments should be kept separate from the goals of states, the facilitation of the flourishing of their polities. Polities are not simply made up of citizens, but anyone falling under their legal jurisdiction.

Flourishing is not about justice. But justice, with its apparatus of laws, penalties and reparations, is about remedying what happened in the past and addressing injustices. Certainly, flourishing requires justice; however, justice does not require flourishing. Flourishing is essentially future focussed. Discussions about flourishing orient us to how we want to live, what we can be within the polity. Through those discussions, the recognition of past injustices will need to be addressed because past injustices have present consequences: it will be necessary to enable people to achieve the lives that they desire for themselves in shared solidarity. In such a scenario, it is important to see how legal frameworks (within which we find human rights discourse) coordinate with discussions of flourishing and not in competition with it. These complement each other; they do not compete for normative force.

A further matter is raised by dint of the fact of human rights discourse being a legal framework. We should not expect nor want legal frameworks to enshrine rich ethical perspectives. The state should, as far as possible, refrain from imposing a substantive notion of the good on those falling within its power. Our self-conceptions of our own flourishing are just that sort of substantive notion of the good. Facilitating the exploration and self-constitution of the individuals within its power is not the same thing as imposing a substantive notion of the good on those individuals. The multiplicity of conceptions of flourishing such individuals can determine means that the state has little to no role in advocating or endorsing some specific conception of the good.

We have seen that only when individuals have the material and social conditions that allow them to imagine, explore and wholeheartedly endorse a conception of their own lives can they flourish. Those social and material conditions depend on state policies in many different ways. A state's failing to support those conditions might not be a violation of human rights, but it is nevertheless a ground for normative criticism.

**Acknowledgements** We wish to thank Franziska Felder and Kelly Somers for their help with this chapter and thank Kristin Blom of the Dag Hammarskjöld Foundation for the source of the oft-quoted but rarely sourced remark by Dag Hammarskjöld on the aims of the UN.

## References

Aminath Didi, Karen Soldatic, Carolyn Frohmader, and Leanne Dowse. 2016. "Violence Against Women? Is Australia Meeting Its Human Rights Obligations?" Australian Journal of Human Rights 22(1): 159–77.

Ashford, Elisabeth. 2007. "The Duties Imposed by the Human Right to Basic Necessities." In Freedom from Poverty as a Human Right, edited by Thomas Pogge. Oxford: Oxford University Press, 183–218.

Avery, Scott. 2018. Culture Is Inclusion: Indigenous Disability in Australia. Sydney: First Peoples Disability Network.

Beitz, Charles. 2009. The Idea of Human Rights. Oxford: Oxford University Press.

Benhabib, Seyla. 2013. Dignity in Adversity: Human Rights in Troubled Times. Cambridge: Polity Press.

Berghs, Maria. 2012. War and Embodied Memory: Becoming Disabled in Sierra Leone. London: Routledge.

Block, Pamela, Devva Kasnitz, Nakema Nishida, and Nick Pollard (eds.). 2016. Occupying Disability: Critical Approaches to Community, Justice and Decolonising Disability. New York: Springer.

Brysk, Alison, and Gershon Shafir (eds.). 2004. People Out of Place: Globalisation, Human Rights and the Citizenship Gap. London: Routledge.

Charlton, James. 2000. Nothing About Us Without Us: Disability Oppression and Empowerment. Los Angeles: University of California Press.

Council of Australian Governments. National Disability Strategy (2010–2020). 2011. Canberra: Australian Government.

Crenshaw, Kimberle. 1991. "Mapping the Margins: Intersectionality, Identity Politics, and Violence Against Women of Color." Stanford Law Review 43: 1241–299.

de Sousa Santos, Boaventura. 2002. Toward a New Legal Common Sense. London: Butterworths Lexus Nexus.

Encalada, Alberto Vásquez. 2019. "Transforming Disability Law and Policy in Peru: The Role of Civil Society." In Global Perspectives on Disability Advocacy and Activism: Our Way, edited by Karen Soldatic and Kelley Johnson. London: Routledge, 232–44.

Fitts, Michelle, and Karen Soldatic. 2020. "Who's Caring for Whom? Disabled Indigenous Carers' Experiences of Australia's Infrastructures of Social Protection." Journal of Family Studies. https://doi.org/10.1080/13229400.2020.1734478.

Flynn, Eiolonoir, and Anna Arstein-Kerslake. 2014. "Legislating Personhood: Realising the Right Support to Exercise Legal Capacity." International Journal to Law in Context 10(1): 1–59.

Frankfurt, Harry. 1987. "Identification and Wholeheartedness." In Responsibility, Character, and the Emotions: New Essays in Moral Psychology, edited by Ferdinand David Schoeman. Cambridge: Cambridge University Press.

Frankfurt, Harry. 1988. The Importance of What We Care About: Philosophical Essays. Cambridge: Cambridge University Press.

Fraser, Nancy. 1995. "From Redistribution to Recognition? Dilemmas of Justice in a Post-Socialist Age." New Left Review 2: 68–93.

Fraser, Nancy. 2007. "Feminist Politics in the Age of Recognition: A Two-Dimensional Approach to Gender Justice." Studies in Social Justice 1(1): 23–35.

Fraser, Nancy. 2013. Fortunes of Feminism: From State-Managed Capitalism to Neoliberal Crisis. London: Verso.

Gilroy, John. 2019. "Understanding the NDIS: The Scheme Does Not Yet Address All the Needs of Indigenous People with Disabilities." The Conversation. December 12, 2019. https://theconversation.com/understanding-the-ndis-the-scheme-does-not-yet-address-all-the-needs-of-indigenous-people-with-disabilities-57572.

Griffin, James. 2008. On Human Rights. Oxford: Oxford University Press.

Hammarskjöld, Dag. 1954. "Address by Secretary-General Dag Hammarskjöld at University of California Convocation, Berkeley, California, Thursday, May 13, 1954." United Nations. https://ask.un.org/loader.php?fid=11125&type=1&key=6bf400a0db526933d8577cce49f39ad2.

Kant, Immanuel. 1996 [1785]. "Groundwork for the Metaphysics of Morals." In Practical Philosophy, translated by Mary Gregor. Cambridge: University of Cambridge Press.

Kayess, Rosemary, and Philip French. 2008. "Out of Darkness into Light? Introducing the Convention on the Rights of Persons with Disabilities." Human Rights Law Review 8(1): 1–34.

Kreide, Regina. 2007. "Neglected Injustice: Poverty as a Violation of Social Autonomy." In Freedom from Poverty as a Human Right, edited by Thomas Pogge. Oxford: Oxford University Press, 155–82.

Lear, Gabriel Richardson. 2009. "Happiness and the Structure of Ends." In A Companion to Aristotle, edited by Georgios Anagnostopoulos. London: Blackwell, 387–403.

Lobel, Diana. 2017. Philosophies of Happiness: A Comparative Introduction to the Flourishing Life. New York: Columbia University Press.

Marcus, Herbert. 1964. One-Dimensional Man: Studies in the Ideology of Advanced Industrial Society. London: Routledge.

McCallum, Ron. 2019. Born at the Right Time. Sydney: Allen & Unwin.

Meyers, Stephen. 2014. "Global Civil Society as Megaphone or Echo Chamber? Voice in the International Disability Rights Movement." International Journal of Culture, Politics and Society 27(4): 459–76.

Michael, Michaelis. 2006. "How Should We Think of Human Rights?" The Human Rights Defender 15(2): 6–7.

Mladenov, Teodor. 2018. Disability and Post Socialism. London: Routledge.

National Disability Insurance Agency. 2020. "Understanding the NDIS." Australian Government. February 17, 2020. https://www.ndis.gov.au/understanding.

Nussbaum, Martha C. 2001 [1986]. The Fragility of Goodness. Cambridge: Cambridge University Press.

Richter, Zahari. 2019. "Queer-crip.blog: A Virtual Ethnographic Comparison of Social Media Movement-Building Techniques Used by Queer and Disabled Activists." In Global Perspectives on Disability Advocacy and Activism: Our Way, edited by Karen Soldatic and Kelley Johnson. London: Routledge, 193–204.

Smith, Ben. 2016. "Intersectional Discrimination and Substantive Equality: A Comparative Theoretical Perspective." The Equal Rights Review 16: 73–104.

Soldatic, Karen. 2019. Disability and Neoliberal State Formations. London: Routledge.

Soldatic, Karen, and Anne Chapman. 2010. "Surviving the Assault? The Australian Disability Movement and the Neoliberal Workfare State." Social Movement Studies 9(2): 139–54.

Soldatic, Karen, and Kelley Johnson. 2019. "Introduction." In Global Perspectives on Disability Advocacy and Activism: Our Way, edited by Karen Soldatic and Kelley Johnson. London: Routledge, 1–12.

Soldatic, Karen, Liam Magee, Paul James, Shuman Partorejdo, and Jakki Mann. 2020. "Disability and Migration in Urban Australia: The Case of Liverpool." Australian Journal of Social Issues. https://doi.org/10.1002/ajs4.93.

Spivak, Gayatri Chakravorty. 1988. "Can the Subaltern Speak?" In Marxism and the Interpretation of Culture, edited by Cary Nelson and Lawrence Grossberg, 271–315. London: Macmillan.

Tremain, Shelley. 2002. "On the Subject of Impairment." In Disability/Postmodernity: Embodying a Disability Theory, edited by Mairian Corker and Tom Shakespeare, 32–47. London: Bloomsbury Publishing.

Tremain, Shelley. 2019. "Feminist Philosophy of Disability: A Genealogical Intervention." The Southern Journal of Philosophy 57(1): 132–58.

T. S. Eliot Quotes. BrainyQuote.com, BrainyMedia Inc, 2020. https://www.brainyquote.com/quotes/t_s_eliot_109032, accessed October 2, 2020.

Williams, Bernard. 1985. Ethics and the Limits of Philosophy. London: Routledge.

World Health Organization and World Bank. World Report on Disability. 2011. Geneva: World Health Organization and World Bank.

CHAPTER 5

# Disability and the Dilemma of Difference

*Kjersti Skarstad*

## Introduction

Persons with disabilities are among the most marginalized people in the world, experiencing graver and more human rights violations than their nondisabled peers (Elwan 1999; World Health Organization and World Bank 2011). The dilemma of difference posits that there are two ways of dealing with such discrimination: treat persons with disabilities similarly to others (integration) or provide "special" treatment (separation) to alleviate the specific challenges of the marginalized group. The dilemma occurs because both integrated and targeted equality approaches run the risk of exacerbating inequality. Identical policies may avoid stigmatization, but are inefficient in tackling group-specific challenges and hence what is often termed as the "special" needs of the group in question. Targeted policies grapple with the challenges head on, but can increase stigmatization by demonstrating group differences (Minow 1990; Jenness 2003).

K. Skarstad (✉)
Bjørknes University College Oslo, Oslo, Norway



F. Felder et al. (eds.), *Disability Law and Human Rights*, Palgrave Studies in Disability and International Development, https://doi.org/10.1007/978-3-030-86545-0_5

The dilemma of difference is a philosophical question with clear policy and legal implications. At the philosophical (conceptual) level, the dilemma of difference is mainly a question about what equality is. By extension, this understanding has consequences for the practical approaches seen as suitable for achieving equality. In this chapter, equality is understood as having the same human rights as others,[1] and I show how the dilemma of difference can be reinterpreted as a question of how we can perceive human beings as different, yet equal in human rights. While the dilemma is often posited as a choice between "equal" or integrated approaches, and "special" or different treatment, I argue that—due to our differences—both integrated and targeted approaches are necessary tools to achieve equality in practice. Differential treatment is thus equal treatment if the treatment is a (legitimate) measure to obtain equal rights in practice.

I start by discussing how the dilemma has historically played out in the context of disability and human rights and how it remains a challenge. Closely connected to how we understand disability rights, is how we understand disability. I thus focus on the debate about whether to have disability-specific human rights provisions—including having a disability human rights convention—and whether to see disability as difference or normalcy. Both of these debates tap into how we perceive the universality (and hence equality) of human rights. I show that an underlying assumption of the debate is the erroneous belief that sameness in individual characteristics implies sameness in rights and vice versa.

The United Nations (UN) Convention on the Rights of Persons with Disabilities (CRPD) specifies what implementing human rights for persons with disabilities entails as an integral part of the human rights system. The CRPD takes a pluralist approach valuing individual differences. The convention focuses on both *sameness* of human rights (equality) and the different measures necessary to ensure that equality is achieved for persons with disabilities in practice. I argue that by showing how we should take both sameness and difference into account, the CRPD moves beyond and provides a new framework for understanding the dilemma of difference.

Using the CRPD as a framework, the main part of this chapter argues that integrated and targeted approaches should not be seen as opposites,

[1] Because human rights are rights one has by virtue of being human, it follows that they are equally (or universally) shared among all human beings.

but as complementary in achieving equality of human rights. Group-specific human rights provisions and measures are not a threat to equality or indicate relativeness of human rights; rather, they are necessary to ensure that human rights are universally applied. By separating (and understanding the difference) between human rights ideals and practice, the dilemma of difference can be better dealt with. Human rights ideals are universal (the same for all), but differences between individuals entail a difference in how these ideals are achieved in practice. Hence, to avoid disability-specific human rights limitations, human rights need to be subject to disability-specific support. At the political level, the concept of equality implies mainstreaming practices, understood as fully taking the rights of persons with disabilities (and others) into account in general policies as well as having targeted policies or measures combating specific human rights challenges.[2]

## The Dilemmas

The dilemma of difference is the notion that inequality can be exacerbated both by treating members of minority groups the same (meaning identical) as members of the majority and by treating them differently (Minow 1985, 1990; Jenness 2003; Norwich 2007). Separation or segregation of a minority group may reinforce stigma, minority feelings of inferiority, and majority feelings of superiority (Minow 1990, 160). Yet, integration also risks perpetuating hierarchy: if differences are not acknowledged, inequalities cannot be dealt with efficiently and will continue to exist. The dilemma of differences is often discussed within a legal context, this chapter takes a philosophical approach and looks at the broader framework in which the law operates.

The dilemma occurs in different variants for all discriminated groups. In the context of disability, the choice of whether to have disability-specific human rights provisions—including having a disability human rights convention—and whether to see disability as difference or normalcy, are examples of the dilemma of difference. Each of these will now be presented and discussed.

[2] See Skarstad and Stein (2018) for an explanation of this understanding of the concept of mainstreaming.

### *Universal or Disability-Specific Human Rights Provisions*

Persons with disabilities have experienced and are still experiencing graver human rights violations than persons without disabilities. In light of the dilemma of difference, the options available to remedy the situation can be framed this way: (1) Should the international response be on *sameness*, emphasizing existing human rights conventions and provisions for this group? Or (2), should the response be focusing on *difference*, creating a convention including specific provisions focusing particularly on disability human rights challenges?

The CRPD was enacted in 2006. Up until that year, the rights of persons with disabilities were not explicitly mentioned in any of the existing human rights conventions.[3] However, by definition, human rights are rights that we have only by virtue of being human. This is inscribed in all the human rights covenants. Thus, as human beings, persons with disabilities were and are clearly covered by all the existing human rights conventions. As such, it may seem paradoxical that there should be a separate disability human rights convention—it should have been unnecessary. A separate convention could perhaps even be harmful—it could lead to the view that persons with disabilities are a distinct group with different interests than the rest of the society, potentially intensifying their marginalization. A separate convention could also lend support to the view that human rights cannot be universal in the sense of applying equally to all groups, and hence that human rights are relative rather than universal.

Another argument supporting the sameness option is that a disability human rights convention could create incentives for the existing human rights committees to delegate issues pertaining to persons with disabilities to the disability convention committee instead of integrating disability human rights issues in their own work. This would lead to a more fragmented human rights system.

An underlying premise of the arguments against a disability-specific human rights convention is that the existing human rights instruments were fully capable of integrating disability human rights concerns. Yet, empirical evidence shows that this has not been the case. While persons with disabilities have experienced overwhelming human rights abuses, the

[3] A notable exception is the rights of children with disabilities in the Convention on the Rights of the Child.

UN human rights systems paid close to no attention to such abuses up until the creation of the CRPD (Quinn et al. 2002). To illustrate, from 1993 to 2002 only four disability-related complaints were declared admissible by the human rights bodies, and only 7% of the Human Rights Committee's concluding observations mentioned the human rights of persons with disabilities, of which only 3% made critical statements or recommendations (ibid., 71). This situation persisted, despite documentation showing that persons with disabilities experienced human rights violations at a substantially higher rate than nondisabled persons (Elwan 1999). When issuing a General Comment on nondiscrimination in 1989, the Human Rights Committee eschewed the opportunity to make explicit that persons with disabilities are comprised within the "other status" category of the International Covenant on Civil and Political Rights (Mégret 2008a).

Among the few notable exceptions to the UN's pre-CRPD silence on the equal rights of persons with disabilities are the Standard Rules on the Equalization of Opportunities for Persons with Disabilities and the Vienna Declaration and Program of Action, both issued in 1993. Of signal importance is also the 1991 General Recommendation on disability by the Committee on the Eliminiation of All Forms of Discrimination against Women, the 1994 General Comment on disability by the Committee on Economic, Social and Cultural Rights, and the General Comment on the Rights of Children with Disabilities by the Child rights committee in 2006.[4]

Despite these exceptions, the human rights challenges of persons with disabilities have overall been ignored. Combined with the fact that persons with disabilities experienced and experience massive human rights violations, the argument that a disability human rights convention could do more harm falls on its own merits. Recent empirical research also shows that the effect of the CRPD has been a dramatic increase in the overall quantitative incidence of disability rights being referenced by the UN treaty bodies.[5]

[4] The Convention on the rights of the child from 1989 includes the rights of children with disabilities in two articles, but fails to include their rights on an equal basis with others, see Peters (2007) and Quinn et al. (2002).

[5] In the seven years before the CRPD was enacted (2000–2006) disability was mentioned in 16% of the treaty bodies concluding observations, compared to 62% in

However, although empirical facts show that creating a disability convention, and hence focusing particularly on the human rights challenges of persons with disabilities, was necessary, the dilemma of difference remains. How should the convention be constructed and interpreted? A convention merely stating the obvious—that human rights pertain equally to persons with disabilities would be less effective in grappling with disability-specific challenges, whereas focusing on such challenges could lend support to the view that disability rights are just specific to persons with disabilities and thus not human rights proper. This would also make the convention less efficient; if governments see disability human rights as "human rights light," they are less likely to prioritize disability human rights protection.

An underlying premise of the sameness approach is that human rights challenges can be solved in the same way for all individuals. This seems unlikely. It is hard to believe that the same human rights system that has excluded persons with disabilities for so long can offer equal human rights protection to this group without any modification of the premises of the system.

The convention ended up containing all human rights—civil, political, economic, social as well as cultural. It specifies that human rights apply equally to persons with disabilities and how governments can ensure that this is realized in practice. But the convention goes further than merely stating that all rights apply equally to persons with disabilities. It contains, as we shall look more into later, novel features. For example, as the first international human rights convention, the CRPD states that there is a distinct human right to be included in the community (article 19). This has been seen as representing a relativization of human rights (Mégret 2008b).

### *Disability as Normalcy or Difference*

Closely connected to how we understand disability rights, is how we understand disability. The dilemma of difference literature tells us that if disability is understood as a difference, it may be easier to give disability-specific support—focusing on the specific needs of a group. Yet this may exaggerate difference and create further stigma. Focusing on disability

the eight years after the enactment of the convention (2007–2014), see Skarstad and Stein (2018).

as normalcy may make it easier to understand disability as natural part of humanity thus reducing stigma. Yet by obscuring real differences, persons with disabilities may not receive the help that they need.

Historically, persons with disabilities have been seen as different in the sense of being an aberration or deviation. In much of Western political theory, persons with disabilities have been portrayed in limiting, depreciating, and discriminatory ways (Arneil 2009). Much of political theory deprecates disability by describing persons with disabilities as categorically different from others (Arneil 2009; Skarstad 2018a). This has particularly been the case for persons with intellectual disabilities. They have been seen as not having the required autonomy for having rights (Fiala-Butora 2015). The stronghold of this idea is evident by the many laws and policies around the world that have disability-specific limitations to the right to self-determination. The underlying logic seems to be that because persons with disabilities are different (in, particularly self-determination, capabilities) they are seen as justifiably having limited (and hence non-equal rights) rights.

Within disability studies, the discriminatory way of seeing persons with disabilities has been framed as the medical model. The name refers to how disability traditionally has been understood as a medical, and hence a decontextualized individual problem. By viewing disability as a medical problem, one fails to perceive disability as a social-political concept. As such, it limits the social response to disability as one focused on medical correction and material compensation (Oliver 2009; Stein 2007; Wasserman et al. 2013). In its most aggressive form, it uses perceived biologically atypical medical conditions to objectify persons with disabilities (Stein 2007). In these cases, persons with disabilities are not seen as individuals, but as patients being predefined by, and hence acting according to, their medical conditions.

Given the way in which seeing persons with disabilities as different has traditionally equaled that they should not be given the same rights, there is no wonder that the focus has been on sameness within human rights and disability studies. Within these scholarly fields, the dilemma of difference is thus not mainly between whether to focus on impairment as a relevant difference or not but about whether something is lost by focusing extensively on sameness.

Some political and human rights theorists have shown how disability is a normal and common human feature. They have for example emphasized that vulnerability and dependency—traits usually associated with persons with disabilities—are universal human features, that everyone at any point can become disabled, and that everyone will indeed have disabilities in certain parts of their lives (Arneil 2009; Fineman 2008).

Within disability studies, the medical model has been contrasted against the social model. The latter emphasizes how social and structural barriers, rather than the impairment, lead to exclusion (Oliver 2009; Oliver and Barnes 2012). However, one prominent critique against the social model defenders has been that by emphasizing disability as a socially created difference, they underplay the actual medical realities of living with impairments (Shakespeare 2014).

Although much has been written on the social model within disability studies, the model has so far been expressed as requiring only formal equality—treating all persons the same—or as requiring only that people should have equal opportunities (the equal opportunity model) (Degener 2017; Kayess and French 2008; Stein 2007). The formal equality model ignores that different persons have different starting points due to for example historical differences and discriminatory structures persisting from such historical differences. The equal opportunity model, however, considers this by requiring that all persons (regardless of their background and status) be supported in a way that creates equal chances to participate and exercise rights. The model thus lends support to a difference approach with the aim of "levelling the playing field" so that everyone can compete on the "same" terms. However, the equal opportunity model also has its limitations. It assumes that leveling the playing field is possible; yet differences are not solely the result of historic circumstances. As an example, persons with intellectual disabilities are not solely worse off when it comes to making their own decisions because of historical discrimination or lack of support; they have an actual cognitive impairment making it harder for them to consider options and make decisions. Ignoring needs arising from individual differences will not be helpful to those who need assistance.

Hence, the critique is that these models will not be efficient in helping persons with disabilities with their disability-specific challenges. Despite accommodation and removal of discriminatory structures, differences may exist. Basing equality on the notion of "sameness" may not only ignore the need for specific support; it may also be oblivious to the standard that persons with disabilities are compared—that is, who they are to be similar to. Persons with disabilities, or anyone else, should not feel pressure to become like someone else to obtain the same rights (Rioux and Riddle 2010).

A first step out of this Gordian knot is (as we did when discussing in section "Universal or Disability-Specific Human Rights Provisions") to try to identify the underlying premises of the arguments. In this case, some of the problems seem to occur because there is an assumption that sameness in rights must imply sameness in individual characteristics and vice versa (e.g., persons with disabilities do not have the same level of autonomy or decision-making skills, therefore they cannot have the same right to self-determination). Yet, such an understanding of rights does in fact put qualification criteria on human rights, violating the central human rights premise that human rights are not earned, they are rights we have only by virtue of being human (Skarstad 2018a). Moreover, disability is incorrectly seen as a difference that is relevant for the extent to which someone has rights. Instead, I will argue, it may be relevant for how we achieve rights in practice.

## Sameness and Difference as Reflected in the CRPD

Enacted as a response to massive human rights violations coupled with insufficient human rights frameworks to address them, the CRPD became the first international convention to explicitly address and protect the human rights of persons with disabilities. The CRPD clearly states that persons with disabilities have all human rights to the same degree as everyone else and explains how these rights are to become a reality for persons with disabilities.

At first glance, the convention may confusingly seem to contain elements lending support to both the sameness (understood as identical treatment) and difference approach to disability. As an example, article 1 of the CRPD states that "[p]ersons with disabilities include those who have long-term physical, mental, intellectual or sensory impairments which in interaction with various barriers may hinder their full and effective participation in society on an equal basis with others." The focus is thus on how society can accommodate and include all individuals to obtain the same rights in practice. Yet, the convention does not refute that persons with disabilities have a difference—an impairment. It is the *interaction* between social barriers and impairments that creates disability.[6] Moreover, the article on health contains a duty to "Provide those health services *needed by persons with disabilities specifically because of their disabilities*, including early identification and intervention as appropriate, and services designed to minimize and prevent further disabilities" (article 25b, emphasis added).

As the first UN human rights convention, the CRPD includes a set of general principles and general obligations that guide the interpretation of all its articles (Lord and Stein 2009). One of its general principles is "Respect for difference and acceptance of persons with disabilities as part of human diversity and humanity" (article 3d). Thus, persons with disabilities are both described as different and as an intrinsic part of "humanity." Disabilities are not perceived as deviations or aberrations. Persons with disabilities are described in positive terms. This is evident for example by article 8 and preamble para. m requiring States Parties to recognize and promote positive contributions to society by persons with disabilities.

Equality and nondiscrimination are general principles of the convention. They are evoked consistently throughout the substantive articles of the CRPD, as seen by the repeated use of the wording "on an equal basis with others" (CRPD Committee 2018). Yet each article also specifies how the right should be fulfilled for persons with disabilities specifically. Also, the CRPD's definition of discrimination includes lack of reasonable accommodation,[7] which can be understood as a disability-specific form of discrimination (CRPD Committee 2018).

Among the convention's general obligations is the duty that States Parties "take into account the protection and promotion of the human rights of persons with disabilities in all policies and programmes" (article 4c). The CRPD thus contains a duty to mainstream the human rights of persons with disabilities (Skarstad and Stein 2018). The protection of the rights of persons with disabilities should be integral to general policies. At the same time, the convention contains new and disability-specific provisions. Article 19 states that there is a right to live independently and being included in the community. According to the article, States Parties

[6] The CRPD conceptualizes rather than strictly defines disability: As society is constantly evolving, so too are disabling barriers and what is considered a disability.

[7] "'Reasonable accommodation' means necessary and appropriate modification and adjustments not imposing a disproportionate or undue burden, where needed in a particular case, to ensure to persons with disabilities the enjoyment or exercise on an equal basis with others of all human rights and fundamental freedoms" (CRPD, Article 2).

are to "take effective and appropriate measures to facilitate full enjoyment by persons with disabilities of this right and their full inclusion and participation in the community."

Hence, at first glance, the convention's inclusion of provisions pointing to both sameness and difference, even within the same articles, may seem confusing. However, the combination of both "sameness" and "difference" is not really a paradox; it simply reflects a specific understanding of equality where both "sameness" and "difference" are taken into account to fully achieve human rights. The CRPD addresses the continuing human rights violations and exclusion experienced by persons with disabilities by specifying what implementing human rights for this group entails as an integral part of the human rights system (Skarstad and Stein 2018). By showing how we should take both sameness and difference into account, the CRPD moves beyond the dilemma of difference.

## The Substantive Equality Model of the CRPD

Essentially, the dilemma of difference is about how we understand equality. The CRPD represents a substantive understanding of equality. Persons should be treated in a way that makes them attain the same human rights outcomes as others. To achieve this, structural and indirect discrimination must also be addressed and power relations have to be taken into account (CRPD Committee 2018). The CRPD demands that societies must be reconstructed to ensure the equal rights of persons with disabilities by ensuring their full inclusion and participation in society (Skarstad and Stein 2018). Both sameness and difference approaches have to be applied, depending on context and whether they lead to equality of outcome.

The substantive equality model of the CRPD goes further than other international human rights conventions. For example, although both the Convention on the Elimination of All Forms of Racial Discrimination (CERD) and the Convention on the Elimination of All Forms of Discrimination against Women (CEDAW) require States Parties to change prevailing social attitudes, the CRPD additionally requires States Parties to foster respect for persons with disabilities in all levels of the education system (Mégret 2008a).

The substantive equality model is often contrasted to, but does in fact also encompasses and extends the formal equality model and the equal opportunity model.[8] It does so by including both sameness and difference measures and by solving some of the tensions that occur within the formal and equal opportunity models. As noted, the problem with the equal opportunity model is that it falsely assumes that leveling the playing field so that people can compete on the same terms is possible in all circumstances; it thereby ranks individuals in a competitive framework (Rioux and Riddle 2010). When individuals are ranked, it is always according to a certain standard or norm. Although not usually explicitly acknowledged, the equal opportunity model often entails comparing different groups to an ableist male standard or norm. Yet as Rioux and Riddle (ibid., 48) point out, "[i]n most cases [persons with disabilities] cannot, and should not, be expected to overcome natural characteristics and be like the 'norm'." Leaving the dominant framework in society untouched and requiring assimilation from persons with disabilities is unfair.

A good (substantive) model of equality needs to take a pluralist perspective as its starting point. This entails valuing all individuals and people's different abilities and talents. This is clearly the case of the CRPD, which for the first time in human rights law, includes a general principle on "respect for differences" (article 3d). This clear pluralist starting point also benefits especially other discriminated groups such as women and minorities.[9]

As noted, closely connected to how we understand disability rights, is how we understand disability. The CRPD's human rights-based model of disability is a substantive equality model and an elaboration of the "social model of disability" which emphasizes how social and structural barriers, rather than the impairment, lead to exclusion (Oliver 2009; Oliver and Barnes 2012). An impairment does not predefine an individual—its consequences vary according to social context. Disabilities or impairments can never be a legitimate ground for the denial or restriction of human rights (CRPD Committee 2018).

In the human rights-based model, the necessary social reconstruction implied by the social model is understood within the context of human rights. As the CRPD demands substantive equality—alteration of norms

[8] The CRPD includes equality of opportunity as a general principle.

[9] See e.g. Stein (2007) for examples. Another novelty of the CRPD is the explicit protection against intersectional discrimination. Having the rights of children and women as a general principle and specifying their rights in several articles, the CRPD offers a stronger framework for human rights protection of women and children (with disabilities).

and reasonable accommodation, and thus differential treatment where necessary, the human rights-based model offers a more comprehensive approach of how justice for persons with disabilities can be achieved (Degener 2017; Kayess and French 2008). Hence, while the social model of disability has been criticized for not entailing substantive equality, the human rights-based model of disability of the CRPD clearly does.[10]

The definition of discrimination in the CRPD parallels that of the CERD and CEDAW in that "any distinction, exclusion or restriction on the basis of disability which has the purpose or effect of impairing or nullifying the recognition, enjoyment or exercise, on an equal basis with others, of all human rights and fundamental freedoms in the political, economic, social, cultural, civil or any other field" is discrimination (CRPD, article 2). However, as noted, the CRPD also includes denial of reasonable accommodation as discrimination (CRPD, article 2). Notably, and in contrast to the CEDAW which states "on a basis of equality between men and women" (CEDAW, article 1), the CRPD uses the term "on an equal basis with others." Hence, the situation of persons with disabilities is not to be compared with another specific group (e.g., persons who do not have a disability), but the general population, all of which are to have the same human rights. This underlines the pluralist perspective of the convention.

While many human rights conventions use the term "equality before the law," the CRPD uses the term "equality under the law." According to the CRPD committee, the former term simply refers to the possibility to engage in legal relationships, while the term used in the CRPD refers to the right to use the law for personal benefit (CRPD Committee 2018), hence to be an active citizen and positively engage.

## Equality of Human Rights

The CRPD clearly integrates both sameness and difference approaches, and provides a substantive understanding of equality. However, further explanation is needed if we are to understand how the CRPD represents

[10] The human rights-based model is also a social model as it sees disability as socially constructed. What the human rights-based model adds is first and foremost that persons with disabilities have the same rights as others and as such it creates a human rights-based framework for understanding and solving the challenges and discrimination that persons with disabilities face.

a framework for moving beyond the dilemma of difference. A substantive model of equality seeks equality of outcome. However, it is not always clear what this outcome should be. As a first step, it is thus crucial to consider and be specific on what kind of outcome it is that individuals should be equal to. Secondly, conceptual clarity is also needed on when difference is legitimate and on what has to be the same for all.

The wanted outcome should not be similarity between people in terms of skills or merits. The outcome we want to achieve is (equality in) human rights and hence that all individuals can flourish and develop their specific talents and abilities. To reach this goal, different methods (both similar and different/targeted approaches) have to be applied, and they need to be combined. What measure(s) are legitimate in a given case have to be judged according to whether it leads to better human rights protection.[11] To reach equal human rights in practice for a minority group can entail different approaches and measures than those that benefit the majority. This is not a threat to equality or indicates relativeness of human rights; rather, it is a necessity to make sure that human rights are universally applied.

To understand this properly, and hence to deal better with the dilemma of difference, we must understand the difference between ideals and practice. The starting point for human rights conventions is that all human beings have (the same) human rights, and that they accordingly ought to be treated with the same dignity and respect. Human rights conventions seek to say something about what treating someone with dignity and respect entails regarding specific rights and obligations (Skarstad 2018a). Human rights are thus ideals that inform how we should treat each other. Each individual should be treated according to the same moral standards (human rights). Yet in practice, because different human beings have different abilities and challenges, the fulfillment of human rights may require different approaches for different groups—that is, treating everyone according to the same overarching ideals may entail differential treatment in specific cases (Skarstad 2018a).

In sum, the human rights (ideals) are the same for all, the standard that we all should be equal to are those human rights ideals, and to achieve them in practice will require slightly different approaches for different groups and in different contexts.

[11] In accordance with human rights law, criteria such as proportionality and legitimate aim are also necessarily relevant.

This understanding follows from the plurality approach. If we fully take into account and value that individuals are different (in abilities, challenges, and talents) yet have the same human rights, the next step is to see that there must be (slightly) different ways of achieving the same human rights for different people. We all have the same rights, but (due to our differences) there are different ways of achieving them. This entails that human rights cannot be subject to disability-specific limitations, but has to be subject to disability-specific support (Skarstad 2017).

Although not giving final answers, separating between ideals and practice and seeing the wanted result as equality in human rights ideals, provides a way out of the dilemma of difference in two important ways. Firstly, it creates a new framework for evaluating whether a specific measure or approach is legitimate (it should be judged according to whether it leads to [equality of] human rights). Secondly, it provides conceptual clarity about when and what have to be the same (human rights ideals) and when and what can be different (individuals, measures).

Based on this understanding, we can better make sense of the dilemmas identified in section "The Dilemmas" of this chapter. One of the dilemmas was whether the focus should be on normalcy or difference. Focusing on sameness in capacities of persons with disabilities and their nondisabled peers has been seen as a strategy for obtaining the same rights but at the cost of not receiving disability-specific support. One pertinent example is the way in which the right to self-determination has been withheld from persons with intellectual disabilities on the notion that they do not have the same capacity for autonomy (self-determination). The way out of the dilemma is to recognize that the level of autonomy a person currently has is not relevant for whether the person has the right to self-determination (individuals differ); what matters is that all persons should be treated according to the (same) autonomy ideal. The CRPD gives answers to what treating everyone according to the autonomy ideal entails. Article 12 firstly states that persons with disabilities enjoy the right to self-determination on an equal basis with others in all aspects of life. It then specifies that States Parties have to "take appropriate measures to provide access by persons with disabilities to the support they may require in exercising their legal capacity" (self-determination) (article 12.3).

Hence, individual levels of autonomy and capacities are not relevant for whether someone has the right to self-determination. Instead, the focus has to be on finding the correct measures and methods to ensure that the (equal) right to self-determination can become a reality. Ensuring the equal right to self-determination is thus a practical task.

Ensuring that everyone has the right to self-determination can mean that in cases where the individual does not understand the issue or cannot express preferences—or needs and wants—the individual's general interests, personality, and lived experiences should be used to infer what the individual's decision would be (Skarstad 2018b). Not giving such support in such cases means that someone else makes the decision for the individual, substituting the individual's decision. Avoiding decision-making support is to fail to protect the right to self-determination for all. Hence, the example shows that giving disability-specific support or having disability-specific provisions is not an option but a necessity in terms of ensuring (equality of) human rights in practice.

In other words, disability-specific human rights provisions or measures are ways of enabling universal rights for persons with disabilities. In the same manner, specific support or measures targeting the human rights challenges of for example women, children, people of color, sexual minorities, ethnic minorities, and persons belonging to several of these categories are ways of enabling universal human rights for these people. For example, prenatal care is a way of enabling the universal right to health for women who are to give birth, and protecting ethnic minorities from racial violence is a way of ensuring that the right to physical integrity applies universally. In the same manner, decision-making support is a necessity for ensuring the universal right to self-determination for all.

Understanding disability-specific provisions as integral to ensuring universality of rights also offers a solution to the critique of the social model as not considering the actual medical realities of living with impairments (Shakespeare 2014). The human rights-based model reinterprets the potential medical treatment of painful impairments and rehabilitation as parts of the right to health for persons with disabilities and others (Skarstad 2018a). Hence, the equality of human rights approach dismantles the dilemma of difference debate considering universal or disability-specific human rights provisions. These are not opposite strategies to choose between, instead, disability-specific human rights provisions are integral to the universalist approach.

Human rights are an evolving project and have throughout history been criticized for not equally encompassing the rights of all groups (e.g., the rights of women, indigenous people, children, sexual and racial minorities, and persons with disabilities) (Ishay 2008). Scholars have for example criticized the understanding of human rights as being informed by a view of the human being as a white nondisabled male (Crenshaw 1989; Nussbaum 2006). The view of the human being and hence the concept of human rights is thus under constant evolvement (and improvement). The development of new human rights instruments reflects this (Donnelly 2013). The different human rights conventions are not (or does not have to be) a threat to the universality of human rights, but are ways of making the human rights project more inclusive—and hence more true to its core premise of applying equally to all human beings.

Although focusing specifically on disability, the CRPD benefits all by broadening the concept of human rights to more fully include all human beings. It broadens the scope and understanding of what human rights entails in general. Article 19—Living independently and being included in the community—can be understood in this light. This article and the CRPDs broad demand on ensuring the right to "[f]ull and effective participation and inclusion in society" (article 3c), are novel and are necessarily responses to the extensive experience that persons with disabilities have of being excluded from society. However, exclusion and social isolation (even when living in a community) are not only experienced by persons with disabilities, and have detrimental effects on all. The CRPD builds on the knowledge that to realize human rights, persons must be included in society. That is, individuals must be embedded in just social relations and participate in meaningful social practices (Lord and Stein 2013; Skarstad 2018a; Nussbaum 2006; Taylor 1985). Only this way can individuals flourish and develop their potential. The CRPD thus draws on new insights relevant to all human beings and human rights.

## Conclusion and Policy Implications

The CRPD specifies what implementing human rights for persons with disabilities entails as an integral part of the human rights system. Human rights are the same for all, but disability-specific measures are necessary to ensure that human rights apply equally to persons with disabilities in practice. Using the CRPD as a framework, I have shown how separating between ideals and practice provides a way out of the dilemma of difference. Human rights ideals are universal, but differences between individuals may entail a difference in how the human rights ideals are achieved. Hence, applying different approaches to different groups is not a paradox, but a necessity for the universal application of human rights.

At the political level, this means that achieving equality is not a choice between integrated or targeted approaches; rather, the rights of persons with disabilities (and others) should be taken fully into account in general policies as well as having targeted policies or measures combating specific human rights challenges. Both types of policies are ways of making sure that the interests of a vulnerable group are attended to by the wider society. Combining these political strategies is thus the way political systems can realize the equal human rights of vulnerable groups. This approach does not reduce the increased stigma that may occur from targeted policies by itself. Stigma may, however, be reduced, if it is more generally understood that targeted policies are a necessity for achieving equality—not only for persons with disabilities, but for all of us.

## References

Arneil, Barbara. 2009. "Disability, self image, and modern political theory." *Political Theory*, 37 (2), 218–42.

Crenshaw, Kimberle. 1989. "Demarginalizing the intersection of race and sex: A black feminist critique of antidiscrimination doctrine, feminist theory and antiracist politics." *The University of Chicago Legal Forum*, 1989 (1), 139–67.

CRPD Committee. 2018. General Comment No. 6. Article 5: Equality and non-discrimination (Adopted 9 March 2018).

Degener, Theresia. 2017. *A new human rights model of disability, the United Nations convention on the rights of persons with disabilities*. Berlin: Springer, 41–59.

Donnelly, Jack. 2013. *Universal human rights in theory and practice*. Ithaca: Cornell University Press.

Elwan, Ann. 1999. *Poverty and disability: A survey of the literature*. Social Protection Advisory Service.

Fiala-Butora, János. 2015. *Reconstructing personhood: Legal capacity of persons with disabilities*. Dissertation, Harvard Law School.

Fineman, Martha Albertson. 2008. "The vulnerable subject: Anchoring equality in the human condition." *Yale Journal of Law & Feminism*, 20 (1), 8–40.

Ishay, Micheline. 2008. *The history of human rights: From ancient times to the globalization era*. Berkeley: University of California Press.

Jenness, Valerie. 2003. "Engendering hate crime policy: Gender, the 'dilemma of difference,' and the creation of legal subjects." *Journal of Hate Studies*, 2 (1), 73–92.

Kayess, Rosemary, and French, Phillip. 2008. "Out of darkness into light? Introducing the convention on the rights of persons with disabilities." *Human Rights Law Review*, 8 (1), 1–34.

Lord, Janet E., and Stein, Michael Ashley. 2009. "Social rights and the relational value of the rights to participate in sport, recreation, and play." *Boston University International Law Journal*, 27, 249–281.

Lord, Janet E., and Stein, Michael Ashley. 2013. "Contingent participation and coercive care." In Bernadette McSherry and Ian Frecelton (eds.), *Coercive Care: Rights, Law and Policy*. New York: Routledge, 31–49.

Mégret, Frédéric. 2008a. "The disabilities convention: Towards a holistic concept of rights." *The International Journal of Human Rights*, 12 (2), 261–78.

Mégret, Frédéric. 2008b. "The disabilities convention: Human rights of persons with disabilities or disability rights?" *Human Rights Quarterly*, 30 (2), 494–516.

Minow, Martha. 1985. "Learning to live with the dilemma of difference: Bilingual and special education." *Law and Contemporary Problems*, 48 (2), 157–211.

Minow, Martha. 1990. *Making all the difference: Inclusion, exclusion, and American law*. Ithaca/New York: Cornell University Press.

Norwich, Brahm. 2007. *Dilemmas of difference, inclusion and disability: International perspectives and future directions*. Oxon: Routledge.

Nussbaum, Martha. 2006. *Frontiers of justice: Nationality, disability, species membership*. Cambridge, MA: Harvard University Press.

Oliver, Michael. 2009. *Understanding disability: From theory to practice*. 2nd edn. Hampshire: Palgrave Macmillian.

Oliver, Michael, and Barnes, Colin. 2012. *The new politics of disablement*. New York: Palgrave Macmillan.

Peters, Susan J. 2007. "Education for all? A historical analysis of international inclusive education policy and individuals with disabilities." *Journal of Disability Policy Studies*, 18 (2), 98–108

Quinn, G., et al. 2002. *Human rights and disability: The current use and future potential of United Nations human rights instruments in the context of disability*. New York/Geneva: United Nations Publications.

Rioux, M. H., and Riddle, C. A. 2010. "Values in disability policy and law: Equality." In *Critical perspectives on human rights and disability law*. Leiden: Brill Nijhoff, 37–55.

Shakespeare, Tom. 2014. *Disability rights and wrongs revisited*. London: Routledge.

Skarstad, Kjersti. 2017. *Realizing the human rights of persons with disabilities: From political ideals to political practices*. Dissertation, University of Oslo.

Skarstad, Kjersti. 2018a. "Human rights through the lens of disability." *Netherlands Quarterly of Human Rights*, 36 (1), 24–42.

Skarstad, Kjersti. 2018b. "Ensuring human rights for persons with intellectual disabilities? Self-determination policies and the use of force in the case of Norway." *The International Journal of Human Rights*, 22 (6), 774–800, 20.

Skarstad, Kjersti, and Stein, Michal A. 2018. "Mainstreaming disability in the United Nations treaty bodies." *Journal of Human Rights*, 17 (1), 1–24.
Stein, Michael. 2007. "Disability human rights." *California Law Review*, 95 (1), 75–121.
Taylor, Charles. 1985. *Philosophical papers: Volume 2, philosophy and the human sciences*. Cambridge: Cambridge University Press.
Wasserman, David et al. 2013. "Disability and justice." In *Stanford Encyclopedia* (Online: https://plato.stanford.edu/entries/disability-justice/).
World Health Organization and World Bank. 2011. *World report on disability*. Malta: World Health Organization.

CHAPTER 6

# Forms of Equality, Faces of Discrimination: CRPD Article 5, Article 12, and the Disability's Difference Debate

*Leslie P. Francis*

Article 5 of the Convention on the Rights of Persons with Disabilities (CRPD) provides that all persons with disabilities are "equal before and under the law and are entitled without any discrimination to the equal protection and equal benefit of the law" (United Nations 2006). Achieving the promise of this provision has been controversial. Some claim Article 5 is primarily aspirational. Others argue that fair and practical strategies can enable states to provide all people with freedom from discrimination through equal protection and equal benefit from the law. This chapter considers how Article 5, coupled with Article 12 provisions on equal recognition before the law, can be practically understood in an

L. P. Francis (✉)
University of Utah, Salt Lake City, UT, USA
e-mail: francisl@law.utah.edu



F. Felder et al. (eds.), *Disability Law and Human Rights*, Palgrave Studies in Disability and International Development, https://doi.org/10.1007/978-3-030-86545-0_6

unjust world. Key to my account is a civil rights interpretation of "entitled without discrimination to the equal protection and equal benefit of the law."

My account begins with the debate over whether someone's having a disability means that their welfare is diminished. Addressing this debate is critical to understanding why claims to disability justice should not be based on assertions that people with disabilities have diminished welfare but instead on disability civil rights. I disentangle three different aspects of the debate over whether disability diminishes welfare and demonstrate how they mount up to particularly problematic judgments about persons with intellectual disabilities. Next, I set out the difference between human rights accounts, civil rights accounts, and welfarist accounts of disability rights and explain briefly why a civil rights approach is preferable as a ground for disability justice. I then argue for a civil rights interpretation of Articles 5 and 12 of the CRPD. Finally, I illustrate the practical effect of this account with examples from health care, especially decisions regarding health care and people with mental illness or intellectual disability.

My argument draws from my earlier work with Anita Silvers. We conceptualized the basic themes together. Her untimely death prevented her participation in the argument's actual realization; its present form is entirely mine and should not be taken for her views. I dedicate it to her memory.

## Differences: Good or "Bad"?

Extensive recent debate has addressed whether disability necessarily diminishes welfare. Spurred by Elizabeth Barnes's book (2016), recent discussion has been framed in terms of whether physical disability is "mere" difference or "bad" difference. Writers such as Guy Kahane and Julian Savulescu (2016) claim that disability is significantly likely to harm people's lives and therefore addressing discrimination at the social level will not erase differences in individuals' prospects for a good life. Characterizing disability as "bad" difference, if accurate, makes securing disabled people's hopes for equality impossible, quixotic, or at best dauntingly hard. Moreover, "bad" difference proponents take the "mere" difference characterization proposed by advocates of equality for all to be nothing but a psychologically and politically reassuring ploy.

This debate proceeds along multiple, albeit related dimensions. The dimension emphasized by Barnes is the scope of judgments about whether differences are bad. She thinks that disability is not globally bad for a person; to be disabled is just to be a different person than one would be were one not disabled. But disability may be locally bad for the person, for example causing pain. Local bads are part of every life, disabled or not. Global badness is not a feature of every life; lives can be globally good even when they encounter a variety of local bads. Indeed, people typically encounter a variety of local bads over the course of their lives. Global judgments about the badness of a life are especially pernicious when tied to judgments about the worth of the life or the status of the person.

Another related dimension is epistemic. Judgments of whether disability is globally bad, or associated with a variety of local bads, may be subjective, made from the perspective of the disabled person. Or, they may employ some supposedly objective comparator such as a functional assessment. Selection of comparators is problematic, as controversy about "normal species typical" functioning attest. Critics argue that selection relies on ineluctably normative judgments about functions worth measuring. Disability rights advocates are especially critical of judgments about species-typical norms used to set standards for nondiscrimination (Satz 2006). Differences between how people with disabilities judge the quality of their lives and how others judge these lives are notorious. For example, many studies address negative attitudes of health care providers toward disability and their effects on the treatment people with disabilities receive (Bickenbach 2016).[1]

Still another dimension is causal, about the impact of conditions on how people's bodies and minds function. Especially important here is the debate over whether limitations in functioning should be attributed to causes external to the person. People function differently in worlds of ramps, stairs, or waterways, or printed texts, calculation, or visualization. The social model of disability holds that changing world design and social structures alters functional capabilities and thus is central to remediation of bad local differences such as confinement. For example, the CRPD Committee on the Rights of Persons with Disabilities concluded that the failure of the city of Linz, Austria, to make tram information available in

[1] Tracy and Iacono (2008), for example, argue that involving people with developmental disabilities as tutors for medical students can change attitudes and favorably influence the health care these patients receive.

audible form violated Article 5(2) of the CRPD prohibition of discrimination on the basis of disability (Committee on the Rights of Persons with Disabilities 2014).

For intellectual disabilities especially, these three dimensions deliver cumulative damage. Diminished intellectual functioning is supposed to bring diminished abilities to judge one's good. Changes in the world, some believe, will not help. Moreover, when intellectual functioning is thought paradigmatic of being human, its loss has thereby been judged to be globally, rather than locally, bad for the person.[2] From these features of intellectual disability, two important consequences have been inferred: the need for protection and its concomitant deprivation of rights.

Protectionism, however, is not always benign. Apparent concern for the welfare of people with disabilities may mask conflicts of interest or disparaging attitudes. Protectors may abuse their power or impose their views on people they believe are unable to make their own judgments. A Supreme Court decision well known in the United States, involving a municipality's refusal to issue a permit for a group home for people with intellectual disabilities, illustrates this. The municipality's reasoning—that the home would be located near a school and its residents needed protection from the students—was a thinly veiled pretext for rejecting the disabled as neighbors. Nonetheless, the Court majority refused to adopt a standard of heightened scrutiny for disability-based categorizations. It presumed that disability difference may give rise to well-intentioned paternalism in many circumstances although did not do so in the actual case before it. The Court reasoned that the state may need to act protectively when disability is involved and so should not have to offer more carefully tailored justifications:

> Because mental retardation is a characteristic that the government may legitimately take into account in a wide range of decisions, and because both State and Federal Governments have recently committed themselves to assisting the retarded, we will not presume that any given legislative action, even one that disadvantages retarded individuals, is rooted in considerations that the Constitution will not tolerate.

[2] Notably, Barnes confines her account to physical disabilities, making no judgments about badness and intellectual disability.

> Our refusal to recognize the retarded as a quasi-suspect class does not leave them entirely unprotected from invidious discrimination. To withstand equal protection review, legislation that distinguishes between the mentally retarded and others must be rationally related to a legitimate governmental purpose. This standard, we believe, affords government the latitude necessary both to pursue policies designed to assist the retarded in realizing their full potential, and to freely and efficiently engage in activities that burden the retarded in what is essentially an incidental manner.[3]

The dissent conversely saw diversions from ableist norms as engendering fear, bigotry, segregation, and eugenics. Writing for the dissent, Justice Marshall forcefully questioned the benignity of differential treatment of the disabled:

> Fueled by the rising tide of Social Darwinism, the "science" of eugenics, and ... extreme xenophobia ... leading medical authorities and others began to portray the "feeble-minded" as a "menace to society and civilization ... responsible in a large degree for many, if not all, of our social problems." A regime of state-mandated segregation and degradation soon emerged that in its virulence and bigotry rivaled, and indeed paralleled, the worst excesses of Jim Crow. (ibid., 461f.)

The result, on Justice Marshall's view, was a structure of legal analysis—lower level rational basis scrutiny—that let rights deprivations pass unnoticed or subjected them to less probing examination than they required.

## Human Rights, Civil Rights, or Welfare?

A civil rights approach frames disability rights in terms of nondiscrimination and the furtherance of inclusion. A human rights approach instead frames rights in terms of claims rooted in some feature that is shared exclusively by human beings. In an earlier discussion, Anita Silvers and I argued that a civil rights approach provides a more secure foundation than a human rights approach for rights to health care of persons with disabilities (Silvers and Francis 2017). The problem we saw is that human rights, if founded in species norms, risk marginalizing people with disabilities. Our argument began with how human rights traditions justify

[3] See City of Cleburne v. Cleburne Living Center. 1985. 473 U.S. 432, 442.

human exceptionalism: all and only humans have human rights because of some characteristic that humans supposedly share but nonhuman animals do not. We then cautioned about the selection of these characteristics. Locating the characteristic as mental, broadly construed, demeans those who cannot exercise the requisite rational capacities. Locating the characteristic as biological privileges species-typical functioning. Instead, we argued through a lens of pragmatism, rights press "political institutions to recognize what is necessary for each of their members to lead flourishing lives within them (…) expanding equality among different kinds of individuals who happen to be interacting with one another" (ibid., 138).

Justice is not perfect, we further contended. Instead, it should be viewed as a work in progress for a nonideal world. Efforts to achieve justice take place in worlds of resource constraints and inequitable distribution. Efforts to achieve rights must recognize these factors, starting with "social resources needed to meet basic interests that are critical to individuals' interactive flourishing" (ibid.). These limits must also be challenged as new ways for accommodating difference are explored. This is a civil rights frame because it is grounded in achieving increased inclusion of human difference, rather than normative accounts of what is special to being human.

Such a civil rights frame also does not require taking a side in the "bad difference" debate discussed above. Civil rights judgments are not based on contentions that some differences are worse than others, or bad in themselves. Welfarist frames, by contrast, are rooted in assumptions that disability brings disadvantages that must be made up for in some way if equality is to be achieved. These frames risk lending force to the concern that the freedom from discrimination prescribed in Article 5 of the CRPD cannot be practically achieved and thus must be judged aspirational.

Philosophers have offered a variety of metrics for measuring welfare. Some use welfare directly. Some of these views postulate that welfare lowered by disability calls for compensation. Richard Arneson (1989) defended equal opportunity for welfare as the metric, taking account of individual choices that reduce welfare and that the individual can be held responsible for making. Arneson criticized using equality of resources as the metric (Dworkin 1981a, b) and observed that if disabilities increase resource requirements, people with disabilities should have more resources. For example, people who ambulate with legs and people who ambulate with expensive wheelchairs require different resources to get around in the world or experience the same level of welfare.

G.A. Cohen's "On the Currency of Egalitarian Justice" (1989) has become the classic locus for the view that the badness associated with disability, rather than resulting welfare, gives rise to claims for equalizing benefit:

> My unfortunate person's legs are paralyzed. To get around, he needs an expensive wheelchair. Egalitarians will be disposed to recommend that he be given one (...) before they have asked about the welfare level to which the man's paralysis reduces him. When compensating for disability, egalitarians (...) propose compensation for the disability *as such* (...). (Cohen 1989, 918)

Cohen's view is that egalitarians should favor wheelchair distribution to his "unfortunate person" in virtue of the person's misfortune, rather than considering access to resources or opportunities for welfare. For Cohen, abundant happiness is not "decisive against compensating him for his disability" (ibid.). People with disabilities are unavoidably disadvantaged, Cohen thinks, in ways for which they cannot be held responsible. In these cases of bad luck (in contrast to bad choices), disadvantage calls for compensation. Moreover, the unfortunate person should expect subsidies for efforts at overcoming the disadvantage (ibid., 920).

Welfarist approaches threaten the stability of disability rights in ways akin to human rights approaches. Judgments that disability is ineluctably bad for the person may spur conclusions that disabled lives are not worth living in their current state, deprioritizing care for these people or setting goals of care to correct the disability if possible. Or, judgments about disability badness may yield conclusions about care futility or costs. Or, the idea that people deserve compensation for their misfortunes may convey attitudes that demean.

In sum, the civil rights approach aims to achieve inclusion of difference in the world in which we live. Civil rights approaches emphasize access to public services on terms equal to others. They include accommodation as needed for this access. They do not start with disadvantage or normative ideals of the human. Instead, they initiate efforts to enhance inclusion.

## Conceptualizing Article 5 and Article 12: Rights as Human or Civil?

In this section, I begin the argument that a civil rights understanding of Article 5 and Article 12 can be the basis for interpreting them as practical rather than aspirational. This section first summarizes the provisions of Article 5 and Article 12, followed by accompanying interpretive materials. These materials clearly reject a welfarist frame. Explaining them in civil rights terms is more difficult but critical to their practical deployment.

### *Articles 5 and 12: The Text*

Article 5 provides that people with disabilities are "equal before" and "equal under" the law, "entitled without any discrimination" to "equal protection" and "equal benefit of" the law (CRPD, Art. 5 § 1). States parties must prohibit all discrimination on the basis of disability and guarantee all persons with disabilities "equal and effective legal protection against discrimination on all grounds" (ibid., § 2). Effective protections include appropriate steps to ensure reasonable accommodation (ibid., § 3). Moreover, steps to "accelerate or achieve de facto equality of persons with disabilities" are not discrimination against others who are not disabled (ibid., § 4).

Article 2 defines critical technical terms, especially "discrimination," which includes a denial of "reasonable accommodation":

> "Discrimination on the basis of disability" means any distinction, exclusion or restriction on the basis of disability which has the purpose or effect of impairing or nullifying the recognition, enjoyment or exercise, on an equal basis with others, of all human rights and fundamental freedoms in the political, economic, social, cultural, civil or any other field. It includes all forms of discrimination, including denial of reasonable accommodation;
>
> "Reasonable accommodation" means necessary and appropriate modification and adjustments not imposing a disproportionate or undue burden, where needed in a particular case, to ensure to persons with disabilities the enjoyment or exercise on an equal basis with others of all human rights and fundamental freedoms; (…).

Article 12 explains "equal recognition before the law" (CRPD, Article 12 § 1). It requires that persons with disabilities be recognized as legal persons and "enjoy legal capacity on an equal basis with others in all aspects of life" (ibid., § 2). As legal persons with full legal capacity, persons with disabilities have legal rights to make decisions just as others do: imposing age-restricted limitations on legal capacity for everyone is not a violation of Article 12, but imposing differential age-restricted limits based on disability would be.[4] As people with intellectual disabilities may require assistance in exercising legal capacity, Article 12 also requires states to provide access to needed supports, appropriate and effective safeguards to prevent abuse, and effective measures to ensure property rights and control of financial affairs (ibid., §§ 3–5).

### *Interpretive Materials: Article 5*

The CRPD establishes a Committee on the Rights of Persons with Disabilities to receive reports from states parties about the status of implementation (CRPD, Articles 34, 35). Under the Optional Protocol to the CRPD, now formally confirmed by 96 states parties, the Committee is also authorized to monitor implementation and to examine individual complaints with regard to alleged violations of CRPD requirements by states parties to the Protocol. The Committee has issued comments to clarify the obligations in Articles 5 and 12. Article 12 comment, "General Comment No 1" (2014) explains "equal recognition before the law." Article 5 comment, "General Comment No 6" (2018), explicates equality and nondiscrimination. Comment 6 clarifies that "Articles 5 and 12 are fundamentally connected, because equality before the law must include the enjoyment of legal capacity by all persons with disabilities on an equal

[4] In the United States, the Individuals with Disabilities Education Act requires states receiving federal funding to provide a free public education for all children with disabilities between the ages of 3 and 21, 20 U.S.C. § 1412 (a)(1)(A). Many states do not provide public education before age 5 and students typically graduate from high school by age 18. Some might suggest by analogy that for people with developmental disabilities, legal status could vary by age as well. The alternative, seemingly required by Article 12, is that legal status may not vary by age; instead, after the age of majority appropriate legal supports should be available for those who need them.

basis with others." My discussion begins with Comment 6, even though it was issued later, because Article 5 is the more overarching.

Comment 6 starts with concern that states parties are continuing "to approach disability through charity and/or medical models" (ibid., I.2). The Committee judges an underlying problem for CRPD implementation is that "laws and policies are commonly not regarded as disability-based discrimination because they are justified as being for the protection or care of the persons with a disability, or in their best interest" (ibid., I.3). In calling for comments on the initial published draft of Comment 6, the Committee also noted that the perpetuation of negative stereotypes about persons with intellectual or psychosocial disabilities was particularly troubling, as was the imposition of supposedly beneficial measures on this group (Committee on the Rights of Persons with Disabilities 2017).[5]

Arguing that Comment 6 can be construed in civil rights terms is more difficult. The language of "human rights" is the term used throughout the comment as the frame for achieving disability rights. For example, Comment 6 begins by observing that, although improved, "laws and regulatory frameworks often remain imperfect and incomplete or ineffective, or reflect an inadequate understanding of the human rights model of disability" (Comment 6, I.3). Two points are key to my argument that human rights as understood in Comment 6 can be glossed in civil rights terms: use of equality and nondiscrimination, and understanding equality as accommodation of difference.

The core concepts of equality and nondiscrimination that shape Comment 6 are grounded in "the inherent dignity and worth and the equal and inalienable rights of all members of the human family as the foundation of freedom, justice and peace in the world" (ibid., II.6). Dignity is not linked to a special biological or intellectual feature of humans; rather, it is instantiated in nondiscrimination and equality with "the wording 'on an equal basis with others', which links all substantive rights of the Convention to the non-discrimination principle" (ibid., II.7). Human rights are invoked in opposition to the medical model of disability and in support of nondiscrimination and equality.

In Comment 6, nondiscrimination is glossed as meaning "on an equal basis with others" (ibid.). Being on an equal basis requires not only formal equality, treating similars similarly, but also substantive equality

[5] The call also noted that women and children with disabilities were subjected to misplaced paternalism.

which addresses structural and indirect discrimination and takes power relations into account—all matters external to the person (ibid., III.10). Substantive equality addresses "dilemmas of difference," acknowledging that differences among human beings must be recognized socially for equality to be achieved (ibid.). Thus understood, substantive equality is a "new model of equality," inclusive equality (ibid. III.11) that emphasizes accommodation and intersectionality. It has four dimensions. First is fair redistribution of resources to address socioeconomic disadvantage. Second is recognition to combat stigma and stereotyping and support dignity and intersectionality. A third dimension is participatory, reaffirming people as members of social groups. The final dimension is accommodation of difference as a matter of dignity (ibid.). The idea is that people with disabilities "will not be granted more or fewer rights or benefits than the general population" but that states will "take concrete specific measures to achieve de facto equality for persons with disabilities to ensure that they can in fact enjoy all human rights and fundamental freedoms" (ibid., V.17).

Comment 6 also specifies interpretations of equality before and under the law. Equality "before" the law means nondiscrimination in the administration of justice. It is the entitlement to equal treatment in the application of law (ibid., V.14). Differential application of a law based on disability would violate this requirement; an example might be the U.S. Supreme Court case described above in which the municipality had applied a zoning regulation differently to a home for people with disabilities than for other aggregate homes under the pretext that the home's residents needed protection. Equal "under" the law means being equally able to engage in legal relationships and to use the law for benefit (ibid.). Under Comment 6, "equal benefit" of the law means enjoying legal rights on an equal basis and includes accessibility, reasonable accommodations, and individual supports needed to exercise rights, as provided in Article 12.

Comment 6 further explains nondiscrimination in terms of four distinct kinds of protections against four different forms of discrimination. First is direct discrimination—that is, treating people with disabilities less favorably than others similarly situated for a reason related to a prohibited ground. Second, indirect discrimination occurs when otherwise neutral laws, policies, or practices have a disproportionate negative impact. Third is denial of reasonable accommodation, for example not allowing space for an accompanying person in a theater or other place of entertainment.

Finally, harassment such as intimidation or other violations of dignity must be addressed for nondiscrimination to be achieved.

In addition, Comment 6 emphasizes that states parties must prohibit discriminatory denial of health care services. It also insists that it is discrimination to violate the right "to receive health care on the basis of free and informed consent" (ibid., L.66). Here, Comment 6 cross-references the statement in Comment 1 that realization of Article 12 rights requires that people with disabilities "have opportunity to develop and express their will and preferences (...) and to make choices and to have control over their everyday lives, on an equal basis with others (...)" (Comment 1, IV.44).

Rooted in nondiscrimination and equal benefit under law, Comment 6 attacks problematic forms of differentiation and exclusion. It uses the language of human rights to spell out these requirements forcefully. But it does not depend on grounding human rights in a special characteristic of human beings that some humans may not share. Instead, it construes inclusion in broad and novel ways. This is arguably a civil rights frame, emphasizing how social factors exclude, rather than a human rights frame as traditionally understood to emphasize special features of humanity.

### *Interpretive Materials: Article 12*

Comment 1 begins with the statement that Article 12 does not "set out additional rights for people with disabilities; it simply describes the specific elements that States parties are required to take into account to ensure the right to equality before the law for people with disabilities, on an equal basis with others" (ibid., I.1). The role of Article 12, Comment 1 states, is to "further describe (...) the content of this civil right" in "areas in which people with disabilities have traditionally been denied the right" (ibid.). Of primary concern is determination of legal capacity and deprivation of the rights as legal subjects of people determined to lack capacity.

According to Comment 1, Article 12 prohibits restriction of legal capacity "on an unequal basis with others" (ibid.). Status as a person with a disability may not be grounds for denying legal capacity. Legal capacity is both passive and active; it involves being both a holder of rights and an actor with rights (ibid., II.12). Practices such as guardianship, conservatorship, and forced mental health treatment deny an individual the right to full legal capacity in a manner that is equal to others. On some interpretations of Comment 1, so does any exercise of surrogate decision-making or substituted judgment based on a determination of incapacity.[6]

Legal capacity—recognition under law—differs from mental capacity, however. Individuals have different decision-making skills, depending on factors including social and environmental conditions. For the Comment, the problem in many jurisdictions is that functional assessments of mental capacity are conflated with legal capacity for people with disabilities only. This is discriminatory denial of legal capacity.

Instead, according to Comment 1, the approach should be providing supported decision-making for the exercise of legal capacity. Support may take many different forms, although all forms must recognize autonomy. Some support involves universal design and accessibility, for example providing information in understandable format or utilizing communication aids. Process-based support may involve advance planning for people who anticipate potential cognitive declines or mental illness; the entry into force of advance directives should be specified in the directive. Recognition of difference—as also described in Comment 6—means that support is not the same for everyone. Rather, support should be tailored in type and intensity and some people may choose not to have support at all. Moreover, in order to avoid determinations of incapacity rejected by Comment 1, it would seem that supported decision making must be available to anyone with a disability on terms equal to others.

Support raises concerns about abuse, including undue influence, threats, deception, or manipulation. Protection against abuse is critical but must respect the autonomy of the person with disabilities. Defaulting to the best interest standard fails to recognize autonomy; instead, the touchstone for support must be the best effort to ascertain the rights, will, and preferences of the person.[7] Like others, people with disabilities will take risks and make mistakes; it treats them unequally to prevent them from making mistakes when others are not similarly protected (Comment 1, III.27). So, for example, it is not discrimination to prevent everyone from making an expensive and irrevocable purchase on credit but it would be discrimination to prevent only persons with intellectual disabilities from

[6] For a criticism of Comment 1 along these lines, see Freeman et al. (2015).

[7] A problematic example of substituting the best interests standard for autonomy is the reasoning in A.-M.V v. Finland (2015).

such purchases. Similarly, it is not discrimination to restrict legal capacity based on circumstances such as bankruptcy or a criminal conviction (ibid., IV.32).

supported decision making must be available to all and should not hinge on mental capacity assessments. There must be no financial barriers or communicative barriers. Legal recognition of the support person must be readily available; states must facilitate creation of supports, especially for people who are isolated and may not have ready access to supports. All support must be based on the will and preferences of the person being supported. There must be adequate safeguards for assuring that the actions of a supporter are in accord with the will and preferences of the person being supported and a mechanism for challenging the actions when they are not. Supported persons must be able to refuse support and change or terminate the support relationship at any time. Finally, support may not be a justification for limiting other rights, such as the right to vote, the right to marry, or the right to found a family (ibid., III.29).

These rights are not aspirational; they go into effect with ratification of the CRPD. However, several of these key provisions have been highly controversial, especially in health care: the apparent complete rejection of any role for surrogate decision-makers, the rejection of the best interest standard, and the right of the person to refuse support at any time. In the concluding section, I explore how a civil rights frame can be helpful in understanding their practical implementation in the example of health.

## Practical Application: Article 25, on Health, Through a Civil Rights Lens

Article 25, on health, is a specific example of how Articles 5 and 12 play out for a substantive right. It thus provides an illustrative test case for the practical implementation of the Article 5 requirement of equality before the law. Article 25 requires that persons with disabilities "have the right to the enjoyment of the highest attainable standard of health without discrimination on the basis of disability." This is not a right to the best health or even to the best health care. It is a right to the best attainable standard *without discrimination*. More specifically, Article 25 requires

- the same range, quality, and standard of free or affordable health care provided to others

- health services needed specifically because of disabilities, including identification and prevention
- provision of services as close as possible to home communities, including in rural areas
- health services of the same quality and ethical standards given others, including standards of informed consent
- nondiscrimination in the provision of health insurance and, where permitted, of life insurance
- prohibition of discriminatory denial of health care, health services, or food or fluids on the basis of disability.

Four specifications are explicitly comparative: free or affordable health care, quality and ethical standards including informed consent, insurance, and care denials. A society that provided very low levels of these specifications for anyone would not discriminate on the basis of disability, although that society would likely violate rights for everyone (Bickenbach 2016). Two specifications are linked to the disparate impact of policies on people with disabilities, who might need services that others do not need and services closer to home.

Complete rejection of capacity evaluation and surrogate decision-making is the most controversial aspect of Comment 1 and it may be inconsistent with nondiscrimination requirements of Article 25. People may lose the ability to make decisions temporarily because of accidents or illness. In such cases, a capacity evaluation may determine that they are unable to express their wishes for themselves. For persons without disabilities, the standard practice is to turn to a substitute decision-maker, if one has been chosen by the person, or to someone else that it seems most likely the person would have chosen, such as a spouse, child, parent, or other close relative. The substitute's responsibility is to give effect to the known wishes of the patient or, if the patient's wishes are not known, to try to extrapolate what they would have been in the present circumstances. If wishes are unknown, the last step is to consider the best interests of the person, as understood subjectively in light of the person's situation and whatever can be known about them. This process does not assume that the person lacks capacity for the longer term, or that the lack of mental capacity should be translated into a change in legal status. Rather, it is a way of dealing with an immediate situation as it is assumed the patient would have wanted. Advance directives are desirable in such situations, especially directives that select a surrogate decision-maker, but they are frequently unavailable, especially for people who do not imagine themselves in such emergent circumstances.

To reject this process for disability altogether would seem to fail to place persons with disabilities on an equal basis with others, leaving them without emergency decision-making mechanisms available to others (Szmukler et al. 2014). Scholten and coauthors (2019) criticize what they call the "radical CRPD model" for prohibiting any substituted judgment and requiring supported decision making at all times. More ethically challenging, however, are situations in which people with mental illness experience fluctuating or sudden changes in status (Jeste et al. 2018). Some people use psychiatric advance directives to specify the care they would, or would not, wish to receive should their status change; some research indicates that people use these directives to choose among forms of care rather than to reject treatment altogether (Jeste et al. 2018; Werner and Chabany 2016). The statement in Comment 1 that choices about supported decision making may be revoked at any time would seem to allow present preferences to extinguish prior directives, except when no coherent expression of present preferences occurs. But people may want to bind themselves for later, believing that their later occurrent preferences may not reflect their longer-term autonomous choices. Szmukler (2019) conceptualizes this situation as a conflict between the person's expressed will and present preferences and argues that Comment 1 is mistaken to privilege preferences over autonomous choices.

Whether earlier decisions should be overridden by the choices of present selves is not a problem unique to mental disability, however. Considerable debate in bioethics attends whether the present self, the prior self, or a conceptualization of longer-term values should prevail (DeMarco and Lipuma 2016). "On an equal basis with others," it would seem, should mean that persons with disabilities are not treated differently or discriminated against in this debate. If advance directives are to be recognized when they clearly reflect the will of the person, on an account of what this will is and how it is to be determined, they should be recognized for people with disabilities (Szmukler 2019).

Comment 1 rejects capacity determinations because of their misuse in other circumstances, especially to compel treatment (de Almeida 2019). Judgments of capacity loss have grounded institutionalization and eugenics, in the infamous words of Justice Holmes that "three generations of imbeciles are enough."[8] People with mental disabilities and mental illness have suffered from segregation and deinstitutionalization without sufficient supports or services. Discrimination and unequal benefits have been so pervasive that it is understandable why concerns would be raised about the use of methodologies such as capacity determination that have proved so pernicious. However, a reminder of civil rights models under circumstances of injustice is the need for continuing scrutiny to avoid introducing new forms of injustice and exclusion, even as we address existing ones.

## Conclusion

Article 5 of the CRPD provides that persons with disabilities are equal before and under the law and are entitled without any discrimination to the equal protection and equal benefit of the law. Article 12 instantiates these requirements for people with disabilities as legal actors and Article 25 does so for health care. These articles and interpretive comments can be read in civil rights terms that explain how they are achievable rather than merely inspirational. This civil rights reading can illuminate challenges to implementation of nondiscrimination in health care and the need to avoid creating new forms of exclusion through the failure to address longstanding abusive practices.

## References

A.-M.V. v. Finland, European Court of Human Rights, Fourth Section, Application no. 53251/13 (15 October 2015). http://hudoc.echr.coe.int/eng?i=001-158615.

Arneson, Richard. 1989. "Equality ad Equal Opportunity for Welfare." *Philosophical Studies* 56(1): 77–93.

Barnes, Elizabeth. 2016. *The Minority Body*. New York: Oxford University Press.

Bickenbach, Jerome. 2016. "Disability and Health Care Rationing". In *The Stanford Encyclopedia of Philosophy* (Spring 2016 Edition), edited by Edward N. Zalta. https://plato.stanford.edu/archives/spr2016/entries/disability-care-rationing.

Cohen, G.A. 1989. "On the Currency of Egalitarian Justice". *Ethics* 99(4): 906–944.

[8] See Buck v Bell. 1927. 274 U.S. 200.

Committee on the Rights of Persons with Disabilities. 2014. *Communication no. 21/2014*. https://juris.ohchr.org/Search/Details/2087.

Committee on the Rights of Persons with Disabilities. 2017. "Call for Submissions: Draft General Comment on the Right of Persons with Disabilities to Equality and Non-Discrimination (article 5) (April 2017)". https://www.ohchr.org/EN/HRBodies/CRPD/Pages/CallPersonsDisabilitiesEqualityResponsability.aspx.

Committee on the Rights of Persons with Disabilities. 2018. "General Comment No. 6 (2018) on Equality and Non-Discrimination (26 April)". https://tbinternet.ohchr.org/_layouts/15/treatybodyexternal/Download.aspx?symbolno=CRPD/C/GC/6&Lang=en.

de Almeida, José Miguel Caldas. 2019. "The CRPD Article 12, the Limits of Reductionist Approaches to Complex Issues and the Necessary Search for Compromise". *World Psychiatry* 18(1, February): 46–47.

DeMarco, Joseph P., and Samuel H. Lipuma. 2016. "Dementia, Advance Directives, and Discontinuity of Personality". *Cambridge Quarterly of Healthcare Ethics* 25(4): 674–685.

Dworkin, Ronald. 1981a. "What Is Equality? Part 1: Equality of Welfare". *Philosophy and Public Affairs* 10: 185–246.

Dworkin, Ronald. 1981b. "What Is Equality? Part 2: Equality of Resources". *Philosophy and Public Affairs* 10: 283–345.

Freeman, Melvyn Colin, Kavitha Kolappa, Jose Miguel Caldas de Almeida, Arthur Kleinman, Nino Makhashvili, Sifiso Phakathi, Benedetto Saraceno, and Graham Thornicroft. 2015. "Reversing Hard Won Victories in the Name of Human Rights: A Critique of the General Comment on Article 12 of the UN Convention on the Rights of Persons with Disabilities". *Lancet Psychiatry* 2(9): 844–850.

Jeste, Dilip V., Graham M.L. Eglit, Barton W. Palmer, Jonathan G. Martinis, Peter Blanck, and Elyn R. Saks. 2018. "Supported Decision Making in Serious Mental Illness". *Psychiatry* 81(1): 28–40.

Kahane, Guy, and Julian Savulescu. 2016. "Disability and Mere Difference". *Ethics* 126(3): 774–788.

Satz, Ani B. 2006. "A Jurisprudence of Dysfunction: On the Role of 'Normal Species Functioning' in Disability Analysis". *Yale Journal of Health Policy, Law, and Ethics* 6(2): 221–267.

Scholten, Matthé, Astrid Gieselmann, Jakov Gather, and Jochen Vollmann. 2019. "Psychiatric Advance Directives Under the Convention on the Rights of Persons with Disabilities: Why Advance Instructions Should Be Able to Override Current Preferences". *Frontiers in Psychiatry* 10(2019): 631.

Silvers, Anita, and Leslie P. Francis. 2017. "Human and Civil Models of Rights: Health and Ill Disabled and Access to Healthcare". In *Human Rights and Disability: Interdisciplinary Perspectives*, edited by John-Stewart Gordon, Johann-Christian Põder, and Holger Burckhart. Abington, UK: Routledge.

Szmukler, George. 2019. "'Capacity', 'Best Interests', 'Will and Preferences' and the UN Convention on the Rights of Persons with Disabilities". *World Psychiatry* 18(1): 34–41.

Szmukler, George, Rowena Daw, and Felicity Callard. 2014. "Mental Health Law and the UN Convention on the Rights of Persons with Disabilities." *International Journal of Law and Psychiatry* 37(3): 245–252.

Tracy, Jane, and Teresa Iacono. 2008. "People with Developmental Disabilities Teaching Medical Students—Does It Make a Difference?" *Journal of Intellectual & Developmental Disability* 33(4): 345–348.

United Nations. 2006. *Conventions on the Rights of Persons with Disabilities*. Geneva: United Nations.

Werner, Shirli, and Rachel Chabany. 2016. "Guardianship Law Versus Supported Decision-Making Policies: Perceptions of Persons with Intellectual or Psychiatric Disabilities and Parents". *American Journal of Orthopsychiatry* 86(5): 486–499.

CHAPTER 7

# The Right to Autonomy and the Conditions that Secure It: The Relationship Between the UNCRPD and Market-Based Policy Reform

*Laura Davy and Celia Green*

## Introduction

The international disabled people's movement has organized around the principle of personal autonomy, advocating for greater control and decision-making for people with disability over their own lives and over the services they receive. Autonomy means self-determination and self-government; the freedom to live by your own rules and choices

L. Davy (✉)
Australian National University, Canberra, Australia
e-mail: l.davy@unsw.edu.au

C. Green
University of New South Wales, Sydney, NSW, Australia
e-mail: celia.green@unsw.edu.au



F. Felder et al. (eds.), *Disability Law and Human Rights*, Palgrave Studies in Disability and International Development,
https://doi.org/10.1007/978-3-030-86545-0_7

(Christman and Anderson 2005). A history of institutionalization and segregation, and of people with disability having little rights, voice or power over the course of their own lives, has made personal autonomy a vital goal for the disability rights movement.

The call for autonomy has shaped both the United Nations Convention on the Rights of Persons with Disabilities (CRPD) and recent international trends in the way that disability support is funded and administered. But the benefits of this policy shift to an autonomy paradigm have been both incomplete and varyingly distributed. In the Australian context, the key example of this is the National Disability Insurance Scheme (NDIS). The NDIS, which was introduced in 2013 and fully rolled out nationally as of 2020, is the biggest reform of the national social services landscape since the introduction of Medicare, Australia's universal health care scheme, in 1984. The NDIS promises choice and control to people with disability, but this vision has been realized only incompletely, with some groups experiencing even greater inequities under the new system than they did under the flawed system the NDIS was designed to improve on.

In this chapter we will firstly describe the principle of personal autonomy that has emerged within the CRPD. We then discuss the global shift towards individual funding arrangements in disability support and the marketization of social services, and the rhetorical and actual place of the concept of autonomy within these social reforms. The development and implementation of Australia's NDIS is used as an example of the complex interplay between different and contested understandings of autonomy in public policy. We argue that in advocating for equitable public service delivery for people with disability it is important to distinguish the more expansive concept of autonomy that can be derived from the CRPD from the narrower concept that features in accounts of the benefits of market-based service delivery.

This chapter will not discuss the specific legal innovations introduced by the CRPD in the areas of legal capacity and decision-making in any detailed manner. Other scholars (some of whom are included in this volume) are better placed to tease out these crucial issues. This chapter instead focuses on the new support paradigm that underpins these innovations—the push embodied in the CRPD towards improving the relational, material and structural conditions of everyday life that provide the necessary groundwork for individual selves to enact autonomy in the first place.

This, in our view, is a necessary prior discussion that debates centering on individual cognitive capacities often neglect.

## The Conception of Autonomy in Classical Philosophy and Law

The principle of personal autonomy plays a crucial role in Enlightenment humanist philosophy, the political imaginary of liberal democratic states, and the tradition of human rights. For liberal thinkers from Immanuel Kant and John Stuart Mill to John Rawls, it is *the* crucial human good; as Mill states, 'The only freedom which deserves the name, is that of pursuing our own good in our own way' (1871, pp. 28–29). This capacity to pursue one's own conception of the good and therefore to be an agent over one's own life is seen to be central to human personhood. To violate the personal autonomy of another human being is to commit a harm against their personhood. Even the philosopher Isaiah Berlin, who is notoriously sceptical of many conceptions of autonomy, describes its enormous appeal as a concept in his essay 'Two Concepts of Liberty':

I wish to be a subject, not an object; to be moved by reasons, by conscious purposes, which are my own, not by causes which affect me, as it were, from outside. I wish to be somebody, not nobody; a doer—deciding, not being decided for, self-directed and not acted upon by external nature or by other men as if I were a thing, or an animal, or a slave incapable of playing a human role, that is, of conceiving goals and policies of my own and realizing them. (Berlin 1958/1971, p. 131).

Claiming the right to autonomy, with its attendant connotations of emancipation and empowerment, has therefore been central to the equality struggles of many groups including slaves, women, colonized peoples and Indigenous peoples. But it has also always been a concept fraught with contradictions, assumptions and exclusions for these marginalized groups.

Classical liberal conceptions of autonomy have faced critiques from numerous sources (feminist, postcolonialist, poststructuralist and so on) for failing to recognize individual and group diversity, and the very different barriers that different groups face in exercising their capacity for personal autonomy. Liberal theory describes autonomy as an innate characteristic of rational agents (Rawls 1980), a capacity that demands non-interference from others as a matter of respect for their personhood (Nedelsky 1989). Philosophical models of autonomy have tended to focus on so-called 'internal' or psychological conditions of autonomy such as independence of mind (Dworkin 1988), the ability to make up one's own mind free of the distorting influence of other people's values, beliefs or will. These accounts have been derided for, at their most individualistic and disembodied, depicting a 'retreat into an inner citadel' of the self (Berlin 1958, 1971, p. 135). On some accounts, if a being cannot conform to certain standards of rationality and cognitive capacity, they are not persons, so interfering with their agency does not perpetuate a harm (Feinberg 1989; Frey 2005).

Feminist theorists have challenged this conception of autonomy, arguing that it falls into the trap of atomic individualism—there is little space in this conception of the person for acknowledging any deep forms of dependency and relationality (Nedelsky 2011; Kittay 1999). Rather than being an innate attribute, they claim that autonomy is a capacity that can only be enacted by relationally embedded and materially supported persons. The internal conditions of autonomy include positive prerequisites for knowing and pursuing your own sense of the good, like self-confidence and self-trust (Nedelsky 2011). These internal conditions in turn rest upon certain relational conditions being met. Human beings need to be recognized by others in order to build a positive self-identity—it is through connection, care and our relationships with others that we come to value ourselves and our plans. As one of the authors has argued elsewhere, autonomy is a capacity that can only be enacted through relations of support, advocacy and enablement (Davy 2015).

Whether and how people can exercise autonomy is in large part determined by the structural features of the society in which they live. The ability to choose freely and to practice self-determination depends on the presence of suitable options. Control over one's own life depends, for many people, on the existence of both formal and informal forms of advocacy to support the voices of those who would otherwise not be heard or might be ignored. Participation, the ability to take part in the social, economic and cultural life of one's community, depends on social attitudes and institutions that welcome those who wish to join in. For many of the philosophers who first wrote on autonomy, the kind of material security that allows an individual to be a self-sufficient free agent is taken for granted. But the reality for people with disability in our society, particularly for people with intellectual disability and people with complex support needs, is that it will require major social investment just to meet the basic material conditions of autonomy such as housing, appropriate health services and personal safety and security.

A version of the liberal ideal of personhood underpins much of contemporary law, including human rights law, because of its heritage in and its conceptual entanglement with Enlightenment humanism. That which 'grounds' or justifies human rights has often been viewed as the human traits of autonomy, rationality and free-will; traits that historically certain groups (women, men without property, people of colour, Indigenous peoples) have been viewed as incapable of possessing. But as Celermajer and Lefebvre (2020) observe, over the years and as a result of sustained struggle and agitation, successive groups have pressed for their inclusion within the human rights project and have been acknowledged as subjects entitled to rights.

The way that rights and personhood are understood has been changed by this process of inclusion. In the quest for universalism, human rights frameworks have traditionally tended to abstain from fleshing out a conception of human flourishing that addresses the identity or life contexts of actual people (Quinn and Arstein-Kerslake 2015, p. 37). This has been changing through successive international human rights instruments, however, through the increasing importance of social and economic rights and the tailoring of rights frameworks to minority groups such as women, children, and now, people with disability. The CRPD aims to tailor existing human rights norms to the real-life situations of people with disability. By necessity, making these rights realizable for people with disability across global contexts and through the provision of active support involves an unparalleled level of concrete prescription about the duties of state parties than human rights treaties have offered thus far.

## The Conception of Autonomy Described Within the CRPD

The CRPD has 'modified, transformed and added to traditional human rights concepts in key respects' (Kayess and French 2008, p. 32), and particularly, we argue, in terms of fleshing out the structural and relational conditions that generate individual flourishing. It goes further than other human rights instruments have so far in spelling out a conception of human flourishing based on the lives of people with disability in today's society and the challenges and barriers they encounter in the world around them. No doubt this is at least in part because of the unprecedented level of civil society involvement in its negotiation. The CRPD was negotiated not just by state representatives, but also by representatives of people with disability with lived experience of these everyday challenges and barriers. The rights enshrined in the CRPD cover broad themes at the forefront of the disability rights movement: independent living in the community, employment, education, participation in social and political life, legal capacity and active consultation with people with disability in laws and policies that concern them. These are group rights to be enjoyed by people with disability as a minority group within mainstream society as well as individual rights, and importantly, they are also preconditions for individual autonomy, because they address the individual's place and value within her community.

The preamble of the CRPD insists on the equal personhood of people with disability with others in society and recognizes 'the importance for persons with disabilities of their individual autonomy and independence, including the freedom to make their own choices'. But in crafting an international convention designed to promote the personhood and rights of people with disability, the CRPD had to do more than apply existing rights frameworks to another minority group. According to Quinn and Rekas-Resalbo (2016), it also provides guidance to states on how to embed the conditions of support that would enable people with disability to exercise these rights. The CRPD starts with an aspect of human flourishing, such as individual autonomy and freedom of choice, then crafts rights that aim to embed the conditions of support that would augment capacity for self-determination for persons with disability (Quinn and Arstein-Kerslake 2015).

This has often meant the transformation of 'formerly essentially non-interference based rights (or "negative" rights) into positive state obligations' (Kayess and French 2008, p. 32). For many people with disability, basic civil and political rights will not be realizable unless or until various social and economic rights are implemented. For example, the right to freedom of expression has traditionally been considered a civil and political right, and is included in the International Covenant on Civil and Political rights. But Article 21 of the CRPD, in which this right is discussed, places responsibility on states to ensure that the conditions for the practical exercise of this right are available. It includes positive obligations such as to provide information intended for the general public in accessible formats, and accepting and facilitating the use of sign languages,

Braille, augmentative and alternative communication, and all other modes and formats of communication used by people with disability.

This is clearly evident in the parts of the CRPD that address the right to equal recognition before the law. Quinn and Rekas-Resalbo (2016, p. 299) describe Article 12 as achieving a sort of 'iconic status' in embodying the CRPD shift from viewing people with disability as objects that need to be managed by others to subjects who can author their own lives. The concept of legal recognition, in the context of how the law interacts with people with disability, has largely played out in terms of determining the capacity or incapacity of an individual to make legally binding decisions. Article 12(3) of the CRPD, however, stipulates that 'States Parties shall take appropriate measures to provide access by persons with disabilities to the support they may require in exercising their legal capacity', shifting the focus from assessments of an individual's personal cognitive characteristics to the various social and environmental supports that might influence their capacity to make decisions. In other words, the right to legal capacity entails a simultaneous right to be supported to realize and exercise this capacity.

Capacity is not assumed to be a quality of an individual alone, but is conceptualized in the CRPD as a quality that may be embedded in relationships or institutions. This means that the right to equal recognition before the law is not just a matter of governments refraining from discrimination against people with disability, but of taking concrete steps to provide a supportive, accessible environment that enables people with disability to exercise legal capacity. The Committee on the Rights of Persons with Disabilities suggests a number of specific supports that should be provided to ensure the access of people with disability to legal capacity on an equal basis with others in General Comment 1 on Article 12. These include the assistance of advocates and other support people, the provision of information in multiple formats, and the recognition of diverse, non-conventional methods of communication.

Quinn and Arstein-Kerslake take this further by making a strong case for the indivisibility and interdependence of CRPD rights, linking Article 12 to Article 19, the right to live independently in the community: 'community embeddedness augments capacity. Inappropriate institutionalisation in the past shredded this natural connectedness with community and played a part in degrading decision-making capacities' (2015, p. 51). People with disability living in institutional settings often have all minor day to day decisions, such as when and what to eat and when to sleep made for them, meaning that they are living a life stripped of the scaffolding required for developing their personal autonomy. As Kayess and Sands observe: 'Segregation and the denial of autonomy are central to the nature of institutions. Institutions deny the autonomy to choose where to live and with whom to live, deny autonomy in daily decision-making, and isolate and segregate people with disability from the community' (2020, p. 22). Article 19 is therefore 'as much about individual choice, security and being a participating member of the community on an equal basis with others as it is about the bricks and mortar of housing' (Kayess and Sands 2020, p. 23). Living in conditions of social connectedness and participation with others is in fact essential to developing personal will and preferences about one's life and developing the ability to express and enact personal preferences and plans. The CRPD has encoded the key goal of the disability rights movement within international law, solidifying the impetus for state parties to implement policy that promotes inclusion and support rather than segregation and control.

## Autonomy and Global Shifts in Disability Support Services Delivery

The development and now implementation of the CRPD is just one of the major global influences on contemporary disability policy and practice placing autonomy front and centre. Over the past couple of decades there has been a transnational shift (albeit focused within capitalist democracies of the global North) in which governments provide funding directly to people with disability rather than to disability service providers. These changes promise increased control, flexibility and 'personalisation' for service users, all key aspirations within the disability rights movement.

This shift towards individualized funding is part of an even broader political trend away from collective social welfare provision and towards the use of markets to deliver welfare services. In the name of efficiency and responsiveness, governments in many countries around the world have adopted techniques more commonly associated with the private sector (Carey et al. 2018a). Public service markets have been created through governmental techniques such as competitive tendering, commissioning, and in the case of disability services, the payment of individual budgets to service users. The disability care and support sector has been a major focus of this trend. Many countries have adopted new individualized funding models for people with disability, including the UK, parts of

North America, most members of the European Union, Norway, Iceland, Israel, Australia and New Zealand.

In the disability context, these models have variously been referred to as person-centred support, self-directed care, cash for care, personalized allocations, personal budgets, case and counselling, and individualized funding (see for example Dickinson and Glasby 2010; Malbon et al. 2019; Needham 2011). These models all have a slightly different focus or delivery mechanism depending on the context in which they are employed. However they are all underpinned by concepts of autonomy, self-determination and individual freedoms (Fleming et al. 2019; Malbon et al. 2019) with the key idea being that individuals should be empowered to have choice, control and flexibility in making their own decisions to spend money on the services that best suit their needs. Individualized funding became particularly popular within the independent living movement, as it enables some people with disability to live in their own home, work, attend social events, and organize their own support services to facilitate those activities, for example by hiring personal assistants.

There are various mechanisms by which individualized funding has been administered in different states, but personal budgets for disability care and support tend to be administered through either a direct payment or an intermediary service (Fleming et al. 2019). In direct payment models the funds are given directly to the person with a disability who then self-manages their service or care budget to meet their individual needs and take into account their life circumstances. Direct funds may be used to employ personal carers or assistants or to purchase services from both private or public service provider organizations (Carter Anand et al. 2012). Self managed direct payments often require a significant administrative component for the person receiving the funds (or for a support person such as a family member) and may therefore be more likely to be utilized by people with sensory or physical disabilities rather than people with intellectual or learning disability (Fleming et al. 2019). 'Managed' personal budgets, micro-boards or brokerage models aim to provide similar choice and control for individuals but use a third party that takes responsibility for administrative tasks and may also provide support or guidance to enable people to manage their personal budgets (Carr 2011).

These various models have been utilized in slightly different ways across a number of industrialized welfare states. The UK and Australia have seen the advent of individualized budgets for people with disability which may be personally managed or involve a broker. In the UK the Community Care (Direct Payments) Act 1996 marked a significant turning point for the way people with disability were able to access care funding by allowing them personal control of their care money (Needham and Dickinson 2017). Although early uptake of direct payments was low and was mainly utilized by those with physical disabilities, as the personalization agenda became more dominant in government policies and formalized in the Care Act 2014, more people with intellectual disabilities have taken up personal budgets (Glasby et al. 2016). Needham and Dickinson (2017) note that alternative funding arrangements such as managed personal budgets (where people still have choice in spending but monies are held by a local agency) and individual service funds where money is held by a third party have contributed to an increasing uptake of personal budgets.

Continental European countries and the Nordic welfare states have also adopted individualized agendas for disability care, although to varying degrees. For example, Germany enacted legislation in 2004 to enable the government to provide direct payments to people with disability and further legislation in 2008 giving people with disability the enforceable right to receive direct payments. These direct payments can take several forms including an 'employment model' to enable people with severe disabilities to organize their own 24 hour individual care and personal budgets where a payment is provided to individual people with disability, to be used for assistant services that help integrate people into society (Junne and Huber 2014). Sweden a state with a history of strong social welfare provision, passed two disability Acts in 1993: the Support and Service for Persons with Certain Functional Impairments Act (LSS) and the Personal Assistance Act (LASS). These Acts relate to three groups—people with autism or severe intellectual disability, people with permanent physical disabilities and people with acquired brain injury. These Acts are both underpinned by principles of empowerment and give people with disability the right to make their own decisions and an entitlement to support services. Recipients of LASS can choose who manages or supports their funds with options including self management, joining a co-operative, management by a private company or management by the municipality itself (Laragy 2010).

Advocates of personalized approaches to service provision have argued that they help create citizen empowerment which results in better personal outcomes and improved systems outcomes such as cost efficiencies and uptake of services. For example, an international review of individualized funding interventions (Fleming et al. 2019) found that their benefits included improved self-belief, self-image and freedom in making choices, and better community integration and flexibility for service users. The ability to access health and social services that otherwise may not have been accessible can be enhanced within personalisation schemes (Lakhani et al. 2016), which can in turn lead to other personal benefits such as increased quality of life (Harkes et al. 2014). An evaluation of the NDIS (Mavromaras et al. 2018b) found that the NDIS had a positive impact on participants' wellbeing, however when compared to levels of wellbeing across the general population, people with disability (both NDIS participants and non participants) report wellbeing levels significantly below the national average.

In discussing the potential positive and negative impacts of this shift in social services delivery, it is important to note the differences between the concepts of personalization and individualization, which have shifting boundaries and definitions in the literature. The term personalization is a general approach to making public services more user-focused that encompasses a number of programmatic and operational approaches to reform (Needham 2011). In the context of disability services, person-centred support can be understood as support that is responsive to the needs, preferences and personal context of the person with disability. It involves 'honoring the person' (Waters and Buchanan 2017, p. 1032) as a unique individual and not just a 'user' or 'consumer' of services. The philosophy of personalization recognizes not just the instrumental importance of services and support, but the importance of support services being empowering and enabling. Individualized budgets are just one of a number of tools that can be deployed towards a personalization agenda.

While the link between exercising personal autonomy and personalized support services—understood as the organization of supports according to the needs and wants of the person with disability rather than what is best for the funding agency or service provider—is quite clear and is likely to be applicable to all people with disability, the advantages of individualized funding seem to be more restricted. As we discuss below in the context of Australian disability services reform, the benefits of individualization and a marketized service environment are all too often distributed along existing axes of advantage. International research indicates that while some people with disability do benefit from these service markets, others do not, and those who are disadvantaged by these changes are often those who already experience complex barriers in their lives. Socio-economic status, gender, disability type and level of support needs and the presence of family and advocates are all factors that influence whether or not people with disability experience positive outcomes from the individualization of support services (see for example Lakhani et al. 2016; Malbon et al. 2017; Mavromaras et al. 2018a).

## Australia's National Disability Insurance Scheme

As discussed in the previous two sections of this chapter, the past couple of decades have been a period of rapid social change for people with disability, resulting in a new human rights treaty and global trends towards individualized funding and service arrangements, both of which emphasize personal autonomy. The conceptions of autonomy that emerge from each of these seismic social shifts have some key similarities but also important points of contrast. The development and implementation of the Australia's NDIS, which has been informed by both developments, provides a rich case study of the interplay between these different understandings of autonomy in public policy.

Autonomy is central to the way the NDIS is framed and communicated by policymakers. The aims of the NDIS, as listed in the National Disability Insurance Scheme Act, include giving effect to Australia's obligations under the CRPD, supporting the independence and social and economic participation of people with disability, and enabling people with disability to exercise choice and control in the pursuit of their goals and the planning and delivery of their support services.[1] Under the NDIS, an individual funding package is provided to eligible participants,[2] which they can then use to purchase the support services of their choice. A personalized package of supports is put in place to assist participants to achieve self-determined (and scheme-approved) goals. NDIS participants may self-manage their own budgets or use an external support coordination service to help manage their plans and budgets.

[1] NDIS Act 2013, objects (1)(a), (1)(c) and (1)(e).

[2] Eligibility is restricted to Australian citizens under 65 years of age with a permanent and significant disability.

Until recently, Australian disability services were largely funded through 'block' grants allocated to approved service providers by state and territory governments. In a report based upon a major national consultation funded by the federal government that was a major impetus for the development of the NDIS, the previous disability service system was characterized as 'irretrievably broken and broke, chronically under-funded and under-resourced, crisis driven, [and] struggling against a vast tide of unmet need' (Australian Government 2009, p. 19). The introduction of the NDIS represented a major reform of the way that support services were delivered, from a primarily 'service-centred' to a 'person-centred' system (Productivity Commission 2011, p. 344), bringing Australia in line with the global trend described in the previous section.

But from its outset, Australian disability advocates have identified some fundamental tensions between the human rights approach that characterizes the NDIS objects, described above, and a range of rules and processes that have been developed in the scheme's implementation, which greatly impact on the degree of autonomy that participants can exercise in practice. Submissions on the draft legislation highlighted potential problems in the power relationship between scheme participants and the managing National Disability Insurance Agency (NDIA), which exercises significant discretion over the criteria and processes for determining eligibility and approving planned supports (Australian Senate Community Affairs Legislation Committee 2013, p. 18). These submissions also expressed concern about the way the needs of carers and family members were sidelined and the way a self-directed and individualized funding system may disadvantage people with intellectual disability (Australian Senate Community Affairs Legislation Committee 2013, p. 25).

Many of these concerns have borne out over the past few years as the NDIS has been implemented. Some NDIS participants do report more choice and control over their services, while others report significant barriers accessing the support they need or little material change in their circumstances (Warr et al. 2017). Traditional fault lines of gender, ethnicity, socioeconomic status and urban/rural Australia are determining factors in who experiences advantage and disadvantage within the scheme. Groups such as women, people from low income backgrounds, Indigenous Australians and people from culturally and linguistically diverse background are less likely to be participants within the scheme, and if they do gain access, they are less likely to receive a support package that meets all their needs (Malbon et al. 2019).

Despite the expansive vision described in the NDIS objects, the concept of autonomy that has emerged within the scheme mirrors the 'classical' conceptions of autonomy in liberal political theory quite closely in its focus on individual choice and control. It should perhaps be unsurprising then that the NDIS falls prey to some of the same pitfalls that classical autonomy theory has been critiqued for. Just as liberal political theory has been criticized for ignoring the vastly unequal starting points and opportunities available to individuals in society, the architecture of the NDIS has also often failed to adequately account for difference and marginalization.

Like many models of free-will and autonomy in philosophy, marketized systems of social support are predicated on assumptions about a certain kind of rational actor who is both well-informed about their options and articulate. Under the NDIS, services that were previously provided by government (either directly or through the block funding of service providers) are putatively now available for purchase by people with disability exercising their personal capacities for choice and control within a mixed marketplace of providers. Service users are encouraged to be savvy consumers, negotiating this complex market environment to make the most of its opportunities. This means the administrative structure of the NDIS favours an ideal norm of the "competent' and 'independent' person with the ability to navigate complex decisions and bureaucracy (Malbon et al. 2019). People with intellectual disability, despite being the majority of participants in the scheme, face particularly strong barriers in navigating the scheme and achieving good outcomes from their support plans (Collings et al. 2016). Those without a support relational network of family and friends to advocate on their behalf find it even more difficult to access, plan and review their supports (Meltzer and Davy 2019).

Freedom of choice also rests on an assumption that the empowered consumer is endowed with the information and resources to pick and choose what they want from at least a few quality options. The emergence of market gaps and thin markets in the NDIS where there are only very limited services and/or providers available to choose from (Carey et al. 2018b) highlights the hollowness of a choice and control rhetoric in the absence of suitable options. For example, people who require complex behavioural and/or communication supports or are in close contact with the criminal justice system are not likely to receive access to the same level of choice and control as those whose needs are more mainstream and palatable for potential providers (Soldatic et al. 2014; Fawcett and Plath 2014).

In focusing on providing individual funding packages to meet individual support needs, the NDIS has limited mechanisms in place to address the structural barriers that people with disability may face in exercising personal autonomy. Addressing these structural barriers is instead the focus of the Australian National Disability Strategy ('the Strategy'), Australia's overarching national disability policy framework and main mechanism for implementing the UN Convention on the Rights of Persons with Disabilities (Australian Government 2011, p. 3). Its vision is 'an inclusive Australian society that enables people with disability to fulfil their potential as equal citizens' (Ibid., p. 8). While the NDIS emphasizes individual choice and control, the Strategy emphasizes participation and supporting people with disability to achieve their potential. It embodies a fuller conception of personal autonomy and human flourishing than the NDIS, but has become a mainly aspirational policy document, with its implementation consisting mostly of small initiatives on the local level rather than the widespread systems level change it was designed to achieve (Australian Senate Community Affairs Legislation Committee 2017). The NDIS has been the primary focus of government attention and investment over the past decade, but is just one action under the overarching Strategy and was never designed to meet the support needs of all people with disability, or to meet needs that can more appropriately be catered to through mainstream public services such as health, transport, education and so on. On the personal level, access to the essential, personalized support that enables a life of dignity and control over how this support is provided and who provides it are essential foundations of a self-directed life—but people need more than personalized support services to live a life of self-direction.

## Conclusion: Enabling Autonomy

To return to the philosophical conceptions of autonomy discussed in the first section of this chapter, and in particular the critiques of these accounts of autonomy from feminist theorists, some of the broader factors that shape individual capacity can be summarized according to the figure below (Fig. 7.1).

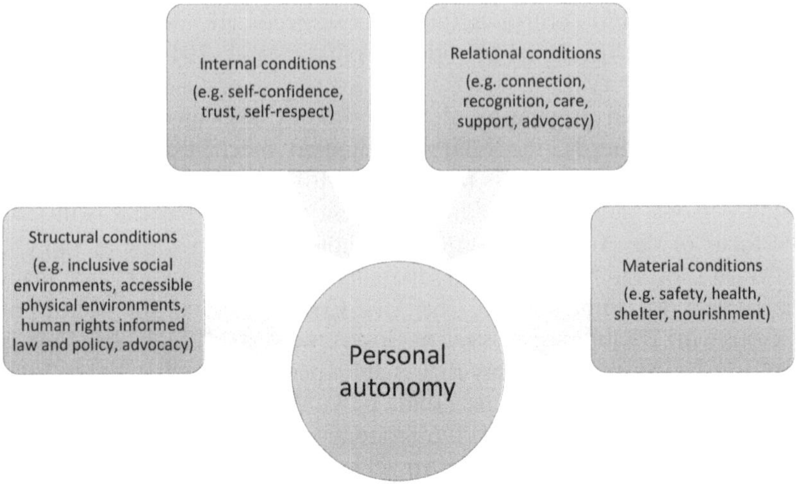


**Fig. 7.1** Conditions of personal autonomy

As depicted, these factors include, firstly, relational conditions such as interpersonal connectedness and recognition from others. This connectedness can take many forms and includes relations of care and support, and for those who require support in articulating their needs, will and preferences, may include formal and informal forms of individual advocacy and communication and decision-making support. Secondly, these factors include material conditions such as safety and security, adequate and appropriate shelter and nourishment, and access to health services. Thirdly, there are important structural conditions that shape an individual's choice horizon, playing a determining role in the degree to which that individual is able to exercise autonomy, and how meaningful their choices can be. These include an inclusive and accessible society that is able to accommodate difference, the implementation of human rights informed policy and legislation, and, at least until discrimination and marginalization are things of the past, group-based and systemic advocacy to agitate for change.

These wider conditions represent the necessary scaffolding to support the development of the fourth cluster of factors that enable autonomy, that is, the personal, internal conditions of autonomy. In philosophy and law these internal conditions have traditionally been conceived quite narrowly in terms of cognitive capacity, but under this schema, informed by feminist autonomy theory, they include traits such as self-confidence, trust and self-respect. These are characteristics of the individual self but are also fundamentally social achievements in that they depend on firstly, the fulfillment of basic physical and relational needs, and secondly, access to a valued identity within the community and opportunities to experience the options out there.

Each of these factors that shape individual capacity for autonomy is captured within the CRPD and fleshed out through particular articles in ways that confront the major inequalities and barriers faced by people with disability. The importance of autonomy as a fundamental principle for the CRPD is recognized alongside non-discrimination and full participation and inclusion in society in Article 3—General principles. The relational factors are acknowledged in Article 23—Respect for home and the family. The importance of material security is acknowledged in Article 28—Adequate standard of living and social protection, and physical safety is highlighted in Articles 15 and 16—Freedom from torture and Freedom from exploitation, violence and abuse. The importance of human rights informed policy and legislation is acknowledged in several articles, including Article 5—Equality and non-discrimination, Article 12—Equal recognition before the law, and 13—Access to justice, while provisions for creating a truly inclusive society and services are addressed in Article 8—Awareness Raising, Article 9—Accessibility, and the articles relating to education, health and mobility. A number of articles are related to each of these factors, including Article 19—Living independently and being included in the community, Article 27—Work and employment, Article 29—Participation in political and public life, and Article 30—Participation in cultural life, recreation, leisure and sport.

The introduction of the NDIS has been particularly significant for a number of reasons. It represents a substantial social investment in a time when many countries, including Australia, have been instituting austerity measures. It places personal autonomy centre stage of Australian disability policy for the first time, on the heels of Australia's ratification of the CRPD. Its primary vehicles for achieving this shift—individual budgets and the creation of a services market—are not particularly innovative in the context of international disability policy and service provision, however, except perhaps in the scale of the government's commitment to new funding. While the logic of human rights and the logic of marketized service provision are not necessarily incommensurable, the discussion of the wider relational, material and structural conditions of autonomy above does highlight the considerable gaps in the conception of autonomy that underpins the international trend of individualization.

It has been argued that the 'right to health' in the CRPD should not be understood narrowly as the right to access health services (Green et al. 2020), and likewise, the principle of personal autonomy, which is prominent within the CRPD, should not be understood narrowly as choice and control over services. There are many barriers to exercising choice and control within individualization schemes which result in inequity, including the difficulties entailed by navigating a complex system, a lack of informal or formal support networks, information barriers, market supply issues and other factors such as an individual's living situation and previous experiences with services. Human variations such as gender, race and class also intersect with barriers to choice and control in the implementation and administration of individualized funding systems. Those with more social, cultural and symbolic capital (such as men, people who speak English well and those with a higher socioeconomic status) are able to derive greater benefit from these service systems (Carey et al. 2019). When these intersections are not addressed there is potential that individualization may not only entrench existing inequalities, but widen them. Aside from these barriers, choice is only one expression of autonomy, and other fundamental conditions of autonomy must be secured before choice can really be a meaningful indicator of autonomy.

Social inclusion has been identified as a key structural factor that needs to be addressed to achieve the same rights and opportunities for people with disability as for non-disabled citizens (Australian Government 2009). However, from the perspective of building social inclusion, individualized funding schemes reinforce a view that the most desirable response to disability policy is provision of services, rather than a focus on broader conditions that act to build empowerment of people with disability such as housing, employment, rights and building community connections (Hallahan 2015). Advocacy is also recognized as a vital prerequisite for people to be able to exercise real choice and control in an individualized funding system as well as an important condition for self-autonomy. However when systems are marketized economic outcomes are prioritized which can result in a frugal approach to what is funded under individual plans. Access to robust advocacy for people without the social or material capital to successfully self-advocate is essential to avoid increasing inequities within an individualized system. Yet, the focus on personalized service provision rather than services that might meet collective needs within schemes such as the NDIS does not prioritize funding for advocacy.

The CRPD has been a powerful political tool for disability advocates, opening up new and more empowering subjectivities for formulating claims on the state and society. It effectively demonstrates the interconnectedness between individual freedom and choice and the fulfillment of social, economic and cultural rights (Quinn 2009). It can be used as a normative benchmark for claiming the basic material conditions of autonomy such as housing, medical attention, safety and security as well as the social conditions of autonomy such as appropriate support services, recognition of legal personhood, inclusive workplaces, education, health and transport systems. This fuller and more expansive concept of autonomy needs to be distinguished from the narrower concept that features in accounts of the benefits of market-based service delivery. The human rights subject is a fundamentally 'open' creature: her conditions of living, the safety and security of her embodiment and the quality of the relationships and social networks around her are all understood to shape her experience of the self, and the ability of this self to be autonomous. Currently, individualized funding systems such as the NDIS are not underpinned by the full gamut of factors that act to shape individual autonomy encompassed in the CRPD. Unless the implementation and administration of individualized support systems are premised on the same principles as are articulated in the CRPD they will fall short of enabling achieving a true vision of human empowerment and autonomy.

## References

Australian Government. 2009. Shut Out: The Experience of People with Disability and Their Families in Australia. National Disability Strategy Consultation Report prepared by the National People with Disabilities and Carer Council, Commonwealth of Australia, Canberra.

Australian Government. 2011. National Disability Strategy 2010–2020, Commonwealth of Australia, Canberra.

Australian Senate Community Affairs Legislation Committee. 2013. National Disability Insurance Scheme Bill 2012 [Provisions], Commonwealth of Australia, Canberra.

Australian Senate Community Affairs References Committee. 2017. Delivery of Outcomes under the National Disability Strategy 2010–2020 to Build Inclusive and Accessible Communities, Commonwealth of Australia, Canberra.

Berlin, I. 1971. 'Two Concepts of Liberty', In I Berlin (ed), Four Essays on Liberty, Oxford University Press, London. (Original work published 1958).

Carey, G., Malbon, E., Olney, S., & Reeders, D. 2018a. 'The Personalisation Agenda: The Case of the Australian National Disability Insurance Scheme', International Review of Sociology, 28(1): 20–34.

Carey, G., Dickinson, H., Malbon, E., & Reeders, D. 2018b. 'The Vexed Question of Market Stewardship in the Public Sector: Examining Equity and the Social Contract through the Australian National Disability Insurance Scheme', Social Policy and Administration, 52(1): 387–407.

Carey, G., Crammond, B., & Malbon, E. 2019. 'Personalisation Schemes in Social Care and Inequality: Review of the Evidence and Early Theorising', International Journal for Equity in Health, 18: 170.

Carr, S. 2011. 'Enabling Risk and Ensuring Safety: Self-Directed Support and Personal Budgets', The Journal of Adult Protection, 13(3): 122–136.

Carter Anand, J., Davidson, J., MacDonald, G., Kelly, B., Clift-Mattews, V., Martin, A., & Rizzo, M. 2012. The Transition to Personal Budgets for People with Disabilities: A Review of Practice in Specified Jurisdictions (2012). National Disability Authority, accessed October 20 2020, http://nda.ie/Policy-and-research/Research/Research-publications/Personal-Budgets-/The-Transition-to-Personal-Budgets-for-People-with-Disabilities-A-Review-of-Practice-in-Specified-Jurisdictions/.

Celermajer, D., & Lefebvre, A. 2020. 'Introduction', In D. Celermajer & A. Lefebvre (eds), The Subject of Human Rights, Stanford University Press, CA.

Christman, J., & Anderson, J. 2005. 'Introduction', In J. Christman & J. Anderson (eds), Autonomy and the Challenges to Liberalism: New Essays, Cambridge University Press, Cambridge.

Collings, S., Dew, A., & Dowse, L. 2016. 'Support Planning with People with Intellectual Disability and Complex Support Needs in the Australian National Disability Insurance Scheme', Journal of Intellectual & Developmental Disability, 41: 272–276.

Davy, L. 2015. 'Philosophical Inclusive Design: Intellectual Disability and the Limits of Individual Autonomy in Moral and Political Theory', Hypatia: Journal of Feminist Philosophy, 30(1): 132–148.

Dickinson, H., & Glasby, J. 2010. The Personalisation Agenda: Implications for the Third Sector. Working Paper, University of Birmingham, Birmingham, UK.

Dworkin, G. 1988. The Theory and Practice of Autonomy, Cambridge University Press, Cambridge, UK.

Fawcett, B., & Plath, D. 2014. 'A National Disability Insurance Scheme: What Social Work Has to Offer', British Journal of Social Work, 44: 747–762.

Feinberg, J. 1989. 'Autonomy', In J. Christman (ed), The Inner Citadel: Essays on Individual Autonomy, Oxford University Press, NY.

Fleming, P., McGilloway, S., Hernon, M., Furlong, M., O'Doherty, S., Keogh, F., & Stainton, T. 2019. Individualised Funding Interventions to Improve Health and Social Care Outcomes for People with a Disability, 15(1–2): e1008

Frey, R. G. 2005. 'Autonomy, Diminished Life, and the Threshold for Use', In J. S. Taylor (ed), Personal Autonomy: New Essays on Personal Autonomy and Its Role in Contemporary Moral Philosophy. Cambridge University Press, Cambridge, UK.

Glasby, J., & Littlechild, Rosemary. 2016. Direct Payments and Personal Budgets. Policy Press

Green, C., Dickinson, H., Carey, G., & Joyce, A. 2020. 'Barriers to Policy Action on Social Determinants of Health for People with Disability in Australia', Disability & Society, https://doi.org/10.1080/09687599.2020.1815523.

Hallahan, L. 2015, 'Disability Policy in Australia: A Triumph of the Scriptio Inferior on Impotence and Neediness?', Australian Journal of Social Issues, 50(2): 191–208.

Harkes, M. A., Brown, M., & Horsburgh, D. 2014. 'Self Directed Support and People with Learning Disabilities: A Review of the Published Research Evidence', British Journal of Learning Disabilities, 42: 87–101.

Kayess, R., & French, P. 2008. 'Out of Darkness into Light? Introducing the Convention on the Rights of Persons with Disabilities', Human Rights Law Review, 8(1): 1–34.

Kayess, R., & Sands, T. 2020. Convention on the Rights of Persons with Disabilities: Shining a Light on Social Transformation: Royal Commission into Violence, Abuse, Neglect and Exploitation of People with Disability Research Report, UNSW Social Policy Research Centre, Sydney.

Kittay, E. F. 1999. Love's Labors: Essays on Women, Equality and Dependency, Routledge, New York.

Junne, J., & Huber, C. 2014. 'The Risk of Users' Choice: Exploring the Case of Direct Payments in German Social Care', Health, Risk & Society, 16: 631–648.

Lakhani, A., McDonald, D., & Zeeman, H. 2016. 'Perspectives of Self-Direction: A Systematic Review of Key Areas Contributing to Service Users' Engagement and Choicemaking in Self-Directed Disability Services and Supports', Health & Social Care in the Community, 26(3): 295–313.

Laragy, C. 2010. 'Snapshot of Flexible Funding Outcomes in Four Countries', Health & Social Care in the Community, 18(2): 129–138.

Malbon, E., Carey, G., & Dickinson, H. 2017. 'Accountability in Public Service Quasi-Markets: The Case of the Australian National Disability Insurance Scheme', Australian Journal of Public Administration, 77(3): 468–481.

Malbon, E., Carey, G., & Meltzer, A. 2019. 'Personalisation Schemes in Social Care: Are They Growing Social and Health Inequalities?', BMC Public Health, 19, 805.

Mavromaras, K., Moskos, M., Mahuteau, S., & Iskerwood, L. 2018a. Evaluation of the NDIS: Final Report, National Institute of Labour Studies, Flinders University, Adelaide, Australia.

Mavromaras, K., Moskos, M., Mahuteau, S., Isherwood, L., Goode, A., Walton, H., Smith, L., Wei, Z., & Flavel, J. 2018b. Evaluation of the NDIS: Final Report, https://apo.org.au/node/143516.

Meltzer, A., & Davy, L. 2019. 'Opportunities to Enhance Relational Well-being Through the National Disability Insurance Scheme: Implications from Research on Relationships and a Content Analysis of NDIS Documentation', Australian Journal of Public Administration, 78(2): 250–264.

Mill, J. S. 1871. On Liberty, Boston, James R Osgood and Company, Boston, MA.

Nedelsky, J. 1989. 'Reconceiving Autonomy: Sources, Thoughts and Possibilities', Yale Journal of Law and Feminism, 1(1): 7–36.

Nedelsky, J. 2011. Law's Relations: A Relational Theory of Self, Autonomy and Law, Oxford University Press, New York.

Needham, C. 2011. Personalising Public Services: Understanding the Personalisation Narrative (New edition), Policy Press, UK.

Needham, C., & Dickinson, H. 2017. ''Any One of us Could Be among That Number': Comparing the Policy Narratives for Individualized Disability Funding in Australia and England', Social Policy & Administration, 52(3): 731–749.

Productivity Commission. 2011. Disability Care and Support. Inquiry Report. Canberra, Australia.

Quinn, G. 2009. 'Bringing the UN Convention on Rights for Persons with Disabilities to Life in Ireland', British Journal of Learning Disabilities, 37: 245–249.

Quinn, G., & Arstein-Kerslake, A. 2015. 'Restoring the "Human" in "Human Rights": Personhood and Doctrinal Innovation in the UN Disability Convention', In C. Gearty & C. Douzinas (eds), The Cambridge Companion to Human Rights Law: 36–55, Cambridge University Press, Cambridge, UK.

Quinn, G., & Rekas-Resalbo, A. 2016. 'Civil Death: Rethinking the Foundations of Legal Personhood for Persons with a Disability', Irish Jurist, 56: 286–325.

Rawls, J. 1980. 'Kantian Constructivism in Moral Theory', Journal of Philosophy, 77: 515–579.

Soldatic, K., van Toorn, G., Dowse, L., & Muir, K. 2014. 'Intellectual Disability and Complex Intersections: Marginalisation under the National Disability Insurance Scheme', Research and Practice in Intellectual and Developmental Disabilities, 1(1): 6–16.

Warr, D., Dickinson, H., Olney, S. et al. 2017. Choice, Control and the NDIS, University of Melbourne, Melbourne, Australia.

Waters, R. A., & Buchanan, A. 2017. 'An Exploration of Person-centred Concepts in Human Services: A Thematic Analysis of the Literature', Health Policy, 121: 1031–1039.

CHAPTER 8

# At the Intersection of Childhood and Disability: Improving Human Rights Protection for Disabled Children

*Gauthier de Beco*

## Introduction

Disabled children are amongst the most marginalized individuals. As they are at the intersection of childhood and disability, they experience acute forms of marginalization and are surrounded by stereotypes. This chapter examines how to enhance human rights protection for disabled children by the aid of human rights treaties using an example of their right to education.

Disabled children can call upon two human rights treaties, namely the Convention on Rights of the Child (CRC) and the Convention on the Rights of Persons with Disabilities (CRPD).[1] Both human rights treaties

[1] Convention on the Rights of the Child 1989, 1577 *UNTS* 3; Convention on the Rights of Persons with Disabilities 2006, 46 ILM 443.

G. de Beco (✉)
The Law School, University of Huddersfield, Huddersfield, UK



F. Felder et al. (eds.), *Disability Law and Human Rights*, Palgrave Studies in Disability and International Development, https://doi.org/10.1007/978-3-030-86545-0_8

not only have some resemblances but also focus extensively on disabled children. While CRC mentions disability for the first time ever in a human rights treaty, the CRPD has a 'twin-track' approach when it comes to childhood with both provisions on disabled children and provisions that take age into account. Disabled children are probably the group of people most considered in several human rights treaties at once. Despite this level of consideration, the intersection of childhood and age remains scantly addressed in the field of international human rights law.

The CRPD and CRC however approach disabled children differently. Both of them view these children predominantly from the perspective of a single identity, that is, as children first or as disabled people first. This chapter suggests that a joint reading of them can help fill the gap left by each of them individually. It researches how international human rights law operates when both disability and age intersect with each other. It therefore follows the suggestion by de Silva de Alwis (2009, 295) that disabled women and children 'are best protected when the CRPD is read together with the panoply of guarantees set out in other human rights treaties'.

The article builds upon the insights derived from intersectionality, which postulates that discrimination on the basis of multiple grounds can lead to a unique kind of discrimination, termed 'intersectional discrimination'. This term was coined by Crenshaw in two seminal articles, where she explained why race and gender should be treated together rather than separately, if the specific disadvantages suffered by Black women were to be understood (Crenshaw 1989, 1991). She demonstrated why single-axis discrimination is problematic, since those specific disadvantages are greater than simply the sum of their parts. While scholarship on the subject matter in the field of international human rights law has likewise tended to concentrate on race and gender, it has received much less attention with regard to disability.

The chapter proceeds through looking at the provisions of the CRC and CRPD, taking into account their historical background, and evaluating the recommendations of their corresponding treaty bodies, namely the Committee on the Rights of the Child (CRC Committee) and the Committee on the Rights of Persons with Disabilities (CRPD Committee). It thus examines how to mitigate their respective weaknesses and to take the most out of both human rights treaties. The chapter also highlights the utility of such an intersectional approach through an analysis of the right of disabled children to education. It explains how inclusive education has gradually become the goal for the education of disabled children in international human rights law. While this goal has been endorsed in the CRPD, the CRC still contains a number of elements that remain essential with a view to bringing about inclusion.

The chapter is divided into two sections. The first section considers the various kinds of prejudice that can result from the intersection of childhood and disability. The second section investigates how both the CRC and the CRPD protect disabled children and how the proposed joint reading can provide enhanced human rights protection for disabled children. It goes on by examining what remedies can be found for fulfilling their right to education through applying the two human rights treaties together.

## Disabled Children

Disabled children are at the crossroad of two identities that taken together reinforce their marginalized position in society. While vulnerability due to childhood is aggravated by another layer of prejudice for being disabled, young age leads to an exacerbation of the image of disabled people as dependent and inferior. Disabled children therefore face disadvantages that are higher than those faced by both children and disabled people when added up. As they are characterized by childhood and disability, they are an apt example of how intersectionality can have an impact on the particular experience of human rights.

Disabled children not only face a high level of rejection but are also victims of different forms of violence as well as punishment in order to modify their behaviour. Being perceived to bring shame to their families, they are frequently separated from their parents and placed in institutions where they live in bad conditions (UNICEF 2013). Their parents may also experience disadvantages, as disabled children are particularly dependent on them. As a result of increased care responsibilities, they have little or no respite time and may have difficulties in coping with their own life (Inclusion Europe 2011). Facing challenges in combining parenthood and employment, families with disabled children often live in poverty. The parents themselves may be subject to discrimination on the basis of disability, a phenomenon called ‘discrimination by association’.

Disability has its own specificity. It is a diverse characteristic that results from the interaction of different kinds of impairments with physical and social barriers embedded in society. Not only there are many kinds of impairments but considerable variations also exist within certain types of disabilities (Garland-Thomson 2009). Disabled people, therefore, represent a largely heterogeneous group (Siebers 2008). Whatever is done in order to distinguish them, it is impossible to capture the phenomenon as a whole.

This heterogeneity must be put into further perspective, as disabled people (as any group of people) can simultaneously belong to other groups, such as racial minorities, women and children. Any additional characteristic alters the way in which an individual lives a particular kind of impairment. The race, gender, age or other dimensions it brings with it may impact differently upon this individual in terms of human rights (de Silva de Alwis 2009).

A notable example is the lack of education for disabled children (which will be discussed in the next section). In many parts of the world, these children simply cannot go to school because of their disability (UNICEF 2013). In Western democracies, they are often referred to a so-called 'special schools', which generally offer them lower standards of education (UNICEF Innocenti Research Centre 2007). Although the importance of inclusive education has been recognized at the international level, there appears to be no real evolution in the situation on the ground (Moore and Slee 2012). While most State Parties have changed their domestic legislation so that disabled children can enrol in regular schools, there are no or limited resources to make it work.

Barriers are hard to overcome both in low-income countries, where resources are an ongoing challenge, and in high-income countries, where disabled children continue to be segregated. The support provided is either missing or inadequate compared to those children's needs (Inclusion International 2009). Teachers are not equipped to deal with issues related to disability and get considerable pressure to meet all kinds of targets (UNICEF 2013). More generally, these children are seen as unable to fit into the general education system. There is a belief that they may compromise the quality of education, a view exacerbated by the fact that standard tests to measure educational attainment are inappropriate for the purpose of inclusive education (Slee 2011). As a result, disabled children may feel unaccepted by regular schools and are sometimes subject to harassment and bullying (Rioux and Pinto 2010).

While education systems can exert pressure on some groups of pupils, it therefore goes to the extremes with those who are disabled, especially in a landscape characterized by competition and self-entrepreneurship.

The exclusion of disabled children from education highlights these education systems' inadequacy in meeting the varied needs of such children. This inadequacy is usually attributed to those children's lack of capacity or simply the costs involved in creating more convenient settings. It is however the educational environment that leads to the exclusion of disabled children from education by imposing restrictions on certain groups of pupils, but States consider that the barriers emerge because these children are inherently less capable than others. Rather than removing obstacles to inclusive education, they opt then for the segregation of disabled children.

## Human Rights Protection

### *The CRC and CRPD*

International human rights law recognized explicitly over time the human rights of certain historically marginalized individuals. Following the adoption of both the International Covenant on Civil and Political Rights (ICCPR) and the International Covenant on Economic, Social and Cultural Rights (ICESCR),[2] the international human rights framework developed towards the adoption of several group-specific human rights treaties. Thus, the International Convention on the Elimination of All Forms of Racial Discrimination (ICERD), the Convention on the Elimination of All Forms of Discrimination against Women (CEDAW), the CRC and, finally, the CRPD were drafted to provide human rights protection for racial minorities, women, children and disabled people.[3]

Initially, the prohibition of discrimination had the role of reaching out to these groups of people, and therefore it served as a springboard for the adoption of the afore-mentioned human rights treaties. The latter have broadened this prohibition, but they have done so divergently. The ICERD and CEDAW, which came first, elaborate on race and gender discrimination in provisions addressing civil and political rights

[2] International Covenant on Civil and Political Rights 1966, 999 UNTS 171; International Covenant on Economic, Social and Cultural Rights 1966, 993 UNTS 3. With the Universal Declaration of Human Rights, the ICCPR and ICESCR are said to form the International Bill of Human Rights.

[3] International Convention on the Elimination of All Forms of Racial Discrimination 1965, 660 UNTS 195; Convention on the Elimination of All Forms of Discrimination against Women 1979, 1249 UNTS 13.

and economic and social rights (even though CEDAW further provides for 'temporary special measures' to achieve de facto equality for women).[4] The CRC and CRPD, which came later, proclaim a full catalogue of rights relating specifically to children and disabled people. They are therefore fully fleshed human rights treaties that go much further than just prohibiting discrimination on the basis of age and disability.

Disabled children fall within the remit of both the CRC and the CRPD. Finding themselves at the crossroad of two identities, they get particular human rights protection from two fully fleshed human rights treaties that chronologically follow each other.

As the CRPD largely borrowed and expanded upon the CRC, both human rights treaties have several common features. The CRC bridged civil and political as well as economic and social rights (Brett 2009), a move that was replicated in the CRPD (de Beco 2019a). Unlike the ICERD and CEDAW, the CRC (Article 2.1) prohibits discrimination on the basis of a non-exhaustive number of grounds, while the CRPD (Article 5.2) also prohibits discrimination 'on all grounds'.[5] The CRC consists of four general principles which were identified by the CRC Committee, including the principle of the 'best interests' of the child and respect for children's views about all matters affecting them.[6] The CRPD has similarly a number of general principles, which are not only more numerous but also enumerated in the human rights treaty itself (Article 3). Noteworthy is also the fact that the CRPD has been ratified at an extremely rapid pace with 184 parties (at the time of writing),[7] while the CRC has achieved almost universal ratification, that is, all countries except one (namely the US).[8]

Both human rights treaties give disabled children a lot of consideration. Despite this high level of consideration, disabled children fall between two stools. The reason is that both the CRC and the CRPD view these

[4] Article 4(1), CEDAW.

[5] The Preamble, which also refers to 'multiple or aggravated forms of discrimination', lists an non-exhaustive number of grounds (Preamble(p), CRPD).

[6] See Articles 3 and 12, CRC. The two other ones are: non-discrimination (Article 2) and the right to life, survival and development (Article 6).

[7] https://treaties.un.org/Pages/ViewDetails.aspx?src=TREATY&mtdsg_no=IV-15&chapter=4&clang=_en.

[8] https://treaties.un.org/Pages/ViewDetails.aspx?src=IND&mtdsg_no=IV-11&chapter=4&clang=_en.

children predominantly from the perspective of a single identity, that is, as children first or as disabled people first. Disabled children are protected both by a human rights treaty for children and by a human rights treaty for disabled people, but they are actually characterized by both childhood *and* disability. The question is: How is this intersection addressed under international human rights law?

The CRC provides for a whole range of rights attached to children. It promotes their well-being and stresses the role of families in the advancement of the child's rights. The Convention draws particular attention to disabled children. It not only lists disability in the prohibited grounds of its general non-discrimination clause (for the first time ever in a human rights treaty) (Article 2) but it also includes a separate article on disabled children (Article 23).[9] The CRC Committee has been particularly sensitive to issues related to disability and, shortly before the CRPD's adoption, issued a general comment on the situation of disabled children (CRC Committee 2007), which remains a point of reference on the rights of disabled children in international human rights law.

The CRC has nonetheless some drawbacks with regard to disability. It aims more at protecting disabled children than guaranteeing their inclusion in society (Sabatello 2013). Its separate article on disabled children mentions 'special care' as well as 'subject to available resources ... assistance for which application is made' and 'assistance ... free of charge, whenever possible' (Articles 23.1–23.3). This wording reflects the welfarist approach to dealing with disability, which has now been revoked by the CRPD. While it can be regarded as 'the dominant language of the time' (Byrne 2019, 871), it shows the way that was still ahead to regard disability as a human rights issue. The CRC is also quite weak regarding disabled children in comparison with the standards it provides for children in general. It is arguably underpinned by the medical model of disability, which sees disability as a problem with the individual rather than the one related to society.

Notwithstanding its limitations, the CRC has provisions that to some extent compensates for such drawbacks. Its separate article on disabled children provides that the disabled child should live in 'conditions which ensure (...) the child's active participation in the community' (Article

[9] Article 23.1 of the CRC provides that the disabled child must 'enjoy a full and decent life, in conditions which ensure dignity, promote self-reliance and facilitate the child's active participation in the community.'

23.1), thereby showing an inclination towards inclusiveness. Other provisions that do not explicitly refer to disability can also be called upon towards this end (Quinn and Degener 2002), including the requirement to 'provide material assistance and support programmes' in order to protect children's right to an adequate standard of living. The CRC Committee, moreover, slowly but surely moved away from the medical model of disability, especially after issuing its general comment on the situation of disabled children (Byrne 2019). In this general comment, it clarified (concerning its separate article on disabled children) that '[t]he core message (…) is that children with disabilities should be included in the society' (CRC Committee 2007, para. 11). It has also made recommendations on matters especially affecting such children, although not always so in a consistent manner (Skarstad and Stein 2018).

The CRPD's purpose is to 'promote, protect and ensure the full and equal enjoyment of all human rights and fundamental freedoms by all persons with disabilities' (Article 1). It provides that disabled people are rights-holders entitled to exercise their rights with respect for their autonomy. Underscoring the 'various barriers [which] may hinder their full and effective participation in society', the Convention is viewed as inspired by the social model of disability (Kayess and French 2008; Bartlett 2012; Harpur 2012). In contrast to the medical model, the social model considers that disability is a consequence of how society is actually organized, something to be distinguished from the notion of impairment (Oliver 2009).

The CRPD likewise devotes much attention to disabled children. Like the CRC, it not only has a separate article on disabled children (Article 7) but also contains several articles that address issues related to age (Articles 8, 13, 16, and 23). The CRPD thus has a so-called 'twin-track' approach when it comes to childhood, that is, provisions on disabled children as such as well as provisions that take into account age. Its separate article on disabled children reiterates some of the CRC's general principles. It further adds that they should 'be provided with disability and age-appropriate assistance' to enjoy their right to express their views about all matters affecting them (Article 7.3). While this article was nearly left out for the sake of consistency during the negotiation of the CRPD (Quinn 2009), it actually maintains and builds upon the gains of the CRC.

However, the CRPD approaches disabled children in a way that does not fully contemplate the life experience of disabled children. While it protects such children against separation from their parents (Article

23.4), it does not consider the role of families with disabled children (Rimmerman 2015). One of the reasons is the fear that such families would exploit these children and jeopardise their autonomy. While there can be conflicts of interest between them, this does not acknowledge that support to the family itself is key to securing life opportunities for disabled children. The CRPD revolves essentially around the individual, regarding the family more as an obstacle to participation in society than a channel towards disabled people's self-realization. The CRPD Committee yet pointed to the need to 'provide adequate support services to family carers so they can in turn support their child ... to live independently' (CRPD Committee 2017, para. 67).

As both the CRC and CRPD are each in their own way incomplete regarding disabled children, there is a need not only to investigate the synergy between both human rights treaties but also to explore whether it is possible to combine their respective perspectives. While the CRC paved the way with its focus on disability as never done before in the field of international human rights law, the CRPD's gives a prominent place to childhood as testified by its 'twin-track' approach. Given that the two human rights treaties draw particular attention to disabled children, joint reading of these human rights treaties might help fill the gap left by each of them individually. While both of them serve disabled children's interests, the human rights protection they provide to these children is partly lost without such a joint reading (Landsdown 2014). Both the CRC and CRPD indeed have a single identity as perspective in mind that predominates the way in which they approach such children, which is why they need to be applied together.

On the one hand, the CRC provides for 'assistance to parents ... in the performance of their child-rearing responsibilities'.[10] Its consideration of parental involvement speaks to the reality that disabled children mostly rely on their families for their development and that these families must cope with additional costs (World Health Organization and World Bank 2011). Managing disabilities remains a responsibility that rests on parents' shoulders, who receive little assistance themselves. Families with disabled children not only require information on how to cope with a particular disability but also struggle for access to the various services that are needed for supporting their children. Because of their personal

[10] Articles 18(2), CRC. Article 23(2) of the CRC also refers to and assistance to 'those responsible for his or her care'.

struggles and reduced employment opportunities, parents generally face chronic hardship (Rimmerman 2015). They may have to sacrifice full-time employment in order to find time for their children while at the same time facing increased costs due to the particular needs of these very children. The CRC recognizes the dependency of those children, which does not necessarily hinders their autonomy.

On the other hand, the CRPD's objective is to foster participation in society (Article 1), which is particularly important as disabled children have been marginalized for a long time. It calls for relinquishing the kind of 'separate-but-equal' status that has come to epitomize human rights protection for disabled people. It focusses on inclusion and the promotion of independence. The CRPD thus upholds the view that disabled children are rights-holders, guaranteeing the enforcement of their rights via access to justice 'through the provision of procedural and age-appropriate accommodations' (Article 13.2). Its sweeping scope can be seen in its affirmation that disabled people 'include those who have long-term physical, mental, intellectual or sensory impairments' (Article 1), while its Preamble recognizes that disability is 'an evolving concept' (Preamble (e)). The Convention therefore has a dynamic approach to understanding disability, whereas the CRC provides a static definition of a child based on purely biological or medical terms.[11] Hence, it has been suggested that the social model of disability could enrich the way of considering childhood in general and contribute to further discerning its intersection with disability (Sandland 2017).

The CRC was written at a time where inclusiveness was not yet an objective for disabled children. This may explain its outdated terminology in addressing issues related to disability. At the same time, the CRPD's attention to childhood would not have been as extensive had the CRC overlooked disability altogether (as done by previous human rights treaties) (Byrne 2012). The CRPD's drafters subsequently endorsed the new direction of travel regarding disabled children, although they lost somewhat sight of the role of families in so doing. While the CRC should now be read in a different way than when it was adopted, it remains complementary to the CRPD.

A joint reading of the two human rights treaties, which combines their respective perspective, can therefore bear more fruit than applying

[11] By contrast, Article 1 of the CRC defines the child as being 'every human being below the age of eighteen'.

each of these human rights treaties in an isolated manner. While there is some synergy between the CRC and CRPD, such a joint reading can help resolve their inconsistencies in considering the intersectional position of disabled children. The CRC places emphasis on parental involvement in the realization of children's rights, which is crucial with regard to disability, but it does not recognize inclusion for its own sake. The CRPD has '[f]ull and effective participation and inclusion in society' amongst its general principles (Article 3c), but it has little regard for the role of families with disabled children. The problem is that both the CRC and the CRPD do not fully account in their own right for the specific situation in which disabled children find themselves. It is only by adopting an intersectional approach that the full range of human rights protection may be released for those children.

## Education

The right to education is of the utmost importance for all individuals. It works as a multiplier by facilitating the enjoyment of economic and social rights, such as the right to work and right to food, as well civil and political rights, such as the right to vote and freedom of expression. This is particularly true for disabled people whose right to education can empower them to take control of their life and move them out of their marginalized position in society. While this right is generally protected by the CRC as well as the ICESCR,[12] the CRPD provides for the right of disabled children to education in Article 24.

The aim here is to combine the respective perspective of the CRC as well as the CRPD with a view to determine what is expected from States Parties in order to tackle the exclusion of disabled children from education. An assessment of the right of disabled people to education may shed light on what a joint reading of the two human rights treaties could deliver in terms of human rights protection for disabled children.

The education of disabled children spurred heated debate during the CRPD's negotiation process and continues to stir controversy amongst stakeholders. This Convention transformed the original significance of

[12] Articles 28 and 29, CRC; 13 and 14, ICESCR. The CRC repeats most of the standards enunciated in the ICESCR, although it adds several new elements, including measures on vocational guidance (Article 28.1d), drop-out rates (Article 28.1e) and school discipline (Article 28.2).

the right to education by adding a new emphasis on inclusion that was hitherto unknown in the field of international human rights law. By incorporating the goal of inclusive education into international human rights law, the CRPD has redefined this right for disabled people.

Earlier international instruments advanced the goal of inclusive education in a way that would give shape to disabled children's right to education. The World Declaration on Education for All: Meeting Basic Learning Needs (Jomtien Declaration) declared that '[s]teps need to be taken to provide equal access to education to every category of disabled persons as an integral part of the education system' (Article 3.5). In a similar wording, the Standard Rules on the Equalization of Opportunities for Persons with Disabilities (Standard Rules) adopted in 1993 provided that '[e]ducation for persons with disabilities should form an integral part of national educational planning, curriculum development and school organization' (Rules 6.1). Another milestone was the Salamanca Statement and Framework for Action on Special Needs Education (Salamanca Statement) enacted at the UNESCO World Conference on Special Needs Education: Access and Equality held in 1994. The Salamanca Statement (1994, para. 2) stated that 'those with special educational needs must have access to regular schools which should accommodate them within a child-centred pedagogy capable of meeting these needs'. It thus laid down the concept of inclusive education, which would find its way more than two decades later into the CRPD.

The CRC did not take into account these developments, as it was drafted before the Salamanca Statement was adopted. In an interesting interaction, the CRC Committee nonetheless adjusted its understanding of the right to education in relation to disability. In its general comment on the situation of disabled children, which was elaborated precisely when the negotiating parties discussed the matter, the CRC Committee not only supported the adoption of future convention but also declared that '[i]nclusive education should be the goal of educating children with disabilities' (CRC Committee 2007, para. 66). It nonetheless recognized that 'the measure in which the inclusion occurs, may vary' and that '[a] continuum of services and programme options must be maintained in circumstances where fully inclusive education is not feasible to achieve in the immediate future' (ibid.). It therefore expressed the view that exceptions should still be allowed to the rule, which view reflected the persistent disagreement between the negotiating parties.

The consensus however started to emerge that inclusiveness be should the objective for the right of disabled children to education even though special education could still be provided if their needs so required (de Beco 2019b). The drafters eventually decided that inclusive education had to feature as an explicit guarantee for all disabled people.

Article 24 of the CRPD starts by stipulating that '[w]ith a view to realizing [the right of disabled people to education] (...), States Parties shall ensure an inclusive education system at all levels and life long learning' (Article 24.1). It then not only prohibits the exclusion of disabled people from education but also sets out a series of steps to be taken towards the goal of inclusive education.

The Convention requires that States Parties ensure that '[p]ersons with disabilities are not excluded from the general education system on the basis of disability' (Article 24.1). Refusal to enrol on such a basis amounts to direct discrimination (OHCHR 2013). States Parties must also ensure that 'children with disabilities are not excluded from free and compulsory primary education' (Article 24.2a), which echoes the CRC's provision that primary education be made 'compulsory and available free to all' (Article 28.1a). The CRPD goes on by providing that '[p]ersons with disabilities can access an inclusive, quality and free primary education and secondary education ... in the communities in which they live' (Article 24.2b). Infrastructure, including classrooms and toilets, as well as transport to school must therefore be fully accessible to them (UNICEF Innocenti Research Centre 2007; Inclusion International 2009, 82). The Convention also requires that States Parties ensure that disabled children 'receive the support required, within the general education system, to facilitate their effective education' (Article 24.2.d). Disabled children should not just be 'placed' in regular schools, but be offered the necessary support so that they can develop their skills and talents like any other children.

The right of disabled people to education has received increased attention in recent years (de Beco 2014, 2018; Kayess and Green 2016; Byrne 2013). It was the subject of a resolution by the UN Human Rights Council (HRC) in 2014 (HRC 2014). The CRPD Committee adopted a general comment on the issue in 2016, which is entitled 'The Right to Inclusive Education' (CRPD Committee 2016). In this general comment, it not only identified the 'core features' of inclusive education but also indicated what the achievement of inclusive education entails for States Parties to the CRPD (CRPD Committee 2016). It furthermore stressed the need to take measures in order to provide access to education for the benefit of all disabled children. It considered that accessibility involves that '[t]he entire education system must be accessible' (CRPD Committee 2016, para. 8), which applies to 'not just buildings, but all information and communication' and also the '[m]odes and means of teaching' (CRPD Committee 2014, para. 39). As accessibility in respect of education has usually been interpreted as a matter of non-discrimination or as relating to physical and economic obstacles (CESCR Committee 1999), this interpretation of access goes further than what is traditionally understood in the by it field of international human rights law.

Even though the CRC does not refer to disability in relation to education, it can still contribute to realizing the right of disabled children to education. It provides that such children must be assisted in education 'in a manner conducive to the child's achieving the fullest possible social integration' (Article 23.3). Despite the old-dated terminology, this provision can be seen as opposing the segregation of disabled children (Byrne 2019),[13] especially if the CRPD's perspective is brought into play. The CRC further contains several elements that are overlooked in the CRPD, which confirm the need for this intersectional approach. Three of these elements are worth mentioning.

First, the CRC includes a list of values that should inform the 'preparation of the child for responsible life' including 'understanding, peace, tolerance, equality of sexes, and friendship among all peoples, ethnic, national and religious groups and persons of indigenous origin' (Article 29.1d),[14] all of which encourage an attitude of tolerance for all people regardless of any of their characteristic (Lundy and Tobin 2019). This list of values highlights the importance of promoting positive social attitudes towards disabled people in the delivery of education. The CRC thereby adds a normative dimension to the education of disabled children as it points out what the purpose of strengthening 'human diversity' exactly involves for the education system (Article 24.1a), although the list does not explicitly refer to disabled people. The CRC therefore dovetails with

[13] Note that the CRC Committee replaced the term 'integration' by the term 'inclusion' in its general comment on the situation of disabled children (CRC Committee 2007, para. 11).

[14] This list of values was not taken over in the CRPD.

obligation to raise awareness by '[f]ostering at all levels of the education system ... an attitude of respect for the rights of persons with disabilities' provided for in the CRPD (Article 8.2b).

Second, the CRC highlights a number of principles and aims that underlie the right of disabled children to education or facilitate its realization. For instance, it sets out the general principle of the right to life, survival and development (Article 6.2), which is partially reiterated in its separate article on disabled children (Article 23.3). As families with disabled children struggle with worries and rejection, this principle is fundamental in order to enable such children to be educated. Another important issue concerns one of the aims of education set out in the CRC, namely the '[t]development of the child's personality, talents and mental and physical abilities to their fullest potential' (Article 29.1).[15] This serves as a reminder that these 'mental and physical abilities' must be enhanced notwithstanding disability beyond any form of rehabilitation. The CRC Committee further recommends that 'teaching methods should be tailored to the different needs of different children' (CRC Committee 2001, para. 9), which is crucial so that these methods can work for all those who are disabled.

Third, the CRC again underscores the role of families, which is fundamental regarding education. As mentioned earlier, this Convention guarantees that parents are given 'appropriate assistance ... in the performance of their child-rearing responsibilities' (Article 18.2). It reminds States of the family as a trusted source for recognition, assistance and identity-building. It thus acknowledges that schools are not the only entry point into the right to education, but that families provide the context in which children are nurtured and through which they receive education. It is here that awareness and understanding of the different needs of disabled children will also be at its highest. The CRC therefore brings home the fact that parental involvement is crucial not only in the education of their children but in all aspects of life and that a good relationship with families as a whole is imperative for achieving inclusive education. The aspect is sometimes ignored with regard to disability, and this Convention helps fill the gap.

In turn, the CRPD not only focusses expansively on education, but also redefined the significance of the right to education by endorsing the goal

[15] This provision was reiterated in 24.1b of the CRPD in which is added 'creativity'.

of inclusive education. It thereby responded to the persistent exclusion of disabled children from education. In doing so, it adopts a human rights-based approach to dealing with disability, which is missing in the CRC's provisions on disabled children. Rather than providing 'special care' as well as 'subject to available resources ... assistance for which application is made' and 'assistance ... free of charge, whenever possible',[16] the CRPD requires that States Parties ensure that 'individualized support measures are provided ... consistent with the goal of full inclusion'.[17] This Convention brings along a difference in tone in the field of international human rights law both by offering stronger standards for achieving its objectives and by confirming the necessity to need to remove obstacles to inclusive education.

As seen in the analysis above, it is only by applying together the CRPD and CRC that a set of remedies can be spelt out in order to fulfil the right to education for disabled children. These remedies range from the guarantee of access to education and provision of support to the enhancement of skills and abilities and improvement of social attitudes towards disabled people as well as the awareness of the role of families. It will therefore be hard for international human rights law to pursue further the goal of inclusive education without contemplating the intersection between children and disability. While the CRC and CRPD each draw particular attention to disabled children, they do so from their own perspective which should be combined through this joint reading of the two human rights treaties.

## Conclusion

Disabled children suffer from disadvantages that are more than the sum of those experienced by both children and disabled people. As pointed out by CRC Committee, they 'belong to one of the most vulnerable groups of children' (CRC Committee 2007, para. 8). As disabled children face rejection and stigma in a way unique to them, they are amongst the most marginalized individuals. In order to address the intersection of childhood and disability, the present chapter argued for the need to consider their life experience *as* disabled children. This concerns all areas of life but

[16] Articles 23(2) and (3), CRC.

[17] Article 24(2)(e), CRPD.

particularly that of education which they are denied because education systems fail to meet their needs.

Disabled children can call upon two group-specific human rights treaties: the CRC and the CRPD. Even though the latter treaty is more advanced in its way of approaching disabled children than the former treaty, this chapter has argued that there is an added value in applying them together. They should not be seen as opposed but as complementary to one another. As illustrated with the analysis of the education of disabled children, such an intersectional approach can be particularly useful in fully grasping the intersection of childhood and disability. The chapter has revealed that there are therefore gains to be made in showing more dedication to this intersection in the field of international human rights law. So doing will still require that the UN treaty bodies cooperate in order to have an open dialogue and to attain mutually acknowledged standards. This could lead to the adoption of common general comments, as already done at different occasions by the CRC Committee (CMW Committee and CRC Committee 2017a, b; CEDAW Committee and CRC Committee 2014). It is welcome in this regard to note that the CRPD and CRC Committees have likewise decided to work on a common general comment on the situation of disabled children.[18]

Finally, engagement with the intersection of childhood and disability is still limited in the field of international human rights law. This is a missed opportunity, as both the CRC and the CRPD focus on disabled children, and there is probably no other group that is covered to such an extent by different human rights treaties. Further exploration of how to improve human rights protection for such children would not only allow develop strategies tailored to their specific situation but also foster a better appreciation of intersectionality in international human rights law more broadly.

## References

Bartlett, P. 2012. The United Nations Convention on the Rights of Persons with Disabilities and Mental Health Law. *Modern Law Review* 75: 752–78.

[18] The author is grateful to the CRC and CRPD Committee members who have provided him with this information.

Brett, R. 2009. Rights of the Child. In *International Protection of Human Rights: A Textbook*, ed. C. Krause and M. Scheinin. Turku: Åbo Akademi University.

Byrne, B. 2012. Minding the Gap? Children with Disabilities and the United Nations Convention on the Rights of Persons with Disabilities. In *Law and Childhood Studies*, ed. M. Freeman. Oxford: Oxford University Press.

Byrne, B. 2013. Hidden Contradictions and Conditionality: Conceptualisations of Inclusive Education in International Human Rights Law. *Disability & Society* 28: 232–44.

Byrne, B. 2019. Article 23. Children with Disabilities. In *The UN Convention on the Rights of the Child: A Commentary*, ed. J. Tobin. Oxford: Oxford University Press.

CESCR Committee. 1999. *General Comment No. 13: The Right to Education (Art. 13).*

CEDAW Committee and CRC Committee. 2014. *Joint General Recommendation No. 31 and General Comment No. 18 on Harmful Practices.*

CMW Committee and CRC Committee. 2017a. *Joint General Comment No. 4 and No. 23 on State Obligations Regarding the Human Rights of Children in the Context of International Migration in Countries of Origin, Transit, Destination and Return.*

CMW Committee and CRC Committee. 2017b. *Joint General Comment No. 3 and No. 22 on the General Principles Regarding the Human Rights of Children in the Context of International Migration.*

CRC Committee. 2007. *General Comment No. 9 on the Rights of Children with Disabilities.*

Crenshaw, K. 1989. Demarginalising the Intersection of Race and Sex: A Black Feminist Critique of Antidiscrimination Doctrine, Feminist Theory and Antiracist Politics. *University of Chicago Legal Forum. Feminism in the Law: Theory, Practice and Criticism* 4: 139–67.

Crenshaw, K. 1991. Mapping the Margins: Intersectionality, Identity Politics, and Violence against Women of Color. *Stanford Law Review* 43: 1241–99.

CRC Committee. 2001. General Comment No. 1 on the Aims of Education.

CRPD Committee. 2014. *General Comment No. 2. Article 9 on Accessibility*, para. 39.

CRPD Committee. 2016. *General Comment No. 4 on the Right to Inclusive Education.*

CRPD Committee. 2017. *General Comment No. 5 on Living Independently and Being Included in the Community.*

de Beco, G. 2014. The Right to Inclusive Education According to Article 24 of the UN Convention on the Rights of Persons with Disabilities: Background,

Requirements and (Remaining) Questions. *Netherlands Quarterly of Human Rights* 32: 263–87.
de Beco, G. 2018. The Right to Inclusive Education: Why Is There so Much Opposition to Its Implementation? *International Journal of Law in Context* 14: 396–415.
de Beco, G. 2019a. The Indivisibility of Human Rights and the Convention on the Rights of Persons with Disabilities. *International & Comparative Law Quarterly* 68: 141–60.
de Beco, G. 2019b. Comprehensive Legal Analysis of Article 24 of the Convention on the Rights of Persons with Disabilities. In *The Right to Inclusive Education in International Human Rights Law*, ed. G. de Beco, J. Lord, and S. Quinlivan. Cambridge: Cambridge University Press.
de Silva de Alwis, R. 2009. Mining the Intersections: Advancing the Rights of Women and Children with Disabilities within an Interrelated Web of Human Rights. *Pacific Rim Law & Policy Journal* 18: 293–322.
Garland-Thomson, R. 2009. Disability, Identity, and Representation, In *Rethinking Normalcy*, ed. T. Titchkosky and R. Michalko. Toronto: Canadian Scholar's Press.
Harpur, P. 2012. Embracing the New Disability Rights Paradigm: The Importance of the Convention on the Rights of Persons with Disabilities. *Disability & Society* 27: 1–14.
HRC. 2014. The Right to Education of Persons with Disabilities.
Inclusion Europe. 2011. *Children's Rights for all! Implementation of the United Nations Convention on the Rights of the Child for Children with Intellectual Disabilities*. http://www.eenet.org.uk/resources/docs/6130.pdf.
Inclusion International. 2009. *Better Education for All When We Are Included Too. A Global Report. People with an Intellectual Disability and Their Families Speak Out on Education for All, Disability and Inclusive Education*. http://ii.gmalik.com/pdfs/Better_Education_for_All_Global_Report_October_2009.pdf.
Kayess, R., and French, P. 2008. Out of Darkness into Light? Introducing the Convention on the Rights of Persons with Disabilities. *Human Rights Law Review* 8: 1–34.
Kayess, R., and Green, J. 2016. Today's Lesson Is on Diversity: A Reflection on Inclusive Education. In *Routledge Handbook of Disability Law and Human Rights*, ed. P. Blanck and E. Flynn. London: Routledge.
Landsdown, G. 2014. Children with Disabilities. In *Human Rights & Disability Advocacy*, ed. M. Sabatello and M. Schulze. Philadelphia: Pennsylvania University Press.
Lundy, L., and Tobin, J. 2019. Article 29. The Aims of Education. In *The UN Convention on the Rights of the Child: A Commentary*, ed. J. Tobin. Oxford: Oxford University Press.

Moore, M., and Slee, R. 2012. Disability Studies, Education and Exclusion. In *Routledge Handbook of Disability Studies*, ed. N. Watson, A. Roulstone, and C. Thomas. London: Routledge.

OHCHR. 2013. *Thematic Study on the Right of Persons with Disabilities to Education*.

Oliver, M. 2009. *Understanding Disability: From Theory to Practice*. New York: Palgrave Macmillan.

Quinn, G. 2009. Disability and Human Rights: A New Field in the United Nations. In *International Protection of Human Rights: A Textbook*, ed. C. Krause and M. Scheinin. Turku: Åbo Akademi University.

Quinn, G., and Degener, T. 2002. *The Current Use and Future Potential of United Nations Human Rights Instruments in the Context of Disability*. New York/Geneva: UN.

Rimmerman, A. 2015. *Family Policy and Disability*. Cambridge: Cambridge University Press.

Rioux, R., and Pinto, P. 2010. A Time for the Universal Right to Education: Back to the Basics. *British Journal of Sociology of Education* 31: 621–42.

Sabatello, M. 2013. Children with Disabilities: A Critical Appraisal. *International Journal of Children's Rights* 21: 464–87.

Sandland, R. 2017. A Clash of Conventions? Participation, Power and the Rights of Disabled Children. *Social Inclusion* 5: 93–103.

Siebers, T. 2008. *Disability Theory*. Ann Arbor: University of Michigan Press.

Skarstad, K., and Stein, M. 2018. Mainstreaming Disability in the United Nations Treaty Bodies. *Journal of Human Right* 17: 1–24.

Slee, R. 2011. *The Irregular School: Exclusion, Schooling and Inclusive Education*. London/New York: Routledge.

UNICEF. 2013. *The State of the World's Children: Children with Disabilities*. New York: UNICEF.

UNICEF Innocenti Research Centre. 2007. *Promoting the Rights of Children with Disabilities*. New York: UNICEF. http://www.un.org/esa/socdev/unyin/documents/children_disability_rights.pdf.

World Conference on Special Needs Education. 1994. *Salamanca Statement and Framework for Action on Special Needs Education: Access and Equality*. http://unesdoc.unesco.org/images/0009/000984/098427eo.pdf.

World Health Organization and World Bank. 2011. *World Report on Disability*. Geneva: WHO.

CHAPTER 9

# The CRPD and Mental Health Law: The Conflict About Abolition, the Practical Dilemmas of Implementation and the Untapped Potential

*Kay Wilson*

The entry into force of the Convention on the Rights of Persons with Disabilities ('CRPD') in 2008 was a landmark in the recognition and development of disability rights in international human rights law. However, the application of the CRPD in the mental health context raises a number of unique challenges arising from: the complicated nature

K. Wilson (✉)
Melbourne Law School, University of Melbourne, Melbourne, VIC, Australia
e-mail: kayw1@unimelb.edu.au



F. Felder et al. (eds.), *Disability Law and Human Rights*, Palgrave Studies in Disability and International Development,
https://doi.org/10.1007/978-3-030-86545-0_9

of mental impairment[1]; entrenched negative social attitudes with respect to mental impairment; and the political and ethical concerns of States Parties to respond to the risks of harm to self and others occasionally posed by persons with mental impairment. Accordingly, the implementation of the CRPD in the mental health context has been dominated by over a decade of unresolved conflict between the CRPD Committee (the international body responsible for monitoring the implementation of the CRPD), certain scholars and disability advocates (whom I call 'abolitionists') and States Parties over what the CRPD *means* for persons with mental impairment and *whether* and *how* States Parties ought to comply with it.

In summary, the conflict relates to whether the CRPD requires the abolition of mental health law.[2] That is, the repeal of the power of the state to detain in hospital and give psychiatric treatment to persons with mental impairment without their consent in certain circumstances. Instead, abolitionists propose that persons with mental impairment should be offered various formal and informal supports to assist them in considering whether they want to be admitted to hospital and to undertake psychiatric or other treatment on a voluntary basis (Gooding 2017, 121–127). In rare cases where a person's will and preferences cannot be determined, a supporter or facilitator may need to make a decision for the individual in accordance with 'the best interpretation of his or her will and preferences' (Committee on the Rights of Persons with Disabilities 2014; Arstein-Kerslake and Flynn 2016, 477) rather than his or her objective medical best interests. More recently, abolitionists have become divided

[1] The terminology which refers to persons with mental impairments has always been problematic and contentious. By persons with mental impairment I mean persons with psychiatric conditions including schizophrenia, bipolar disorder, depression, anxiety disorders, eating disorders, obsessive–compulsive disorder and post-traumatic stress disorder which may be treatable by psychiatric intervention, rather than persons with cognitive impairments such as intellectual disability, autism and dementia. While I have no difficulty with the idea that society can disable persons, 'persons with disabilities' seems too general. I have instead chosen 'mental impairment' as opposed to 'mental illness' or 'psycho-social' disability, in this paper because it is the term used in the *Convention on the Rights of Persons with Disabilities*, open for signature 30 March 2007, UNTS 2515, (entered into force 3 May 2008), Art 1 ('CRPD').

[2] While the term 'mental health law' applies to all laws that relate to mental health, this chapter is particularly concerned about legal provisions which permit the involuntary detention and psychiatric treatment of persons with mental impairment, whether contained in a stand-alone Mental Health Act or dispersed within other legislation.

between whether the abolition of mental health law means the absolute banning of legal coercion of any kind,[3] or whether some forms of legal coercion may be permitted by the CRPD provided they do not discriminate against persons with mental impairment, that is, they are 'disability neutral' (Stavert 2018, 28; Gooding and Flynn 2015, 261; Flynn and Arstein-Kerslake 2017, 57). Nonetheless, most abolitionists still oppose involuntary detention and psychiatric treatment (ibid.).

However, the call for the abolition of mental health law has been criticised by States Parties, medical experts, certain scholars and some persons with mental impairments as not realistically taking into account the effect of severe mental impairment on a person's decision-making and as potentially depriving persons with mental impairment from access to much needed medical care (which millions of people chose voluntarily) and in the most serious cases endangering their own lives and health and in some instances that of others. Many of the underlying concerns of the abolitionists can be taken into account by legal and systemic reforms which aim to decrease coercion and increase decision-making and social support for persons with mental impairments. At present there are two main approaches. The first is a Mental Capacity with Support Model which aims to use supported decision-making to improve a person's mental capacity so that they can make autonomous decisions (which have to be respected by law) and when a person lacks capacity to use their will and preferences to guide decisions made on their behalf. The second is a Support Except Where there Is Harm Model, that is, to support persons to make their own legally binding decisions, except where they are likely to harm themselves or others. Of these, as I have argued elsewhere, I prefer the Mental Capacity with Support Model (Wilson 2018, 2020).

In this chapter, I set out a broad overview of the conflict stemming from the call for the abolition of mental health law and some of the practical problems and dilemmas involved in implementing the CRPD in the mental health context. Would the abolition of mental health law really be good for persons with mental impairment? Are there other ways of responding to the abolitionists criticisms? I also comment on the untapped potential of the CRPD to improve the lives of persons with mental impairments beyond the abolition debate by systemic and social reforms to support persons with mental impairments and build a more

[3] See for example Dhanda (2016) and Minkowitz (2017).

mentally healthy world. My focus is on mental health policy in western high-income countries, as it is difficult to compare countries with different mental health systems and cultural understandings of mental impairment.

## A Brief Overview of the Conflict Between Abolitionists and States Parties over the Future of Mental Health Law

The conflict between abolitionists and States Parties over the future of mental health law began during the CRPD negotiations. The CRPD is unique among international human rights treaties in that it was negotiated between States Parties with strong involvement from civil society, especially Disabled Persons Organisations. While there are different accounts of the negotiation of the CRPD from various people who participated in it,[4] what is clear is that the negotiations with respect to the abolition of mental health law, particularly the right to legal capacity in Article 12, were especially fraught, at one point even threatening to derail the whole convention (Craigie et al. 2019, 165).

The abolitionist's reasons for wanting to abolish mental health law are complex and are a mixture of theoretical and practical concerns derived from the tawdry history of madness and the development of psychiatry which requires far more time and space than is available in this chapter to articulate in full.[5] However, in summary, abolitionists are concerned that by negating the power of persons with severe mental impairment to consent to and refuse hospital admission and psychiatric treatment where they are medically assessed as being at risk of harming themselves or others, mental health law sets up an unhealthy power imbalance between psychiatrists and patients in which persons with mental impairment are not listened to and are treated and forced to stay in hospital against their will. The use of force is by its nature violent (Roper and Gooding 2019, 154). It can involve locked doors and holding people down to administer treatments (ibid., 156). Psychiatric treatments often come with negative side-effects such as weight gain, fatigue and sedation, shaking,

[4] For example, MacQuarrie and Laurin-Bowie (2013) and Duffy and Kelly (2017, 28).

[5] I am not aware of any material which spells it out as comprehensively as my Ph.D. dissertation which has recently been published as a book called Mental Health Law: Abolish or Reform? (Oxford University Press, 2021), especially Chapters 2 and 3.

sexual dysfunction, memory loss and increased risk of heart disease and diabetes (Minkowitz 2007, 419). Cath Roper explains 'the drugs took away sensation, slowed thinking and caused internal alienation which was horrifying, like missing myself, watching myself die' (Roper and Gooding 2019, 156). Fiona Anderson complains that lithium therapy administered to her in 1990 has caused her ongoing chronic pain and kidney dysfunction (Anderson and Chen 2019, 179). Once in hospital, persons are often exposed to other patients with a range of unusual and sometimes harmful behaviours, can be subject to restrictive practices such as seclusion and restraint and, in some instances, even be sexually assaulted by staff (Roper and Gooding 2019, 154).

As peer worker Charlene Sunkel (2019, 52) observes:

> psychiatric facilities often look and function more like prisons than places of care ... in South Africa, persons refusing hospital treatment may be resistant not because of diminished legal or mental capacity (however perceived), but because of the knowledge of what happens in those facilities.

Further, many abolitionists simply object to the idea that mental impairment is a medical condition at all which requires medical treatment, but rather conceptualise their experiences as simply a different form of consciousness (Roper and Gooding 2019, 158; Oaks 2012, 566). It is understandable then that abolitionists have a range of objections to involuntary detention and psychiatric treatment and want to abolish it.

On the other hand, states have always had a role in providing care for people with mental impairment, especially where informal care from family and friends is strained or lacking. The provision of health care has become an important function of the modern state and is of instrumental value because it assists in being able to develop and follow our life plans (Maclean 2009, 28). Access to health care is also a matter of social equity (Sen 1995, 72). Mental impairment can have a serious impact on the person. For example, a woman who tried to cut off her healthy right arm to quiet the voices in her head (Richards 2013, 1), a person who is starving to death who refuses to eat for fear of becoming obese,[6] a woman who believed she would reach an enlightened state if she jumped off a building and landed with her head in the right place (Gooding 2015,

[6] *Re E (Medical Treatment Anorexia)* [2012] EWHC 1639 (COP).

61–62), or persons who harm themselves as a distraction or outlet for their immediate psychological distress and pain, without thinking of the consequences.[7]

States Parties are concerned that persons with serious mental impairments may be so ill that they do not know that they need to be admitted to hospital and treated (which is regarded as a marker of serious impairment) (Amador and Kronengold 2004, 24–25). For example, Kate Richards explains how her psychosis and severe depression interfere with her decision-making:

> when I'm sick I believe the delusional stuff to the same degree that you might know and believe the sky is above and the earth is below. And if someone were to say to me that the delusional thinking is, in fact, delusional, well that's the same as if I assure you now that we walk on the sky. Of course you wouldn't believe me, and that's why it's sometimes so hard for people who are sick like this to accept treatment – to know that they even need treatment. (Richards 2013, 174)

If people with serious mental impairment are left untreated they may continue to deteriorate and either harm themselves through neglect, deliberate self-harm, suicide (Wilson 2018) and in rare cases harm others especially if they abuse drugs and alcohol (Mullen 2006), and can become entangled in the criminal justice system (Grecco and Chambers 2019). People with serious mental impairments may also lose life opportunities that have always been important to them, such as money, careers and relationships, control and stability and can be so consumed by the characteristics of their impairment to the extent that they have difficulty participating in life (Dawson 2009, 23, 32–33).While psychiatric treatments have their drawbacks, many people find biomedical treatments beneficial and respond quickly to medication alone or in combination with talking therapies (Dharmawardne and Menkes 2019, 283). Some people, even those who have resisted medication and therapy initially, come to include it as part of their recovery, even if recovery does not mean a complete absence of symptoms, and they require other forms of social support and lifestyle changes as well (Cohen 2005, 343, 345). For example, activist Patricia Deegan uses hospitalisation and medications

[7] *Nottinghamshire Healthcare NHS Trust (Applicant)* v *RC* (Respondent) [2014] EWHC 1317 (COP), 7 and 37.

along with therapy, self-help, mutual support, friends, religion, work, exercise and spending time with nature as an important part of managing her own recovery (Deegan 1993). Even places where alternatives to traditional psychiatric care are emphasised, such as Trieste in Italy which has a system focussed on complete deinstitutionalisation, voluntariness and community care, have not been able to eliminate the need for involuntary psychiatric treatment completely, even though rates are significantly lower than other European countries (Mezzina 2018). Similarly, while studies of peer respite services have indicated that they can reduce hospital admissions by up to 70%, those who had longer respite (and presumably more serious and complicated issues) still ended up in hospital (Gooding et al. 2018, 37, 42). To not treat a person who cannot access treatment because they are incapable of consenting and where there is concern that they may cause harm to themselves or others, could even be construed as a discriminatory denial of health care.

Unfortunately, the status of involuntary detention and psychiatric treatment was left deliberately unresolved during the negotiation of the CPRD, as states refused to agree to abolish mental health law and disability advocates decided that the CRPD should not mention the issue at all for the fear of giving the retention of mental health law legitimacy (Kayess and French 2008, 30). While Amita Dhanda (2016, 444) has claimed victory for abolitionists in that the CRPD does not contain a positive right permitting States Parties to use involuntary detention and psychiatric treatment, this seems rather hollow given that most states already have a mental health law of some kind, making the issue of abolition rather than permission key to treaty implementation. In the circumstances, a strategically motivated 'negotiated silence' on the future of mental health law, as advocated by Annegret Kampf (2010, 144–146), is a more accurate description of the political decision taken by disability advocates to leave the issue unresolved because State Parties would not agree to their position at that time.

Nonetheless, post-CRPD abolitionists argue that collectively the general principle of non-discrimination (Article 4) and the rights to equality (Article 5), legal capacity (Article 12), liberty (Article 14), bodily integrity (Article 17), health (Article 25) and the ban on torture and cruel and unusual punishment (Article 15), all require the abolition of mental health law. As Melvyn Freeman and colleagues (2015, 844) have remarked:

> countries that originally ratified the CRPD are facing intense pressure to implement far reaching changes that challenge fundamental principles of mental health care and treatment hitherto widely accepted as reflecting a human rights perspective.

The abolition of mental health law has been repeatedly and consistently advocated by the CRPD Committee in its concluding observations to states' reports,[8] General Comment No. 1 (Article 12, Equal Recognition before the Law),[9] the Guidelines on the Right to Liberty and Security of Persons with Disabilities[10] and recently in General Comment 6 (Article 5, Equality and Non-Discrimination).[11]

In particular, in General Comment No. 1, which is probably the clearest and most pointed instruction to states to abolish mental health law, the CRPD Committee has unequivocally and controversially stated:

> State parties' obligation to replace substitute decision-making regimes by supported decision-making requires both the abolition of substitute decision-making regimes and the development of supported decision-making alternatives. The development of supported decision-making systems in parallel with the maintenance of substitute decision-making regimes is not sufficient to comply with article 12 of the Convention [equality before the law/ legal capacity][12];

[8] For example, Committee on Rights of Persons with Disabilities. 2013. Concluding observations on the initial report of Australia, adopted by the Committee at its tenth session CRPD/C/AUS/CO/1 [34], and more recently, Committee on Rights of Persons with Disabilities. 2017. Concluding observations on the United Kingdom CRPD/C/GBR/CO/1) [31] and [55]. George Szmukler (2015, 260) reports that the CRPD Committee has called for the abolition of all substitute decision-making regimes in over 20 state reports.

[9] See Committee on the Rights of Persons with Disabilities 'General Comment No. 1 (2014) Article 12: Equal Recognition before the Law' (11 April 2014) UN Doc CRPD/C/GC/1 [26].

[10] See CRPD Committee. 2015. Guidelines on Article 14 of the Convention on the Rights of Persons with Disabilities: The Right to Liberty and Security of Persons. 14th Session: [6] and [10].

[11] CRPD Committee. 2018. General Comment 6: Equality and Non-discrimination (Article 5), [30].

[12] Committee on the Rights of Persons with Disabilities 'General Comment No. 1 (2014) Article 12: Equal Recognition before the Law' (11 April 2014) UN Doc CRPD/C/GC/1, [24].

The 'substitute decision-making' referred to by the CRPD Committee is where a decision is made for a person by a third party (such as a psychiatrist) which may not reflect his or her will and preferences. For example, consent to hospital admission or psychiatric treatment.[13] States Parties would, however, be able to offer support to a person with mental impairment to make their own decision, or where considerable efforts have been made, allow a third party to make a decision which must be in accordance with that person's will and preferences. Supported decision-making refers to a broad range of formal and informal assistance, including presenting information in an accessible way, advocacy of the patient's point of view and advance care planning, aimed at helping a person to make decisions between good options (Gooding 2017, 118).

The CRPD Committee has also stated more explicitly in General Comment No. 1 (2014, [38]):

> State parties must abolish policies and legislative provisions that allow or perpetuate forced treatment, as it is an ongoing violation found in mental health laws across the globe, despite empirical evidence indicating its lack of effectiveness and the views of people using mental health systems who have experienced deep pain and trauma as a result of forced treatment.[14]

Similarly, the United Nations Special Rapporteur on Torture, Juan E. Méndez, has called for 'an absolute ban on all forced and non-consensual medical interventions against persons with disabilities',[15] including those with mental impairments, although this may not apply where there is a risk of harm to self or others (Gooding 2017, 78). The call for the abolition of mental health law has also been endorsed by Dainius Puras, the Special Rapporteur on the Right of Everyone to the Enjoyment of

[13] CRPD, declarations and reservations, http://treaties.un.org/Pages/ViewDetails.aspx?src=TREATY&mtdsg_no=IV-15&chapter=4&lang=en. Accessed 27 March 2020.

[14] General Comment 1, above n 5, [38].

[15] UNHCR. 2013. Report of the Special Rapporteur on torture and other cruel, inhuman or degrading treatment or punishment, Juan E. Méndez A/HRC/22/53, [89(b)], available at https://www.ohchr.org/_layouts/15/WopiFrame.aspx?sourcedoc=/Documents/HRBodies/HRCouncil/RegularSession/Session22/A.HRC.22.53_English.pdf&action=default&DefaultItemOpen=1. Accessed 27 March 2020.

the Highest Attainable Standard of Physical and Mental Health[16] an independent expert who reports to the United Nations Human Rights Committee. Notably, rather than call for the immediate abolition of mental health law, the Special Rapporteur has instead proposed that States Parties take steps towards the abolition of mental health law such as developing mainstream alternatives to coercion in policy and practice, developing a plan to reduce, with a view to eliminating coercive medical practices in consultation with persons with mental impairment, increasing investment in research and sharing good practices between countries.[17] Nevertheless, the abolition rather than the reform of mental health law remains the ultimate aim.

However, Australia, Canada and a number of other jurisdictions have made interpretive declarations that they do not interpret the CRPD as requiring the abolition of substitute decision-making. Notably, the UK did not make any such declaration. Mary Donnelly (2010, 2) speculates that the reason was 'not because of a plan to abolish compulsory treatment', but because it was never seriously contemplated that the CRPD could require the abolition of mental health law (ibid.; Office of Disability Issues 2011, 40–41). Further, the most recent independent review of mental health law in the UK by Simon Wellesley (2018) has rejected the abolition of mental health law advocated by the CRPD Committee as both undesirable and unnecessary to recognise the UK's human rights obligations under the European Convention on Human Rights (ECHR) and the CRPD, although he proposes a series of reforms to mental health law. Since the CRPD has come into force, no state has gone so far as to abolish substitute decision-making or to implement full-scale supported decision-making in mental health law (Dute 2015, 318–319). As Oliver Lewis observes, it is 'unprecedented in international human rights law for a treaty body to articulate as a norm something that is not reflected in a law anywhere' (Craigie et al. 2019, 165).

Further, not all international and regional human rights bodies have demanded the abolition of mental health law. For example, the Human Rights Committee, which monitors the International Covenant on Civil

[16] UNHRC. 2017. Report of the Special Rapporteur on the right of everyone to the enjoyment of the highest attainable standard of physical and mental health. A/HRC/35/21, [63]–[66].

[17] Ibid., [66].

and Political Rights ('ICCPR'), noted in General Comment 35, contradicting the CRPD Committee, that the deprivation of liberty of persons with disability may be justified where a person is at risk of harming themselves or others.[18] The Subcommittee on the Prevention of Torture and Other Cruel, Inhuman and Degrading Treatment and Punishment has also interpreted the CRPD as not only allowing involuntary detention and psychiatric treatment where persons lack mental capacity and are at risk of harming themselves or others, but points out that a failure to do so may also be a form of discrimination and cruel, inhuman and degrading treatment and punishment.[19] There is an analogy here with denying people who are sick, injured or who have just had surgery access to pain relief, or medical treatment for HIV/AIDs, in which suffering is avoidable with treatment and which are also regarded as cruel, inhuman and degrading treatment.[20] While the Sub-Committee did not provide any specific examples of how the abolition of mental health law could amount to discrimination or cruel, inhuman or degrading treatment, as discussed above, mental impairment can cause severe psychological distress and suffering, including irreparable consequences such as self-harm (e.g. cutting off a limb), accident or suicide attempts, ideation, planning and completion. Similarly, the ECHR permits states to deprive persons of 'unsound mind' of their liberty where it is warranted due to medical necessity.[21] While the European Court of Human Rights has considered the CRPD relevant, it has not joined the call for the abolition of mental health law.[22]

In addition, the call for the abolition of mental health law has divided scholarly opinion. Some scholars, especially those involved in drafting the CRPD and the CRPD Committee, argue that the Abolition with Support

[18] UN Human Rights Committee. 2014. General Comment 35 Article 9 (Liberty and Security of the Person) CCPR/C/GC/35.

[19] Subcommittee on Prevention of Torture and Other Cruel, Inhuman or Degrading Treatment or Punishment. 2016. *Approach of the Subcommittee on Prevention of Torture and Other Cruel, Inhuman or Degrading Treatment or Punishment regarding the rights of persons institutionalized and treated medically without informed consent* CAT/OP/27/2 [14]–[15].

[20] *D v United Kingdom* (1997) 24 EHRR 423.

[21] Article 5(e), European Convention on Human Rights, opened for signature 1950 (entered into force 1 June 2010).

[22] *N v Romania* Application No. 59132/08 decision of 28 November 2017, [141]–[147].

Model is the only way to implement the 'paradigm shift' in rethinking the relationship between persons with disability and the state which is aimed to be produced by the CRPD (Bartlett 2019, 49), in accordance with the letter and the spirit of the CRPD (Minkowitz 2017; Dhanda 2016; Stavert 2018; Gooding and Flynn 2015; Flynn and Arstein-Kerslake 2017). Others are more cautious and critical in interpreting the CRPD as requiring significant reform rather than abolition (Wilson 2018; Davidson et al. 2016; Burch 2017; Scholten and Gather 2017; Del Villar 2015; Bilchitz 2016).

### *What Are Some of the Dilemmas Which Arise from the Call for the Abolition of Mental Health Law?*

The battle between human rights groups seeking the immediate implementation of treaty obligations and fighting for radical change versus stubborn States Parties seeking to avoid their obligations is well-worn trope in international human rights law. However, despite calls for the abolition of mental health law, is the trope accurate with respect to the implementation of the CRPD in the mental health context? I argue that in the mental health context, the trope is complicated by the technical issue of whether the CRPD requires the abolition of mental health law in the first place, and the practical issue of whether the call for abolition of mental health law would be 'good' for persons with mental impairment, or potentially endanger some of their other CRPD rights. Both of these issues turn on whether mental impairment and disability are conceptualised as being medical or social in nature, or a combination of both. I give a brief overview of each of these issues.

### *Does the CRPD Require the Abolition of Mental Health Law?*

As described above, the text of the CRPD does not explicitly prohibit mental health law and States Parties and abolitionists were unable to agree on the abolition of mental health law during negotiations. The discord means that the CRPD contains a number of ambiguities. Of course, it is not uncommon for the drafting of international instruments to be left 'in a fuzzy state for the sake of achieving agreement' (Christian 2015, 7). As noted by Rosemary Kayess and Philip French (2008, 33),

> the CRPD, like all international instruments, is ultimately a negotiated text. It is therefore unrealistic to expect it to reflect a fully coherent or comprehensive exposition of disability rights.

In addition, interpretation during treaty implementation is often conceived of as an ongoing process as parties work together to develop the meaning of the treaty and to translate it into reality (Lewis 2010, 105–106).

Given that abolition is 'barely grazed by the CRPD text' (Kayess and French 2008, 34), the CRPD can be conceptualised as an 'incompletely theorised agreement' which is capable of more than one interpretation. Abolitionists interpret the CRPD based on the British model of social disability which completely rejects the medical model and regards disability as being entirely socially constructed. In other words, disability is created by the failure of society to support and accommodate persons with mental impairments. From this perspective, it is the failure of mental health law to recognise the legal capacity of persons with mental impairments to make their own decisions and the lack of decision-making support available to persons with mental impairments which is to blame. That is, individual autonomy is entirely a result of a person's social and political environment, rather than having any basis in his or her internal mental state (Craigie 2015).

The consequence is that abolitionists take a very selective view of the CRPD by only focussing on some articles (mostly related to liberty and legal capacity) and down-playing others (related to the right to life and health). They see abolition as the only way to implement the CRPD, without taking into account the impact of the mental impairment itself and tend to take the most extreme interpretation of each article. For instance, abolitionists take a very literal and formal view of the meaning of 'equality' and 'non-discrimination'. That is, abolitionists in demanding the abolition of substitute decision-making argue that persons with mental impairment must be treated exactly 'the same' by the law as persons without mental impairment with full mental capacity who can only be given medical treatment voluntarily,[23] even though persons

[23] Committee on the Rights of Persons with Disabilities 'General Comment No. 1 (2014) Article 12: Equal Recognition before the Law' (11 April 2014) UN Doc CRPD/C/GC/1, [7], [13], [15], [32], [33].

with and without mental impairments may not be comparable or similarly situated. Further, the right to health in Article 25(d) is interpreted as mandating the need for informed consent in all circumstances, regardless of whether the person is capable of giving informed consent at the relevant time.[24] Therefore, the differences of persons with mental impairments are (like gender and race) seen as not being 'real' differences justifying different treatment in law, but are simply a result of supposition. As Amita Dhanda (2012, 185) explains 'the paradigm of universal legal capacity is primarily up against barriers of the mind. It is only the existence of these attitudinal barriers which can explain why certain states kept coming back to the paradigm of selective legal capacity and substitution.' In the abolitionist model differences can only be taken into account through the offering of support, which the person with mental impairment is entitled to reject.[25]

Abolitionists also interpret the right to legal capacity in Article 12(4) as requiring the development of 'safeguards' for supported decision-making, rather than as permitting limited involuntary detention and psychiatric treatment in extreme cases. The right to liberty, it is claimed by abolitionists, applies to all forms of preventive detention regardless of whether the person is likely to be at risk of harming themselves or others. Instead, the law should not intervene until a person with mental impairment has committed an actual offence, at which point they should be charged with a crime (Dhanda 2012, 184). Similarly, for abolitionists the right to bodily integrity means absolute control over one's own body and mind in any and all circumstances, rather than as Bernadette McSherry (2008, 122) points out, only as prohibiting unbeneficial and overly intrusive treatment.

However, the British social model of disability is not the only social model of disability to have developed in disability studies, even if it was influential for disability advocates in drafting the CRPD. In fact, Rosemary Kayess and Philip French (2008, 33) have criticised the British social model of disability as an 'uncritical, populist, understanding of the social model of disability'. Similarly, Anne Plumb (2015, 184) has criticised the British social model of disability as being developed with the position of

[24] Ibid., [41].

[25] Committee on the Rights of Persons with Disabilities 'General Comment No. 1 (2014) Article 12: Equal Recognition before the Law' (11 April 2014) UN Doc CRPD/C/GC/1 [19].

people with physical impairments in mind rather than those with mental impairments.

I argue that contrary to claims by the abolitionists, the CRPD is not in fact grounded in the British social model of disability. That is, I argue that a 'critical realist' account which views disability as both real in an objective sense (as opposed to being constituted by 'labels') and as an *interaction* between individual and social/environmental factors, put forward by Tom Shakespeare (2013, 75), presents a far more complex and nuanced approach to understanding the situation of persons with mental impairment. While Shakespeare's critique of the social model of disability is controversial within disability studies, it has still been an influential alternative to and arguably a more fulsome account of the experience of disability. Other theorists which take a similar approach are Michael Bury (1986), Jenny Morris (1991), Julie Mulvany (2000, 589) and Johnathan Burns (2009, 22). Such an approach is also consistent with the text of the inclusive description of disability in the CRPD as being an *interaction* between the different types of impairment and various barriers which may hinder a person's full and effective participation in society and the context of the competing rights described above within the CRPD (Article 1). Further, Andrea Broderick (2015, 77–79) argues that the inclusive description of disability and the preamble of the CRPD were actually drafted to reflect an *interactive* rather than a socially constructivist model of disability, after the Australian delegate pointed out that a purely social and environmental conceptualisation of disability would be unworkable. She also argues that an understanding which leaves out impairment is undesirable and incomplete (ibid.). As I have argued elsewhere, an interactive social model of disability is consistent with a more holistic interpretation of the CRPD which balances rights to liberty and legal capacity with the rights to life, health and maximising the ability of persons with mental impairment to participate in the community (Wilson 2018). A holistic interpretation of the CRPD does not require the abolition of mental health law, although it may require significant legal and systemic reform (ibid.).

### *Is the Abolition of Mental Health Law 'Good' for Persons with Mental Impairment?*

Recognition of the citizenship rights of liberty and autonomy are strongly embedded in Western democracies and have been a core part of the disability rights movement. Within this context the idea that mental health law should be abolished and people should be supported to make their own decisions has a certain appeal. As Terry Carney (2017, 45) asks, what's not to like about the idea of supporting people to make their own decisions?

However, critics of the call for abolition are concerned that it is overly simplistic and does not properly consider the lived reality of mental impairment which is often fluctuating and involves diverse characteristics including hallucinations and delusions, different levels of severity, mental deterioration over time, self-harm and suicide (Davidson et al. 2016; Jeste 2018; Shogren et al. 2017). While there has been much interest in the idea of supported decision-making, further research is needed to test different strategies in practice in the mental health context. Issues like finding appropriate supporters, ensuring that supporters do not manipulate the support process, and determining what to do in the 'hard cases' where persons may have unclear or contradictory 'will' and 'preferences' make implementation difficult (Penzenstadler et al. 2020, 6–7). Further, in some cases support may not be enough to overcome the effect of a person's mental health symptoms (such as extreme apathy, lack of self-regard or delusional beliefs) to assist them in making a serious decision, such as rejecting medical treatment, which may potentially threaten life or health, or put at risk previously cherished life-goals (such as their job, financial position and maintenance of important relationships). Support can also be rejected by the person for whatever reason, regardless of whether they may need it.

Not intervening at all can leave persons with mental impairment in a very bad place. Anne Plumb notes:

> a survivor who wrote on an on-line forum about lighting candles to keep evil influences at bay (her house burned down); a friend of mine who thought he could stop buses by standing ahead of them with his arms outstretched; and I very nearly stepped into a bath of boiling water in the belief that I needed to demonstrate faith in God (aka mystics running over hot coals). Authorities have responded to these risks in ways totally unacceptable to many of us, but should this mean that no-one should intervene? (Craigie et al. 2019, 190)

It is true, as Sascha Callaghan and colleagues (2013, 383) point out, that not all persons with mental impairment who are involuntarily detained and treated are thankful for the intervention in retrospect. Abolitionists tend to view psychiatric treatment negatively and involuntary detention and treatment as always traumatising and unhelpful. But, there is a body of research on people's retrospective thoughts and feelings about involuntary detention and treatment which demonstrates that, contrary to the assertions of abolitionists, not everyone is against involuntary detention and treatment (e.g. Katsakou et al. 2010, 2012; Danzer and Wilkus-Stone 2015, 265–266; Akther et al. 2019; Sunkel 2019). A substantial proportion of persons who have experienced involuntary detention and treatment (between 40 and 80%) report being glad to receive this treatment in retrospect or accept that it was justified, especially if they perceived the admission procedures to be fair (Priebe et al. 2009, 53) and the treatment was successful in causing mental capacity to be regained (Owen et al. 2009, 405).

Further, some persons with mental impairments support involuntary treatment in some cases, so the call for abolition is not representative of all persons with mental impairment. For instance, Graham Morgan, who has been diagnosed with schizophrenia, explains that:

> ...for me, compulsory treatment in the community probably keeps me alive and yet I am aware there is limited evidence that this form of intervention is effective. However, I think there is ample evidence that detention in hospital when desperate, when you cannot bear another day, when the television is beaming horrific messages and instructions into your brain is needed...if left to exercise my legal capacity, I would have died and no peer support, no compassionate friend or loving professional, no aspect of Open Dialogue or eCPR would have made any difference ... . (Craigie et al. 2019, 163)

While some abolitionists, such as Piers Gooding (2017, 13), agree that there may be a minority of cases in which involuntary detention and psychiatric treatment should be permitted, the difficulty for abolitionists is the concern that if they make *any* exceptions, then the freedom of all persons with mental impairments will be at risk. That is because historically changes to mental health law have had little impact on who gets involuntarily detained and treated (Appelbaum 1997, 136). In practice, mental health law may be manipulated by mental health professionals and tribunals 'at the margins' and is moulded to reflect 'widely held moral sentiments' (ibid., 144).

## What Is the Untapped Potential of the CRPD in the Mental Health Context?

While the debate surrounding the call for the abolition of mental health law has overshadowed the implementation of the CRPD in the mental health context, it would be wrong to say that no progress has been made. Significantly, the CRPD and call for the abolition of mental health law have generated widespread agreement that compulsory intervention is overused and should be reduced (Mahomed et al. 2018). Further, the growing numbers of persons with mental impairments in the community, the cost of mental impairments to the economy and the increase of persons with mental impairments receiving disability pensions have also meant that governments have begun to take improving the mental health sector seriously.[26]

The entry into force of the CRPD has sparked widespread mental health and guardianship law reform activity. For instance, all Australian states and territories have conducted reviews and made reforms to their mental health laws in response to the CRPD.[27] The Australian Law Reform Commission also completed a report on Equality, Capacity and Disability in Commonwealth Laws in November 2014. As Sasha Callaghan and Christopher Ryan (2016, 597) observe, each of these reviews and reforms was prompted by the CRPD to make domestic legislation more compliant with human rights. Internationally there have also been a number of post-CRPD reviews and reforms. As noted above, there has been an Independent Review of mental health law in the UK.[28] Northern Ireland has adopted a 'fusion model' which will abolish stand-alone mental health law, but still permit substitute decision-making in the best interests of persons who are assessed to lack mental capacity.[29] The CRPD has led to supported decision-making legislation being enacted

[26] For example, *Royal Commission into Victoria's Mental Health System*, Interim Report, November 2019 (no. 87, 2018–2019); Productivity Commission, *Mental Health Draft Report*, October 2019.

[27] *Mental Health Act* 2013 (Tas); *Mental Health Act* 2014 (Vic); *Mental Health Act* 2014 (WA); *Mental Health Act* 2015 (ACT); *Mental Health Act* 2016 (Qld); *Mental Health Amendment (Statutory Review Act)* 2014 (NSW); *Mental Health (Review) Amendment Act* (SA).

[28] Independent Review of the MHA 1983. 2018. Modernising the Mental Health Act: Increasing Choice, Reducing Compulsion. UK Government, Final Report.

[29] *Mental Capacity Act* 2016 (Northern Ireland).

in Ireland.[30] In Canada, the CRPD has prompted provinces that did not already have supported decision-making, such as Newfoundland and Labrador and Prince Edward Island to create such systems, influenced the development of disability jurisprudence and the CRPD has been part of various reviews, reports and programmes (Hoffman et al. 2016). In New Zealand, the compatibility of the *Mental Health (Compulsory Assessment and Treatment Act) 1992* with the CRPD was reviewed as part of the Disability Action Plan 2014–2018 and the recent Government Inquiry into Mental Health and Addiction (2018) proposes reform to bring mental health law into line with the CRPD (although it appears not to go so far as abolition).

The call for the abolition of mental health law has inspired a number of alternative interpretations of the CRPD which stop short of calling for the abolition of mental health law, but which aim to reduce coercion and to support more persons with mental impairment to make their own healthcare decisions. As foreshadowed in the introduction above, I have identified two alternative types of models which allow for limited involuntary detention and psychiatric treatment (Wilson 2018). The first I call the 'Mental Capacity with Support Model' is in which persons who are medically assessed to lack mental capacity are given support to make their own decisions. The second I call the 'Support Except Where There is Harm' is in which persons with mental impairment are given support in the first instance and are only given treatment without their consent where they are at risk of harm to self or others (ibid.). What these approaches have in common is a new emphasis on recognising and respecting the subjective will and preferences of the individual, albeit to different extents. That is, since the adoption of the CRPD the development of the law has shifted away from the traditional model of care, welfare and protection as reflected in mental health law, and towards liberty, autonomy, self-determination and non-discrimination. In addition, the CRPD may be influencing the development of the 'best interests' test in general medical law which, in recent English cases, has begun to give greater weight to individual wishes and preferences, at times over a person's objective medical best interests.[31]

[30] *Assisted Decision-Making (Capacity) Act* 2015 (Ireland).

[31] For example, X NHS Trust v B [2015] EWCOP 60.

Abolitionists have made a number of criticisms of mental health law and the mental health system, some of which arise from bad experiences of persons with mental impairment in the mental health system (while others are more theoretical issues about whether mental impairment is an impairment at all and issues of liberty and bodily integrity), and from this they have concluded that mental health law should be abolished. That is, from the abolitionist perspective the only answer to these problems is to allow people to be able to refuse hospital admission, treatment and even supported decision-making. But, what happens then if people refuse all assistance? Does the state just abandon them? Abolitionists have framed the issue surrounding the abolition of mental health law as being *whether* the state should intervene against a person's will and preferences. However, an alternative way of viewing it is not *whether* the state should intervene, but to think more about, *when* and *how* the state should intervene and *what* options the state should offer. That is when examined closely many of the criticisms of the mental health system made by abolitionists are really a result of chronic underfunding, crumbling facilities, outdated and disrespectful attitudes, poor communication and a lack of treatment choices. For example, in South Africa a survey of persons with mental impairment indicated that 71% supported involuntary treatment to 'protect' them from their own behaviour at a time where they lacked control of their actions, but they wanted more consultation about involuntary hospitalisation when the police and ambulance arrived and greater involvement in treatment choices (Sunkel 2019). Rather than abolishing involuntary detention and treatment in all cases, abolitionists criticisms should instead be used to strengthen and improve that system to make it more effective by offering a wider range of high-quality services as well as alternatives to traditional psychiatry. Further, reform should go beyond the health system but also to include wider social changes to prevent persons from developing mental impairments in the first place and to support persons with mental impairments in their recovery and ability to participate in the community socially and economically. It even raises the issue of whether greater social support for persons with mental impairments together with services which are more responsive and of the type more people actually want to use might actually decrease the need for coercion and result in greater treatment satisfaction (McSherry and Wilson 2015; Wilson 2018; Craigie et al. 2019, 166; Gooding et al. 2018). An example of this approach is that the Victorian Royal Commission into mental health is working on a new mental health model which emphasises expanding community treatment to avoid involuntary hospital admissions, offering non-hospital-based residential care options, making available a range of treatments beyond medication and bolstering the lived experience workforce including peer supporters.[32] It is also important to remember that the vast majority of persons with mental impairment will never be sectioned under mental health law and receive treatment either on a voluntary basis or no treatment at all (McSherry and Wilson 2015, 66). For them, the debate about whether the CRPD requires the abolition of mental health law is of little relevance, and being able to access the right services at the right time is the key priority.

The CRPD contains a number of other provisions which can provide guidance to States Parties on reform in the mental health sector (apart from the abolition of mental health law). In fact, States Parties may have a general obligation to assist all persons (with and without mental impairment) to partake in the right to the highest standard of mental and physical health, well-being and flourishing (Molas 2016). For instance, Article 8 requires States Parties to raise social awareness of, increase support for and limit non-discrimination against persons with mental impairments. Article 10 requires suicide prevention measures including barriers on bridges, removal of ligature points, arms control and so on (Wilson 2018). Articles 25 and 26 require access to appropriate mental and physical health care, habilitation and rehabilitation, and encourages avoidance of 'diagnostic overshadowing', when physical health conditions are wrongly attributed to a person's mental health condition (Thornicroft 2011). Article 19 requires the provision of suitable housing and appropriate support for people to live in such housing independently, and Articles 24, 27, and 28 require non-discrimination and reasonable accommodation in education and work and an adequate standard of living. That is, States Parties have a general obligation to create societies where everyone's mental health is taken seriously and supported in accordance with their levels of need.

It may also be that in focussing on non-discrimination and citizenship rights, the debate about the abolition of mental health law has ignored other issues that are important to persons with mental impairments. For example, the need to reduce the side-effects of medication and improve

[32] Royal Commission into Victoria's Mental Health System, Interim Report, November 2019 (no. 87, 2018–2019).

the effectiveness and safety of psychiatric drugs (Plumb 2015, 197), workplace reform, improving linkages between health and disability services and the criminal justice system and greater investment in social housing. Greater discussion with a wider range of persons with mental impairment may highlight new ways in which the CRPD can respond to mental health, or result in the development of a new treaty which is mental health specific.

## Conclusion

The implementation of the CRPD has been mired in an ongoing conflict about whether the CRPD requires the abolition of mental health law. While it is tempting to blame States Parties for wanting to 'oppress' persons with mental impairments and for their lack of imagination, the abolition of mental health law raises a number of serious issues for persons with mental impairments. While involuntary detention and treatment can be damaging and traumatising for persons with mental impairment, serious mental impairment left untreated can also be terrible. That said, the call for the abolition of mental health law has served as an important critique of the existing mental health system and highlighted the importance of giving persons with mental impairments greater voice, choice and power in mental health care. There is no doubt that the CRPD and the debate generated by it has been and will continue to be a driver of further legal, social and systemic reform in mental health.

## References

Akther, Syeda et al. 2019. Patients' Experiences of Assessment and Detention Under Mental Health Legislation: Systematic Review and Qualitative Meta-Synthesis. *The British Journal of Psychiatry* 5(37), 1.

Amador, Xavier and Kronengold, Henry. 2004. Understanding and Assessing Insight. In *Insight and Psychosis: Awareness of Illness in Schizophrenia and Related Disorders*, eds. Xavier Amador and Anthony David. Oxford: Oxford University Press, 2nd ed.

Anderson, Fiona and Chen, Bo. 2019. Consent Is More Than Just Yes or No. In *Global Perspectives on Legal Capacity Reform: Our Voices, Our Stories*, ed. Elionoir Flynn. 174, 179. UK: Cambridge University Press.

Appelbaum, Paul. 1997. Almost a Revolution: An International Perspective on the Law of Involuntary Commitment. *Journal of the American Academy of Psychiatry and the Law* 25(2): 135.

Arstein-Kerslake, Anna and Flynn, Eilonoir. 2016. The General Comment on Article 12 of the Convention on the Rights of Persons with Disabilities: A Roadmap for Equality Before the Law. *The International Journal of Human Rights* 20(4): 471.

Australian Law Reform Commission. 2014. *Equality, Capacity and Disability in Commonwealth Laws*.

Bartlett, P. 2019. Will and Preferences in the Overall CRPD Project. *World Psychiatry* 18(1): 48.

Bilchitz, David. 2016. Dignity. Fundamental Rights and Legal Capacity: Moving Beyond the Paradigm Set by the General Comment on Article 12 of the Convention on the Rights of Persons with Disabilities. *South African Journal of Human Rights* 32(3): 410.

Broderick, Andrea. 2015. *The Long and Winding Road to Equality and Inclusion for Persons with Disabilities: The United Nations Convention on the Rights of Persons with Disabilities*. Cambridge: Intersentia.

Burch, Matthew. 2017. Autonomy, Respect, and the Rights of Persons with Disabilities in Crisis. *Journal of Applied Philosophy* 34(3): 389.

Burns, Johnathan Kenneth. 2009. Mental Health Inequity: A Human Rights Approach to Inequality, Discrimination, and Mental Disability. *Health and Human Rights* 11(2): 19.

Bury, Michael. 1986. Social Constructionism and the Development of Medical Sociology. *Sociology of Health and Illness* 8(2):137.

Callaghan, Sascha and Ryan, Christopher. 2016. An Evolving Revolution: Evaluating Australia's Compliance with the Convention on the Rights of Persons with Disabilities in Mental Health Law. *University of New South Wales Law Journal* 31(2): 596.

Callaghan, Sascha et al. 2013. Risk of Suicide Is Insufficient Warrant for Coercive Treatment of Mental Illness. *International Journal of Law and Psychiatry* 36: 374.

Carney, Terry. 2017. Supported Decision-Making in Australia: Meeting the Challenge of Moving from Capacity to Capacity-Building? *Law in Context* 35(2): 44.

Christian, Djeffal. 2015. *Static and Evolutive Treaty Interpretation*. Cambridge: Cambridge University Press.

Cohen, Oryx. 2005. How Do We Recover? An Analysis of Psychiatric Survivor Oral Histories. *Journal of Humanistic Psychology* 45(3): 333.

Committee on the Rights of Persons with Disabilities 'General Comment No. 1. (2014). Article 12: Equal Recognition before the Law' (11 April 2014) UN Doc CRPD/C/GC/1, [26].

Craigie, Jillian. 2015. A Fine Balance: Reconsidering Patient Autonomy in Light of the UN Convention on the Rights of Persons with Disabilities. *Bioethics* 29(6): 401.

Craigie, Jillian et al. 2019. Legal Capacity, Mental Capacity and Supported Decision-Making: Report from a Panel Event. *International Journal of Law and Psychiatry* 62: 160–165.

Danzer, Graha, and Wilkus-Stone. 2015. The Give and Take of Freedom: The Role of Involuntary Hospitalisation and Treatment in Recovery from Mental Illness. *Bulletin of the Meninnger Clinic* 79(3): 255.

Davidson, Gavin et al. 2016. An International Comparison of Legal Frameworks for Supported and Substitute Decision-Making in Mental Health Services. *International Journal of Law and Psychiatry* 44: 30.

Dawson, John. 2009. Concepts of Liberty in Mental Health Law. *Otago Law Review* 12(1): 23.

Deegan, Patricia. 1993. Recovering Our Sense of Value after Being Labeled Mentally Ill. *Journal of Psychosocial Nursing and Mental Health Services* 31(4): 7.

Del Villar, Katrine. 2015. Should Supported Decision-Making Replace Substituted Decision-Making? The Convention on the Rights of Persons with Disabilities and Coercive Treatment under Queensland's Mental Health Act 2000. *Laws* 4: 173.

Dhanda, Amita. 2012. Universal Legal Capacity as a Universal Human Right. In *Mental Health and Human Rights: Vision, Praxis and Courage*, eds. Michael Dudley, Derrick Silove, and Fran Gale. Oxford: Oxford University Press.

Dhanda, Amita. 2016. From Duality to Indivisibility: Mental Health Care and Human Rights. *South African Journal of Human Rights* 32: 438.

Dharmawardne, V. and Menkes, D. 2019. Responding to the UN Special Rapporteur's Anti-Psychiatry Bias. *Australian and New Zealand Journal of Psychiatry* 53(4): 282.

Donnelly, Mary. 2010. *Healthcare Decision-Making and the Law* Cambridge: Cambridge University Press.

Duffy, Richard M. and Kelly, Brendan D. 2017. Rights, Laws and Tensions: A Comparative Analysis of the Convention on the Rights of Persons with Disabilities and the WHO Resource Book on Mental Health, Human Rights and Legislation. *International Journal of Law and Psychiatry* 54: 26.

Dute, Joseph. 2015. Should Substituted Decision-Making Be Abolished? *European Journal of Health Law* 22: 315.

Flynn, Eilionoir and Arstein-Kerslake, Anna. 2017. State Intervention in the Lives of People with Disabilities: The Case for a Disability-Neutral Framework. *International Journal of Law in Context* 13(1): 39.

Freeman, Melvyn Colin et al. 2015. Reversing Hard Won Victories in the Name of Human Rights: A Critique of the General Comment on Article 12 of the UN Convention on the Rights of Persons with Disabilities. *Lancet Psychiatry* 2: 844.

Gooding, Piers. 2015. Navigating the 'Flashing Amber Lights' of the Right to Legal Capacity in the United Nations Convention on the Rights of Persons with Disabilities: Responding to Major Concerns. *Human Rights Law Review* 15: 45.

Gooding, Piers. 2017. *A New Era for Mental Health Law and Policy: Supported Decision-Making and the UN Convention on the Rights of Persons with Disabilities*. Cambridge: Cambridge University Press.

Gooding, Piers and Flynn, Eilionoir. 2015. Querying the Call to Introduce Mental Capacity Testing to Mental Health Law: Does the Doctrine of Necessity Provide an Alternative? *Laws* 4(2): 245.

Gooding, Piers et al. 2018: *Alternatives to Coercion in Mental Health Settings: A Literature Review*. Melbourne Social Equity Institute: University of Melbourne.

Government Inquiry into Mental Health and Addiction. 2018. He Ara Oranga: Report of the Government Inquiry into Mental Health and Addiction. https://mentalhealth.inquiry.govt.nz/inquiry-report/he-ara-oranga/.

Grecco, Gregory G. and Chambers, R. Andrew. 2019. The Penrose Effect and Its Acceleration by the War on Drugs: A Crisis of Untranslated Neuroscience and Untreated Addiction and Mental Illness. *Translational Psychiatry* 9: 320.

Hoffman, Steven et al. 2016. Is the UN Convention on the Rights of Persons with Disabilities Impacting Mental Health Laws and Policies in High-Income Countries? A Case Study of Implementation in Canada. *BMC International Health and Human Rights* 16(1): 28.

Jeste, Dilip V. 2018. Supported Decision Making in Serious Mental Illness. *Psychiatry: Interpersonal and Biological Processes* 81(1): 37

Kampf, Annagret. 2010. Involuntary Treatment Decisions: Using Negotiated Silence to Facilitate Change? In *Rethinking Rights-Based Mental Health Laws*, eds. Bernadette McSherry and Penelope Weller. Oxford: Hart Publishing.

Katsakou et al. 2010. Coercion and Treatment Satisfaction Among Involuntary Patients. *Psychiatric Services* 61(3): 286.

Katsakou et al. 2012. Psychiatric Patients' Views on Why Their Involuntary Hospitalisation Was Right or Wrong: A Qualitative Study. *Social Psychiatry and Psychiatric Epidemiology* 47:1169.

Kayess, Rosemary and French, Philip. 2008. Out of Darkness into Light? Introducing the Convention on the Rights of Persons with Disabilities. *Human Rights Law Review* 8(1):1.

Lewis, Oliver. 2010. The Expressive, Educational and Proactive Roles of Human Rights: An Analysis of the United Nations Convention on the Rights of Persons with Disabilities. In *Rethinking Rights-Based Mental Health Laws*, eds. Bernadette McSherry and Penelope Weller. Oxford: Hart Publishing.

Maclean, Alasdair. 2009. *Autonomy, Informed Consent and Medical Law: A Relational Challenge*. Cambridge: Cambridge University Press.

MacQuarrie, Anna and Laurin-Bowie, Connie. 2013. *Our Lives, Our Voices: People with Intellectual Disabilities and Their Families*. Philadelphia: University of Pennsylvania Press.

Mahomed, Faraaz et al. (2018). Involuntary Mental Health Treatment in the Era of the United Nations Convention on the Rights of Persons with Disabilities. *PLoS Medicine* 15(10).

McSherry, Bernadette. 2008. Protecting the Integrity of the Person: Developing Limitations on Involuntary Treatment. *Journal of Law in Context* 26(2): 111.

McSherry, Bernadette and Wilson, Kay. 2015. The Concept of Capacity in Australian Mental Health Law Reform: Going in the Wrong Direction? *International Journal of Law and Psychiatry* 40: 60.

Mezzina, R. 2018. Forty Years of the Law 180: The Aspirations of a Great Reform, Its Successes and Continuing Need. *Epidemiology and Psychiatric Sciences* 27(4): 336.

Minkowitz, Tina. 2017. CRPD and Transformative Equality. *International Journal of Law in Context* 13: 77.

Minkowitz, Tina. 2007. The United Nations Convention on the Rights of Persons with Disabilities and the Right to Be Free from Non-Consensual Psychiatric Interventions. *Syracuse Journal of International Law and Commerce* 34(2): 405.

Molas, Andrew. 2016. Defending the CRPD: Dignity, Flourishing and the Universal Right to Mental Health. *The International Journal of Human Rights* 20(8): 1264.

Morris, Jenny. 1991. *Pride Against Prejudice: Transforming Attitudes to Disability*. Philadelphia: The Women's Press.

Mullen, Paul E. 2006. Schizophrenia and Violence: From Correlations to Preventive Strategies. *Advances in Psychiatric Treatment* 12: 239.

Mulvany, Julie. 2000. Disability, Impairment or Illness? The Relevance of the Social Model of Disability to the Study of Mental Disorder. *Sociology of Health and Illness* 22(5): 582.

Oaks, David. 2012. Whose Voices Should Be Heard? The Role of Mental Health Consumers, Psychiatric Survivors, and Families. In *Mental Health and Human Rights: Vision, Praxis and Courage*, eds. Michael Dudley et al. Great Britain: Oxford University Press.

Office of Disability Issues. 2011. UK Initial Report on the UN Convention on the Rights of Persons with Disabilities.

Owen, Gareth S. et al. 2009. Retrospective Views of Psychiatric in-Patients Regaining Mental Capacity. *The British Journal of Psychiatry* 195: 403.

Penzenstadler, Louise et al. 2020. Supported Decision Making for People with Mental Health Disorders in Clinical Practice: A Systematic Review. *International Journal of Psychiatry in Clinical Practice* 24(1): 3.

Plumb, Anne. 2015. UN Convention on the Rights of Persons with Disabilities: Out of the Frying Pan into the Fire? In *Madness, Distress and the Politics of Disablement*, eds. Helen Spandler, Jill Anderson, and Bob Sapey. Bristol: Policy Press.

Priebe, Stefan et al. 2009. Patients' Views and Readmissions 1 Year After Involuntary Hospitalisation. *The British Journal of Psychiatry* 194: 49.

Richards, Kate. 2013. *Madness: A Memoir*. Australia: Penguin Group.

Roper, Cath and Gooding, Piers. 2019. This Is Not a Story: From Ethical Loneliness to Respect for Diverse Ways of Knowing, Thinking and Being. In *Global Perspectives on Legal Capacity Reform: Our Voices, Our Stories*, eds. Elionoir Flynn et al. Cambridge: Cambridge University Press.

Scholten, Matthe and Gather, Jakov. 2017. Adverse Consequences of Article 13 of the UN Convention on the Rights of Persons with Disabilities for Persons with Mental Disabilities and an Alternative Way Forward. *Journal of Medical Ethics* 1.

Sen, Amartya. 1995. *Inequality Reexamined*. Clarendan: Oxford University Press.

Shakespeare, Tom. 2013. *Disability Rights and Wrongs*. London: Routledge.

Shogren, Karrie et al. 2017. Supported Decision Making: A Synthesis of the Literature across Intellectual Disability, Mental Health, and Aging. *Education and Training in Autism and Developmental Disabilities* 52(2): 150.

Stavert, Jill. 2018. Paradigm Shift or Paradigm Paralysis? National Mental Health and Capacity Law and Implementing the CRPD in Scotland. *Laws* 7(3): 26.

Sunkel, Charlene. 2019. The UN Convention: A Service User Perspective. *World Psychiatry* 18(1): 51.

Szmukler, George. 2015. Compulsion and 'Coercion' in Mental Health Care. *World Psychiatry* 14: 259.

Thornicroft, Graham. 2011. Physical Health Disparities and Mental Illness: The Scandal of Premature Mortality. *The British Journal of Psychiatry* 199: 441.

Wellesley, Simon. 2018. Independent Review of the MHA 1983. Modernising the Mental Health Act: Increasing Choice, Reducing Compulsion. UK Government, Final Report.

Wilson, Kay. 2018. The Call for the Abolition of Mental Health Law: The Challenges of Suicide, Accidental Death and the Equal Enjoyment of the Right to Life. *Human Rights Law Review* 18: 651.

Wilson, Kay. 2020. The Abolition or Reform of Mental Health Law: How Should the Law Recognise and Respond to the Vulnerability of Persons with Mental Impairment? *Medical Law Review* 28: 30.

CHAPTER 10

# Disability and Forced Migration: Critical Connections and the Global South Debate

*Shaun Grech and Maria Pisani*

## Introduction

Conservative estimates suggest that one billion people (or 15% of the global population) are disabled people, the bulk of whom live in the poorest conditions in the Global South (WHO and World Bank 2011). This number is constantly growing on account of conflict, inaccessible health care, extreme poverty and inequality, as well as shrinking social protection in the continuing age of neoliberal cuts and weakened

S. Grech
The Critical Institute, Attard, Malta
e-mail: s.grech@criticalinstitute.org

M. Pisani (✉)
Department of Youth and Community Studies, University of Malta, Msida, Malta
e-mail: maria.pisani@um.edu.mt



F. Felder et al. (eds.), *Disability Law and Human Rights*, Palgrave Studies in Disability and International Development, https://doi.org/10.1007/978-3-030-86545-0_10

states. The numbers of refugees[1] and migrants is also constantly on the rise due to a range of reasons, including political and economic instability, environmental and climatic factors, poverty and extreme violence. Around 70 million people are forcibly displaced worldwide, and a staggering 37,000 people are forced to flee their homes on account of persecution and conflict every single day (UNHCR 2019b). Some 25.9 million of displaced people are refugees, of whom 85% are located in low- and middle-income countries (UNHCR 2019b). As people forcibly move, displacement is becoming increasingly associated with involuntary immobility and protracted contexts.

Though frequently under-represented in migration discourse, disabled people constitute a substantial number of migrants and refugees on account of the structural or other forces described above as well as impairments developed during the migratory journey. Factors that increase the likelihood of acquiring impairment during this journey include, but are not limited to exposure to rough and dangerous terrain, violent border crossings, extreme weather conditions and perilous work or persecution. Restrictive border/immigration policies and containment measures continue to translate into more perilous routes as people are forced to embark on increasingly dangerous journeys in their attempts to seek refuge, indicating that impairments may be on the rise among these populations.

Disabled migrants and refugees face particular protection risks including a heightened risk of violence, exploitation and abuse alongside barriers in accessing humanitarian assistance and other services that are not adapted, responsive and accessible to their needs. Within such contexts, disabled refugees and migrants are not only among the most disadvantaged but also face higher mortality rates, for example, in disasters (CBM et al. 2019).

Recent measures have started to place disability on the forced migration and humanitarian map, pushing forward policy initiatives and commitments to include disabled people in humanitarian policies and frameworks, largely in response to the UN Convention on the Rights of Persons with Disabilities (CRPD). Article 11 of the CRPD, in particular,

[1] For the purpose of this chapter, the term 'refugee', refers to any individual who feels compelled to leave their home in search of safety and security. Individuals in this position are increasingly forced to take illegalized and dangerous routes.

addresses situations of risk and humanitarian emergencies. Other initiatives have followed, including The Charter on Inclusion of Persons with Disabilities in Humanitarian Action (2016); the European Parliament's 2016 initiative to request the Commission and the Council to provide for special care of disabled people in proposals pertinent to the refugee issue (see EU 2016); the inclusion of disability in the recent Global Compact on Refugees and the Inter-Agency Standing Committee (IASC) Guidelines on Inclusion of Persons with Disabilities in Humanitarian Action published in late 2019. Disability, when mentioned, is often positioned alongside a long list of populations traditionally pitched as 'vulnerable'—those in a weaker position to weather the stresses and shocks of forced migration, and who as a consequence need to be included in humanitarian action. While, as we shall argue later, this approach can be rather disabling, it has helped create at the very least some legitimization of disabled bodies as potential humanitarian subjects in discourse.

Despite these shifts, disabled migrants and refugees continue to be sidelined, if not flagrantly excluded in migration research, theory, policy and humanitarian practice. On the whole, disability is neither mainstreamed nor targeted in humanitarian action (Pisani and Grech 2015; CBM et al. 2019) and is yet to garner the same attention as migrant women, children or unaccompanied minors in the forced migration narrative. At the most basic level, disaggregated data is largely absent and we do not even know how many disabled refugees and migrants there are, meaning they are significantly under-identified (UNHCR 2019a). This in turn impacts humanitarian alertness and preparedness (including training), the responsiveness, accessibility and availability of adapted and specialized services (e.g. rehabilitation, health, social protection, interpreters, etc.), and the ability to monitor the inclusion and effectiveness of programs (CBM et al. 2019; UNHCR 2019a). Even more basically, statistical gaps render this population perpetually invisible in policy and practice, unprioritized and untargeted, while contributing to the intense lack of empirical research (notably qualitative research) that feeds into this cycle of invisibility. The need to build solid evidence based on the situation and realities of these complex and heterogeneous populations in different dynamic contexts is being echoed (see CBM et al. 2019), alongside the need to understand and position these within the structural and other barriers associated with forced migration, and how these are negotiated across space and time (Pisani and Grech 2015). We still lack research on disability within the migratory journey as one of flight, movement and process, as opposed to focussing exclusively on disability as immobility within static contexts (e.g. camps), a reflection of, as we will be emphasizing later, an able-bodied view of forced migration, out of which disabled migrants are perpetually excluded, positioned, somewhat ironically, as motionless and static. We need more information on how disability intersects with involuntary immobility and with mobility (people on the move), dynamics that both form part of the fluid and fragmented journeys marked by intersecting drivers and conditions of flight that migrants and refugees embark on (Squire et al. 2017). The lack of data and information is critical because it renders the barriers faced by disabled migrants and refugees in a range of contexts (protracted and non-protracted) invisible. In turn, the lack of information can stifle advocacy efforts seeking to put disability firmly on the humanitarian map and to push for informed, accessible and responsive services. The need for information becomes even more critical as we consider the struggles of refugees and migrants (Mezzadra and Nielson 2013) who are forced to take increasingly fragmented, drawn out and dangerous journeys, and how these interact with and impact resilience and resistance. This becomes even more complex as we factor in the heterogeneity of the disabled and refugee population. Furthermore, while many NGOs and other stakeholders today have some or other policy on inclusive humanitarian practices, these policies have not to date been subject to critical analyses, in particular how these pan out in practice, and how they impact (or otherwise) the experiences and plans of disabled people and their caregivers (see CBM et al. 2019).

Disability and forced migration are too often ‘treated’ in isolation in epistemological, political and ontological terms. As Smith-Khan and Crock (2019) emphasize, disabled people continue to be the ‘forgotten and invisible refugees’ and we would extend this to also stress that refugees continue to be the forgotten and invisible disabled people. The relationship between disability and forced migration, while evident, complex and urgent, is frequently neither understood nor prioritized. Forced migration studies are still to address disability as a legitimate topic that should be prioritized, just like gender or childhood, instead of a mere sub-population alongside the list of so-called ‘vulnerable’ populations (see below) (Pisani and Grech 2015). This situation is compounded by the fact that disability studies are yet to start engaging with forced migration as a legitimate and core thematic, reinforcing its Eurocentrism (Grech 2011, 2015) and its focus on the ‘condition’ of disabled people within established and familiar contexts, such as those with presumed access to a welfare system in the UK and whose rights and existence are bound to rights and citizenship within the nation-state. Cross-disciplinary interactions between disability and forced migration studies in particular are in short supply, preventing much needed critical engagement and learning across fields and disciplines. The implication is that those working in migration remain unaware of and uneducated in disability, and those working in disability, remain uninformed and uneducated in forced migration.

Importantly, the voices of disabled migrants and refugees are rarely heard, and neither are those of their caregivers. Consequently, what we think we know is based largely on anecdotal evidence (UNHCR 2019a) and the portrayal of disabled refugees as suffering victims-the face of fundraising activities and 'humanitarian porn'—as opposed to a timely, critical and evolving evidence base. The theorizing of migration and any contemplation of policy and practice cannot do without serious consideration of these thinking, agentic bodies and lived, experienced lives. It leaves a policy vacuum, needs are unattended to and theory remains undeveloped and perhaps not only disembodied but also dehumanized.

This chapter responds to this situation and seeks to address some critical issues at the intersection between disability and forced migration. The objective is an admittedly partial exploration of only some issues, but we hope this exploration can serve as a platform for more interdisciplinary engagements and the further inclusion of and legitimization of disability within forced migration and humanitarian discourse and practice and vice-versa.

## Why Should Disabled Refugees and Migrants Matter?

Any serious engagement with, or any claim as to why disabled refugees and migrants deserve epistemological, research, political and practical attention, notably in rights discourse (and indeed a text like this), and why the intersection between disability and forced migration must be understood and prioritized, requires us to first start off with some or other basic understanding of the situations confronted by disabled refugees and migrants. To be clear, these situations are largely heterogeneous, complex and dynamic and can hardly be captured in this chapter.

### *The Numbers Are Far from Small*

The first reason concerns numbers. As highlighted earlier, we do not know how many disabled refugees and migrants there are. However, we can safely speculate that these numbers must be quite dramatic, even if we had to look at some contexts specifically. It is estimated that some ten million of those who are forcibly displaced are disabled people, while in Syria alone, approximately 1.5 million people are now living with permanent impairments as a result of the conflict (UNICEF 2018). In situations where people are forcibly displaced, the incidence of disability is even higher when refugees and migrants do not receive quality, specialized and sustained medical services, hence resulting in secondary impairments alongside trauma (IOM 2016) or a worsening of existing impairments and health conditions. Take for example someone with an untreated gunshot wound, or a person with a disability with no access to regular prescribed medication. Indeed, if we had to take recent happenings, including wars and conflict, whether in Syria or Yemen or the odyssey of the Myanmar Rohingya, the dramatic numbers of people fleeing whether from poverty or persecution, continues to rise. What we are left with are not only multiple sources of impairment in perilous routes but also a range and combination of physical, social, economic and cultural conditions that perpetually force disabled people to move and ensure that they are a substantial number among the migrant population. While some become disabled *en route*, others flee as disabled people. What ties these subjects and instances together is not the often-misplaced obsession with the voluntary-forced dichotomy in migration discourse and policy (see Bivand Erdal and Oeppen 2017). Instead, it is the often-overlooked fact that disabled people are actually in there—*they migrate too*—and are present along this diverse spectrum of migration and respective trajectories. Their presence is in fact greater than most of us think, not least because many disabilities may not be immediately evident, e.g. a deaf refugee or one with low vision, or someone with an intellectual disability. The issue of mental health merits attention. Indeed, this journey is not only physically arduous but also has psychological dimensions, and indeed post-traumatic stress disorder and a host of mental health problems are regularly documented (see Ingleby 2005; Morina et al. 2018). The issue of mental health is interesting, though, since it is rarely defined as or associated with disability, perpetuating the disassociation. The result is also a temporal or rather time-bound approach towards these mental health issues and their understandings, reflected in short-term measures adopted (e.g. brief medicalization) and also a lack of longitudinal research (Bogic et al. 2015) and long-term therapy (Zipfel et al. 2019). Like most situations in refugee lives, they are expected to 'heal' and move on with little or no pressure on the systems supporting them.

### *Exposed: Those Left Behind in Crises*

The second reason as to why attention to disability in forced migration is important is paradoxically because a portion of the disabled population may not readily flee during crises such as environmental disasters and may be the ones left behind. Disabled people are also among those who are most exposed to conflict and emergency situations and marginalized in crisis-impacted communities (IASC 2019). Overall, it is estimated that in situations of disasters, disabled people face a mortality rate of two to four times higher than that of people with no disabilities (IASC 2019). Those with very serious or particular mobility impairments may encounter greater barriers when it comes to fleeing, mobilizing to another area as well as returning and reconstructing their lives. All these become even tougher when critical support from family and friends is scarce or absent, or if this support is fragmented, for example, if family members have been separated, as is often the case within forced migration contexts. Their livelihoods may also be impacted, especially if these depended on the person who left (the main economic provider), alongside the ability to reach health and education facilities if physical support is no longer there (see Passey 2018 for more on this). This means that forced migration affects those left behind, who cannot continue the journey onwards, or who end up entrapped in protracted contexts,[2] also because of inadequate support, for example, someone to push a wheelchair or carry the person on one's back.

[2] UNHCR (2004: 1) defines a protracted refugee situation as 'one in which refugees find themselves in a long-lasting and intractable state of limbo. Their lives may not be at risk, but their basic rights and essential economic, social and psychological needs remain unfulfilled after years in exile. A refugee in this situation is often unable to break free from enforced reliance on external assistance'.

### *Impacts on Caregivers*

In relation to the above, another factor that pushes and justifies attention to disability and forced migration is the fact that disability also impacts those who act as caregivers during the journey and/or in the host country. These may be friends made along the way, or as is often the case, a family member (Handicap International 2015). This care comes at a cost, especially where formal support is absent or fragmented as in humanitarian contexts. The lack or absence of social protection in these contexts is so dramatic that some such as Grech (2019) push for an emphasis on the 'disabled family' in research and practice, not least because the barriers imposed on caregivers ultimately also impact disabled people. These caregivers and their experiences influence how disability is lived and negotiated within the migratory journey, as well as the resources (physical, social, economic, emotional, etc.) available to the disabled migrant or refugee. While literature within fields such as forced migration studies has devoted some attention to care, in particular the gendered impacts of care, these have largely been limited to analysis of the parent/child relationship (Mingot 2019). This is a critical void, given that relationships of support transcend the immediate family and the need for care and support extends into adulthood. This caregiving, importantly, comes at a cost for those providing it in terms of limiting time and opportunity to labour, earn money, search for food or move onwards. It may reduce the time available to search for food, and importantly may also impact the health care of caregivers. This care is also a source of major psychological and physical distress for family members perpetually seeking rehabilitation, access to medication and ensuring the disabled person survives (Handicap International 2015). To restate, the impacts of forced migration merge with care and impact all those caught within the net of care provision, including increasing the likelihood of mental health issues and other health problems (see Bryant et al. 2018).

### *Multiple, Complex and Connected Barriers Meet Unprepared Systems*

Disabled migrants and refugees warrant particular attention because ultimately, they face extraordinary barriers that traverse the social, physical, economic, political and ideological spheres (among others). These barriers include difficulties accessing medication, specialized health care, assistive devices, the loss or fragmentation of family and support networks, problems in finding and performing arduous work and diminishing economic resources, and these barriers become even more potent as they combine. As the literature suggests, barriers are multiple for migrants and refugees overall (see for example Smith-Khan and Crock 2019), but they are further intensified for disabled people because these barriers become tougher to negotiate. They also confront particular protection concerns, including a heightened risk of violence, exploitation and abuse. Within such contexts, disabled refugees and migrants are not only among the most disadvantaged but also face higher mortality rates, especially in disasters and emergencies (CBM et al. 2019; Crock et al. 2013).

Cursory research highlights how disabled refugees and migrants face extraordinary barriers along the migratory journey at least in part because humanitarian responses are not always informed about, trained in, or otherwise equipped to address their needs (IASC 2019). As Holden et al. (2019: 3) stress, learning is still scarce and 'the evidence base on what works to include and deliver outcomes for people with disabilities in humanitarian response—both in terms of specialized services as well as mainstream programming—is extremely limited'. Despite claims to be working towards inclusive humanitarian responses by many, the truth, as the Handicap International (2015) consultation reports, is that disabled people are those consistently 'falling through the cracks' when it comes to humanitarian responses, including programming.

A growing body of literature highlights the scale of these complexly intertwined barriers in practically all spheres—a combination of personal, environmental, structural and importantly institutional obstacles:

> Inaccessible housing (e.g. shelters or tents with steps and narrow entrances and that are overcrowded) and sanitation (e.g. latrines that are not wheelchair accessible)
>
> Water and food that are scarce and/or provided through inaccessible distribution points and with long waiting times leading to unnecessary physical and psychological stress
>
> Heavy food parcels that cannot be easily carried
>
> Lack of adequate food for specific conditions (e.g. diabetes)

Inaccessible and/or unaffordable transportation and long distances to reach some or other distribution or support points or services

Barriers to education, especially one that is culturally relevant, sensitive and equipped (e.g. books in Braille and trained teachers)

Limited or no access to livelihoods, because these often depend on arduous labour and long distances of travel

Unavailability of timely and accessible information e.g. legal rights and information on legal status in Braille, medical services, or support available to access services. Obtaining information is not only time consuming. It is also costly.

Lack of critical support and assistance e.g. culturally sensitive sign language interpreters

Problems in obtaining assistive devices e.g. prostheses, wheelchairs, hearing aids, etc.

Lack of timely and responsive means of medical referral (also related to the lack of basic data on disability collected in humanitarian contexts)

Fragmented access to adequate and personalized health care, particularly specialist health care

Inconsistent or no supply of medication for people with chronic conditions

Dramatic problems in accessing specialized services such as rehabilitation

Limited physical security e.g. in camps or detention, exposing disabled people to multiple situations of risk and even abuse

Confinement and limited freedom of movement

Little or no knowledge on disability by field staff and service providers e.g. camp managers and/or NGOs, including on how to include or target disabled people and also lack of policies on how to do this, compounded by limited or no indicators and monitoring systems

Negative attitudes and discrimination, including by staff and also other refugees

Racism by national service providers

Limited to no access to local Disabled People's Organisations (DPOs), advocacy and other services

Related to the above, national DPOs and others may not be knowledgeable of, close to, or responsive to the situation of disabled migrants and refugees in their own countries. (HI 2015; Holden et al. 2019; Pisani and Grech 2015)

These problems are accentuated for some more than others, and the situation becomes ever so complex when dimensions such as gender, sexual orientation, race and ethnicity, religion, age, geographical location and environmental volatility, legal status and type of impairment among others intersect and are factored in (UNICEF 2017; Pisani and Grech 2015). Research suggests that disabled women are at greatest risk of violence, including sexual violence, rape and exploitation (IASC 2019), and children are at higher risk of abuse and neglect (UNICEF 2017); risks greatly accentuated within the volatile contexts of humanitarian crises. Others face a myriad of complex barriers that may not only lead to discrimination and exclusion but also violence and death, including for example disabled people from religious, ethnic or linguistic minorities, older disabled people, disabled gay, bisexual, transgender or intersex people, for whom protection remains a major concern (UNHCR 2019a). Importantly, they remind us of the huge complexity of the migrant, refugee and disabled populations that calls not only for nuanced and timely information but also for measures that indeed protect and safeguard life and dignity of all in ways that are responsive to the needs of each person.

Overall, these barriers are powerful and become toxic, especially when refugee contexts become increasingly protracted. Disabled people are among those more likely to remain in protracted refugee contexts, and in the absence of possibilities for return, the outcome of such a scenario is that camps become, as Kett and Trani (2010: 15) describe, 'de facto welfare camps'.

In sum, the absence of disaggregated data on the number of disabled people, a lack of consistency in the identification of disabled people, unclear or absent policies on inclusion, lack of preparedness, including training of personnel and services, shortages in funding and lack of evaluation tools and processes among others, not only contribute to the marginalization of disability as a subject of study but also practice in migration and humanitarian affairs. It is paradoxical that while disability theorists in the global North have written so much (and rightly so) about interventions on disabled people through medicalization and diagnosis, disabled refugees and migrants, like many in the Global South, are disabled by a dramatic lack of access to these (Grech 2015).

## Constructions of Disability in the Forced Migration Narrative

Understanding and framing the situation confronting disabled refugees and migrants with precision is difficult if not impossible. However, what ties together some of the points above is that these lives are particularly tough because the barriers and exclusions (including epistemological ones) are bound to how they are constructed within broader discourses on forced migration. Two notable dynamics emerge and which we feel are particularly important: (1) the ableist tones in migration discourse and (2) the positioning of disability within the vulnerable category. As we will be highlighting, while the first marginalizes disability from the migration narrative, the second momentarily draws attention to it, but either on the basis of its perceived lack and/or absence, while drowning agency, also to generate funds within an increasingly competitive and shrinking flow of financial aid. In between, is a spectrum of complex and heterogeneous humanity unfortunately subsumed under or rendered invisible by simplifying and/or homogenizing discourse.

### *Disability Fades: The Ableist View of the Migration Narrative*

Trying to frame and understand the marginality of disability within forced migration requires us to take a step back and understand how forced migration is constructed in discourse, in particular to see who is actually framed as a migrant. From boats abandoned in the Mediterranean to people trying to jump over fences in the US or Europe in search of safety, the images transmitted (e.g. in news media) highlight not only the hardships of the migratory journey that demand extraordinary strength and perseverance but also that this strength and ability to weather such journeys is predicated on strong, normative, able bodies (see also El-Lahib 2015). It is in fact rare to see images of disabled people in the context of forced migration, and when they are seen, they are pitched as vulnerable or used once again as a juxtaposition with an ableist narrative demanding able-bodiedness. This is a journey, as it seems, weathered only by healthy able bodies. Only it isn't. Certainly, the images that make the headlines and that are used to fuel and justify increasingly securitized, militarized and restrictive migration discourse and policies are of a highly agentic, masculinized, racialized and able-bodied young male. This in turn has framed notions of 'deservingness', the quality of reception systems and the provision of support and care (Holmes and Castañeda 2016). Paradoxically, any disabled individual who is able to negotiate and navigate the obstacles and cross the border is positioned as a 'bad migrant', rather than the 'deserving refugee' who remains immobilized, contained and warehoused elsewhere. That said, disabled people often do manage to cross these borders—testimony to the extraordinary determination and agency of human life. Overall, disabled people are rarely framed as migrants or refugee bodies on the move, but instead as static and helpless, perpetually rendered invisible in an ableist view of forced migration massaged by historical and neocolonial representations of vulnerability in the Global South. Ableism is defined here as '... a network of beliefs, processes and practices that produces a particular kind of self and body (the corporeal standard) that is projected as the perfect, species-typical and therefore essential and fully human. Disability then, is cast as a diminished state of being human' (Campbell 2001: 44). In turn, it often reinforces an ableist discourse and response (Hughes 2016) designed for able bodies, including in humanitarian action. The ableist approach and focus on heteronormative productive bodies often means that disabled people continue to slip out of focus. Neoliberalism has much to do with what is framed as the perfect able body, the productive machine and has contributed much to how disabled bodies are framed and often excluded from this narrative—corrected to function and produce, or removed (Grech 2011).

Within an ableist view of forced migration, disabled people if not ignored or rendered invisible, are instead pitched as problematic, either as undeserving or a burden, inadmissible by virtue of the demands and costs imposed by their bodies—bodies devalued in the broader metanarrative of 'compulsory able-bodiedness' (McRuer 2006: 89). Siebers (2008: 8) similarly highlights what he calls an 'ideology of ability' that frames disability as a burden or an object of fear, simultaneously banishing it and turning it into a 'principle of exclusion' (10). Indeed, the admissible refugee, if at all, is limited to one that is willing to work endlessly, be exploited at all times and critically work in areas that require inordinate amounts of (almost inhuman) physical strength. Importantly, though, this body must not demand anything in the way of social protection and must not burden local systems, in particular health care and social protection. These are spaces reserved for citizens, who can actually claim their rights (see below). Soldatic et al. (2015) for example provide a lucid account of how Australia has historically barred entry to disabled immigrants backed by concrete measures taken to prevent their entry, backed by a view of these bodies as a costly and unnecessary burden.

### *Vulnerability and Vanishing Agency*

A second dynamic worth mentioning is that related to vulnerability. Indeed, there are clear patterns, and disability, if not excluded altogether in policy documents on migration or humanitarian issues, is more often than not simply mentioned alongside the list of populations traditionally considered 'vulnerable' (children, women, older adults, etc.). This excerpt from the Global Humanitarian Overview 2019 (OCHA 2019: 59) is illustrative:

> The needs and mental well-being of the most vulnerable — particularly the elderly, persons with disabilities, at-risk women and children and survivors of violence — require a scaled-up and more focussed response.

Disability may not easily stand alone as an area of interest within forced migration, or simply as human beings that migrate, just like others. Instead, disabled people, are often those pitched as victims, weak and dependent, alongside some others, where their own bodies are the problem, and with the implication that these need to be intervened in with an assistance specific to them and their needs for protection on account of their very own vulnerability (Sözer 2019). It is this need for intervention that somehow makes these lives momentarily visible, but only partially, and only by virtue of their lack and absences (whether of functioning or weakness in independence). For example, Mirza (2011) stresses how when toolkits on disability exist in forced migration, they frequently only emphasize screening, prevention and treatment, internalizing disability as a personal ‘problem’ that needs to be fixed or removed—‘aberrations in need of therapeutic intervention’ by others to ‘return them to the natural order of things, either back into the fold of the nation-state or back into the state of normalcy’ (217). The label of ‘vulnerable’ also acts to define who is deserving and who is not, even pitching people against others for any support available in what can perhaps best be understood as a hierarchy of legitimacy through misery. In some instances, it can also become a criterion as to who deserves protection, and who can and should be granted refugee status. This means that the tag vulnerable may occupy a conflicting space of disempowerment and stripping of strength and agency juxtaposed with a possible bargaining position, for example, in the hands of lawyers supporting cases for asylum.

Critically, an approach emphasizing vulnerability leaves the broader system, structures and barriers, which produce so-called ‘vulnerability’ unprobed, while generalizing the needs and demands of disabled refugees and migrants. Yeo (2019: 1) argues how ‘labels of ‘vulnerability’ obscure systemic oppression and distract from the rights and achievements of disabled people’. Critically, as Mainwaring (2016: 289) argues in the context of forced migration, it ‘obscures the agency demonstrated by migrants and refugees and evidenced in their own accounts of their journeys’. The voices of disabled refugees and migrants as agentic bodies therefore continue to be stifled, drowned in a generalizing ‘vulnerable’ narrative of helplessness and hopelessness. We urgently need to understand barriers, lives and experiences through an optic of agency and subjectivity to highlight how disabled migrants and refugees navigate, resist and negotiate these barriers and ultimately survive, because this capacity for survival is what needs to be strengthened. This is not to suggest that there aren’t specific problems confronted by these populations. Indeed, there are many. Instead, what we are suggesting is the need to understand collective experiences and hurdles faced by migrants and refugees in confronting a collective state of human vulnerability (see Mirza 2011). In this regard, we might benefit from an approach that challenges the epistemological isolation of the vulnerability of disabled people as something that needs to be theorized and understood separately from that experienced by others, to move instead towards a reconceptualization of vulnerability as something that is shared simply by virtue of being human, 'our common vulnerability' (Turner 2006: 9). If anything, this will help prioritize agency and the threats to this (and consequently enhanced vulnerability), not by virtue of being disabled or a migrant, but from broader political, historical, economic and other forces that marginalize, oppress and disable. Understanding the situations and barriers confronted by disabled refugees and migrants, while a priority, can only be framed and understood within such discursive and material spaces without ignoring or diminishing their agency.

Disability can hardly be encapsulated in all embracing discourse, but can instead only be remotely understood over time, in its full complexity. This understanding, too, is also constantly renegotiated. While disability may intensify vulnerability to suffering, poverty and other barriers experienced by migrants and refugees, it does not necessarily make them more weak or vulnerable. It also does not mean that this suffering is incremental and dependent on the level of vulnerability. If anything, this scale of vulnerability so to speak will only serve to differentiate further the mass of displaced bodies and pitch those as 'deserving' of help and support (traditionally those constructed as having less agency) against those who are not (strong bodies that demonstrate agency). Consequently, it conditions or may bypass an understanding of actual lived experiences of those on the move, irrespective of who they are and how they are framed, and can also mean that those who are not framed as 'vulnerable' are flagrantly excluded with possibly fatal consequences (Fiddian-Qasimiyeh 2017). We urgently need a critical and also dynamic approach towards vulnerability, repositioning it as a human and shared 'condition', while prioritizing the critical role and strengths of disabled migrants and refugees not merely in surviving but also in resisting and reframing discourse, policy and practice.

## 'Intervening' in Disability: The Weakness of Rights

Speaking about disability and forced migration necessarily demands a conversation about rights and how the discursive and policy context constructs those who fall outside the space of the nation-state, ergo beyond the protection of citizenship and the assumed 'right to rights' (Arendt 1951). Indeed, the legacy of human rights and liberal democratic norms that are celebrated in the global North as a defining character of the 'civilized', are flagrantly abused and ignored in what is an increasingly militarized space, marked by policy measures and discursive practices which contribute to the securitization of the richer countries of the

North that seek to keep the 'immigrant threat' at bay. In 2019 alone almost 1300 migrants and refugees lost their lives in the Mediterranean Sea in their attempts to reach Europe. While the number of crossings continues to decrease due to ongoing collaboration with Libyan border guards in what is widely seen as a violation of basic human rights, the percentage of persons losing their lives has increased as journeys become increasingly dangerous as a direct result of political interventions by the European Union and its Member States (UN Support Mission in Libya and OHCHR 2018). Indeed, the 1951 Geneva Convention, by far the most broadly ratified refugee treaty, is increasingly disregarded with brazen disdain by some of the most wealthy and powerful states. As we write in the midst of the Coronavirus pandemic, we also witness the closing of borders even further, whereby national interests and safety are used as a justification for rights violations and as an excuse to keep these unwanted people out. And once again, so-called 'national interest' takes precedence over human life. Indeed, what we see in such political discourse emphasizing national security concerns, is the perpetual construction and intensification of the forced migrant as 'illegal' (see Pisani 2011), while asylum seekers in and from the Global South are denied the possibility—and right—to access the asylum system and protection. The consequence is that forced migrants must remain in the Global South, often in protracted refugee situations.

Within such discourse, disabled refugees and migrants are particularly disadvantaged. Indeed, even with the CRPD, including its Article 11 in force in the global North, it is not hard to see how the rights of disabled refugees and migrants are regularly violated, and obligations by these States systematically ignored when it comes to the alien other. Over the past years, we have been and continue to be witness to perverse spectacles of militarized border controls and hard-line, punitive and illegal detention for those exercising their right to request asylum or just trying to better their lot. The increasingly rare possibilities for resettlement are further limited for disabled bodies, constructed as a liability, a burden, or even a national security threat (see Pisani and Grech 2015).

There are other critical barriers experienced, and disability does indeed impact a person's chances of qualifying for protection, including difficulties in understanding the asylum process, communicating and presenting a coherent and consistent testimony (Crock et al. 2013). The question that arises is in the absence of refugee protection, how will their rights be protected? The issue, and this has been taken up by others working on disability (see Soldatic and Grech 2014), is how rights travel across borders, if simply being a human is enough to claim one's rights elsewhere, or if being disabled allows one to claim disability rights. The problems with rights and their implementation are many in practice and include: knowledge of these in the first place as well as local policies and laws; support from organizations, especially pro bono legal services; financial aid to cover costs, including transportation to seek legal services; time constraints including the immediate necessity to work; racism among authorities and government services among many others (see also Grech 2015). In practice, and the truth is that disabled refugees and migrants, like many other marginalized Global South subjects have few or no means to seek redress and many slip outside protection, even when they have rights on paper.

The main point, though, that we would like to make is that the right to rights, ultimately is bound to what Pisani (2012) has called the 'citizenship assumption' to highlight how rights, and if and how people are able to claim them (or not), are in fact premised on an assumption of citizenship. This is an area that needs much critical probing, not least because it distils dramatically the power of international instruments such as the CRPD for subjects travelling across borders. Do they remain human when they cross borders? Do their rights as human beings and as disabled people, vanish? Policies on paper are in practice just a start, and not an end in themselves. Protection measures need to be in place to ensure that they remain valid for subjects crossing borders.

## Conclusion

This chapter has looked at some of the intersections between disability and forced migration in an admittedly very partial way. We need urgent research into the lives, situations, conditions and experiences of disabled migrants and refugees across a range of geopolitical contexts. We need in particular a robust evidence base as grounds for assessing the impact of interventions on those affected most directly. Without such analysis, discriminatory exclusions and disabling practices will remain an ongoing feature of migration and refugee policy and practice, and humanitarian measures will have little effect in promoting change and addressing protection needs in a nuanced and informed way. Given that migratory and regulatory frameworks are constantly changing (e.g. in the US and the EU), and borders are perpetually enacted and revised (discursively and materially), this analysis needs to be constant and changing.

Disability needs to be situated and positioned within the forced migration narrative and conversely migration within disability discourse, highlighting stories, barriers, agency and resistance in the process. Descriptive empirical studies on their own will not advance our understanding of disability and forced migration, and more importantly will not develop theory. We require instead genuine interdisciplinary and critical efforts and all the theoretical connections we can make. If the disability is to garner the same attention as women and children in migration discourse and practice, it requires data, nuanced research and importantly for disability to become a political and practice priority. This requires lobbying and advocacy, and DPOs must define and own this process.

We need research and interventions that can transcend the disabled individual, to understand care within forced migration as a dynamic and emerging force, and to reframe disability and implications for policy and practice through a collective narrative (see Grech 2019). We therefore also need to actively seek to transnationalize existing theory on care, including within disability and migration studies.

Finally, we need to move beyond idealistic views of rights and to understand and question their limitations in practice, including their boundedness to citizenship. Only then can we work towards ensuring that these rights are responsive, adapted and protective of everyone, irrespective of where they are.

## References

Arendt, H. (1951) *The Origins of Totalitarianism*. New York: Harcourt, Brace & Co.

Bivand Erdel, M. and Oeppen, C. (2017) Forced to Leave? The Discursive and Analytical Significance of Describing Migration as Forced and Voluntary. *Journal of Ethnic and Migration Studies*, 44(6), 981–998.

Bogic, M., Njoku, A. and Priebe, S. (2015, October 28) Long-Term Mental Health of War-Refugees: A Systematic Literature Review. *BMC International Health and Human Rights*, 15, 29. doi: https://doi.org/10.1186/s12914-015-0064-9.

Bryant, R. A., Edwards, B. et al. 2018. The Effect of Post-Traumatic Stress Disorder on Refugees' Parenting and Their Children's Mental Health: A Cohort Study. *Lancet Public Health*, 3(5), 249–258.

CBM, HI and IDA. 2019. *Inclusion of Persons with Disabilities in Humanitarian Action*. Germany: CBM.
Campbell, F. K. 2001. Inciting Legal Fictions: Disability's Date with Ontology and the Ableist Body of the Law. *Griffith Law Review*, 10(2001), 42–62.
Crock, M., Ernst, C. and McCallum, R. 2013. Where Disability and Displacement Intersect: Asylum Seekers and Refugees with Disabilities. *International Journal of Refugee Law*, 24(4), 735–764.
El-Lahib, Y. 2015. The Inadmissible "Other": Discourses of Ableism and Colonialism in Canadian Immigration. *Journal of Progressive Human Services*, 26(3), 209–228.
European Union. 2016. Proposal for a Regulation of the European Parliament and the Council: Establishing a Common Procedure for International Protection in the Union and Repealing Directive 2013/32/EU. Brussels: EU.
Fiddian-Qasmiyeh, E. 2017. Disrupting Humanitarian Narratives? Representations of Displacement Series. Available online: https://refugeehosts.org/representations-of-displacement-series/.
Grech, S. 2015. *Disability and Poverty in the Global South: Renegotiating Development in Guatemala*. London: Palgrave.
Grech, S. 2011. Recolonising Debates or Perpetuated Coloniality? Decentring the Spaces of Disability, Development and Community in the Global South. *International Journal of Inclusive Education*, 15(1), 87–100.
Grech, S. 2019. Disabled families: The impacts of disability and care on family labour and poverty in rural Guatemala. *Societies*, 9, 76. https://doi.org/10.3390/soc9040076.
Handicap International. 2015. *Disability in Humanitarian Contexts Views from Affected People and Field Organisations*. Paris: Handicap International.
HI. 2015. *Disability in Humanitarian Context: Views from Affected People and Field Organisations*. Paris: HI.
Holden, J., Lee, H. et al. 2019. *Disability Inclusive Approaches to Humanitarian Programming: Summary of Available Evidence on Barriers and What Works*. London: DFID.
Holmes, S. M. and Castañeda, H. 2016. Representing the "European Refugee Crisis" in Germany and Beyond: Deservingness and Difference, Life and Death. *American Ethnologist*, 43(1), 12–24.
Hughes, B. 2016. Impairment on the Move: The Disabled Incomer and Other Invalidating Intersections. *Disability & Society*, 32(4), 467–482.
IASC. 2019. *Guidelines: Inclusion of Persons with Disabilities in Humanitarian Action*. New York: IASC.
Ingleby, D. (Ed.). 2005. *Forced Migration and Mental Health: Rethinking the Care of Refugees and Displaced Persons*. US: Springer.
IOM. 2016. *Disability and Unsafe Migration: Data and Policy, Understanding the Evidence*. Global Migration Data Analysis Centre: Data Briefing

Series. https://publications.iom.int/system/files/pdf/gmdac_data_briefing_series_issue_7.pdf.

Kett, M. and Trani, J. 2010. Vulnerability and Disability in Darfur. *Forced Migration Review*, 35, 12–13.

Mainwaring, C. 2016. Migrant Agency: Negotiating Borders and Migration Controls. *Migration Studies*, 4(3), 289–308.

McRuer, R. 2006. Compulsory Able-Bodiedness and Queer/Disabled existence. In L. J. Davis (ed.), *The Disability Studies Reader* (pp. 161–172). New York: Routledge.

Mezzadra, S. and Neilson, B. 2013. *Border as Method, or, the Multiplication of Labor*. Durham: Duke University Press.

Mingot, E. S. 2019. The Gendered Burden of Transnational Care-Receiving: Sudanese Families Across The Netherlands, the UK and Sudan. *Gender, Place & Culture*, 27(4), 546–567.

Mirza, M. 2011. Disability and Humanitarianism in Refugee Camps: The Case for a Travelling Supranational Disability Praxis. *Third World Quarterly*, 32(8), 1527–1536.

Morina, N. et al. 2018. Psychiatric Disorders in Refugees and Internally Displaced Persons After Forced Displacement: A Systematic Review. *Front Psychiatry*, 9, 433. doi: https://doi.org/10.3389/fpsyt.2018.00433.

OCHA. 2019. *Global Humanitarian Overview 2019*. OCHA.

Passey, M. 2018. How Migration to Europe Affects Those Left Behind. *Forced Migration Review*, FMR57, 35–37.

Pisani, M. 2011. There's an Elephant in the Room and she's "Rejected" and Black. *Open Citizenship*, 2, 24–51.

Pisani, M. 2012. Addressing the 'Citizenship Assumption' in Critical Pedagogy: Exploring the Case of Rejected Female Sub-Saharan African Asylum Seekers in Malta. *Power and Education*, 4(2), 185–195.

Pisani, M. and Grech. S. 2015. Disability and Forced Migration: Critical Intersectionalities. *Disability and the Global South*, 2(1), 421–441.

Siebers, T. 2008. *Disability Theory.* Michigan: University of Michigan Press

Smith-Khan, L. and Crock, M. 2019. 'The Highest Attainable Standard': The Right to Health for Refugees with Disabilities. *Societies*, 9(2).

Soldatic, K. and Grech, S. 2014. Transnationalising Disability Studies: Rights, Justice and Impairment. *Disability Studies Quarterly*, 34(2).

Soldatic, K., Somers, K. et al. 2015. 'Nowhere to Be Found': Disabled Refugees and Asylum Seekers Within the Australian Resettlement Landscape. *Disability and the Global South*, 2(1), 501–522.

Sözer, H. 2019. Categories That Blind Us, Categories That Bind Them: The Deployment of Vulnerability Notion for Syrian Refugees in Turkey. *Journal of Refugee Studies,* 34(3), 2775–2803. doi: https://doi.org/10.1093/jrs/fez020.

Squire, V, Dimitriadi, A. and Perkowski, N. 2017. *Crossing the Mediterranean Sea by Boat: Mapping and Documenting Migratory Journeys and Experiences*. Final Project Report, 4 May. Available at: https://www.warwick.ac.uk/crossingthemed.

Turner, B. S. 2006. *Vulnerability and Human Rights*. University Park, PA: Pennsylvania State University Press.

United Nations. 2018. *Support Mission in Libya & OHCHR. Desperate and Dangerous: Report on the Human Rights Situation of Migrants and Refugees in Libya*. Geneva: United Nations.

UNHCR. 2019a. *Working with Persons with Disabilities in Forced Displacement 2019*. Rome: UNHCR.

UNHCR. 2019b. Figures at a Glance. https://www.unhcr.org/figures-at-a-glance.html.

UNICEF. 2017. *Including Children with Disabilities in Humanitarian Action*. Paris: UNICEF

UNICEF. 2018. No End in Sight to Seven Years of War in Syria: Children with Disabilities at Risk of Exclusion. https://www.unicef.org/eca/press-releases/no-end-sight-seven-years-war-syria-children-disabilities-risk-exclusion.

WHO and World Bank. 2011. *World Report on Disability*. Washington: World Bank.

Yeo, R. 2019. The Regressive Power of Labels of Vulnerability Affecting Disabled Asylum Seekers in the UK. *Disability & Society*. doi: https://doi.org/10.1080/09687599.2019.1639688.

Zipfel, S., Pfaltz, M. C. and Schnyder, U. (Eds.). 2019. *Refugee Mental Health*. Lausanne: Frontiers Media. doi: https://doi.org/10.3389/978-2-88945-840-0.

CHAPTER 11

# Intersections in Human Rights and Public Policy for Indigenous People with Disability

*Scott Avery*

## The Colonial Origins of the Social Inequality of Australia's Indigenous People with Disability

Securing the rights of Indigenous people with disability is a critical social issue confronting Australian social policy. As a marginalized group intersecting larger marginalized groups in society, Indigenous people with disability face social inequalities and multi-faceted forms of discrimination that interact and compound the gravity of their social isolation, even within the Indigenous and disability populations that they are constituent to.

The plight of Australian Indigenous people with disability is peculiar amongst Indigenous peoples worldwide. Australian Indigenous people with disability live in a post-colonized nation and are subjected to the enduring effects of colonization (Moreton-Robinson 2003), including

S. Avery (✉)
Western Sydney University, Sydney, NSW, Australia
e-mail: S.Avery@westernsydney.edu.au



F. Felder et al. (eds.), *Disability Law and Human Rights*, Palgrave Studies in Disability and International Development,
https://doi.org/10.1007/978-3-030-86545-0_11

racism that is both structural and personal (Larson et al. 2007), and is on top of disability-based discrimination that they are also subjected to. Experiencing social, health and economic outcomes at a substantially inferior rate compared to other groups in Australian society (Avery 2018), the burden of social inequity that Indigenous people with disability must bear is extravagantly high compared to other groups in Australia. However, the ability of Indigenous people with disability to secure their rights by leveraging social and political processes within Australia is inhibited by being a numerically acute minority group. Further, whilst the social, health and economic outcomes of Australian Indigenous people with disability appear comparable to those of other peoples with disability from the 'Global South', their plight for social justice on the global stage is obscured by living in a nation that is otherwise characterized as from the 'Global North'.

Understanding the impact of colonization upon Australian Indigenous people first requires an appreciation of how Indigenous social structure embodies a cultural belief system that is inclusive of people with disability. Remnants of this inclusive cultural value system that predate colonization are found in the tracks of a one-legged man on a hunt with his tribe, embedded in the clay at the Lake Mungo heritage site in New South Wales and dating back 20,000 years. The narrative of a one-legged man actively participating on a hunt is emblematic of an Indigenous belief system and worldview of humanity in which people with disability are accepted as part of the normal and unremarkable make-up of their social structure. The culture of inclusion of Indigenous people is still innately practiced by Indigenous peoples today (ibid.). A number of studies have observed that there is no word for 'disability' in Indigenous languages (Ariotti 1999), indicating an 'invisibility of the disability experience' in which their identity as an Indigenous person overshadows how a person's disability may be viewed (King et al. 2014). Expressions of a culture that is inclusive of people with disability is not unique to Australian Indigenous peoples, but have also been observed in the cultural practices of other Indigenous peoples, including amongst Maori people (Te Pou o te Whakaaro Nui 2016) and in some native American Indian cultures (Kapp 2013).

The shock waves of colonization that have reverberated through Indigenous societies are vast and enduring. The assertion of colonization of the Australian continent through violence against the native Indigenous population is well documented, in the recording of massacres and the introduction of foreign diseases which drastically reduced the Indigenous population in the first decade following European contact (Reynolds 2013). Furthermore, the imposition of guns, alcohol, tobacco and sugar as agents of colonization added to the disablement of the surviving population and their future generations.

What is less documented in the history of colonization in Australia is the social order that was concurrently imposed upon the new colony. European colonization of Australia's Indigenous lands and peoples commenced in the late eighteenth and early nineteenth century during a period in history known as 'the Enlightenment', and in the midst of the industrial revolution that was occurring in Europe. Many of the ideals of 'Enlightenment' thinking were imported as foundations for the social and political economy of the new colony. The ideals that were imported through colonization included the emergence of classical free-market theories and concepts of 'human capital' (Smith 1776) that commodified people in industrialized production processes, the counterpart of which was the discarding of those people who were unable to participate in the industrialized production process, giving an origin to a notion of a 'disabled person'. It was, and remains, a social order completely at odds with the Indigenous cultural values of diversity and inclusion.

In the two and a half centuries since the commencement of colonization, Indigenous people with disability have been vulnerable to the worst aspects of social engineering: whether it is the over-incarceration of Indigenous people (Johnston 1991); the institutionalization of people with disability in mental asylums and institutions and the structural violence that occurred within them (Sweet 2017)[1]; the removal of children from their families as part of the assimilation policies known as Stolen Generations and beyond (McGlade 2012; Human Rights and Equal Opportunities Commission 1997) or exclusion from equal participation in a market economy (Hunter 2000). Left unchecked for centuries, the dispossession of Indigenous people with disability from their rights has become institutionalized into the practices of social policy and service systems, as reflected in their current social standing.

[1] See also Commonwealth of Australia—Attorney General's Department. 2019. Royal Commission into violence, abuse, neglect and exploitation of people with disability. Letters Patent.

## Intersectional Inequality, Discrimination and Isolation Experienced by Indigenous People with Disability

In terms of population prevalence, Australia's Indigenous people with disability are numerically a small minority within the total Australian population, but bear a substantially disproportionate load of social inequality. Indigenous people comprise 3.3% of the Australian population,[2] of which it is estimated that 45% of Australian Indigenous people have some disability and/or restrictive long-term health condition. Between 7.3 and 7.7% of the Indigenous population have a disability that is severe or profound, which is a prevalence rate between 1.8 and 2.1 times the rate of severe and profound disability in the non-Indigenous population.[3] There are also material differences in the life expectancy between Indigenous people and the rest of the Australian population, with Indigenous men experiencing 8.6 years shorter life expectancy compared to other Australian men, and Indigenous women experiencing 7.8 years shorter life expectancy compared to other Australian women.[4] This life expectancy outcome is for the Indigenous population as a whole and does not factor the likelihood of a further reduction in the life expectancy for Indigenous people who also have disability, as life expectancy reported in the official datasets is not disaggregated by disability status.

In addition to a heightened prevalence of disability in the Indigenous population compared to other groups, Indigenous people with disability experience social inequality compared to other groups in society. A comparison across groups of social health and well-being outcomes that can be statistically measured has shown that access barriers that Indigenous people with disability face are pervasive across a vast range of systems intended for their support including: accessible housing; disability supports; transport; access to justice; exposure to threatened or actual violence; access to an inclusive education; attaining employment and

[2] Australian Bureau of Statistics (ABS). 2018a. Estimates of Aboriginal and Torres Strait Islander Australians, June 2016. Rel. 3238.0.55.001.

[3] Australian Bureau of Statistics (ABS). 2016. National Aboriginal and Torres Strait Islander Social Survey, (NATSISS) 2014–15. Rel. 4714.0.

[4] Australian Bureau of Statistics (ABS). 2018b. Life Tables for Aboriginal and Torres Strait Islander Australians, 2015–2017. Rel. 3302.0.55.003.

accessing health and health care services (Avery 2018). Further, the inequality in the social, health and well-being outcomes that Indigenous people with disability experience are greater than other groups, including Indigenous people without disability and people with disability who are not Indigenous. These findings provide empirical affirmation of 'intersectionality' (Crenshaw 1991) as an interpretive frame to explain the experiences of Indigenous people with disability as an acutely marginalized group within larger marginalized populations.

In addition to experiencing pervasive social inequality as a form of structural discrimination, Indigenous people with disability experience other multi-faceted discrimination including that which is racially based ('racism'), and disability-related ('ableism'). The prevalence of racism and its adverse impact upon the health and well-being of Australian Indigenous people is well documented (Larson et al. 2007; Ferdinand et al. 2012). In addition to racism and ableism as forms of discrimination that act independently of each other, there is a hybrid category of discrimination that cannot exclusively be explained by racism or ableism alone. This third category of discrimination is referred to in this research as 'intersectional discrimination' (Avery 2018), so named as it aligns with the concept of 'intersectionality' (Crenshaw 1991) as an interpretive frame to explain the experiences of people at the edges of marginalized communities. An illustrative case example of how racism and ableism can interact in intersectional discrimination is an account of an Indigenous man who has cognitive impairment, who experiences harassment in his daily life by people who presume he is intoxicated. These encounters happen as a regular occurrence, such as by security guards when he goes shopping, by service staff at eating places and when he tries to catch public transport. In this real-life scenario, ableist prejudices that conflate intellectual disability with drunkenness are magnified by racist prejudices about the prevalence of alcohol consumption by Aboriginal and Torres Strait Islander people, interacting to produce a vulnerability to discrimination that is not adequately explained by racism or ableism alone. The repetitiousness of these every-day encounters of discrimination has effectively driven him into a life of isolation.[5]

Given the discrimination that Indigenous peoples with disability experience is frequent and has both racial and ableist dimensions, there are

[5] This is a case study was extracted from *Culture Is Inclusion*. Avery, S. 2018. Loc cit, p. 99.

conceivably greater opportunities to detect breaches in their human rights through one of the many of rights mechanisms that these issues traverse. However, the social inequality that Indigenous people with disability face is pervasive and intractable, which indicates that it is harder to address infringements on human rights that multi-dimensional. This is because the international human rights frameworks and domestic social policies that they are translated into are structurally designed with one aspect of human rights in mind. The unidimensional design of rights and policy inadequately addresses the intersectional nuances that affect marginalized people with a stake across two or more aspects of rights. The next part of this chapter explores how the unidimensional design of human rights and social policy falls short in securing the composite right of Indigenous people with disability as an intersectional group.

## The Efficacy of Indigenous and Disability Rights Frameworks in Securing the Composite Rights of Indigenous People with Disability

Whilst the rights entitlements of Indigenous people with disability traverse various international rights instruments, the two principle rights mechanisms within international human rights law that most directly relate to their rights are the *Convention on the Rights of Persons with Disabilities* (CRPD) and the *United Nations Declaration on the Rights of Indigenous Peoples* (UNDRIP). The CRPD and UNDRIP are of similar age, with the CRPD adopted by the United Nations in 2006 and the UNDRIP in 2007. Beyond their tenure and a few other tenuous points of connectivity, the two mechanisms operate separately from each other, and have very different application and effect when translated into domestic social policy.

As an instrument concerned with the rights of persons with disability, the CRPD aims to 'promote, protect, and ensure the full enjoyment of human rights by people with disabilities' (Article 1) and outlaws direct discrimination against individuals with disability. The reference to '*persons*' with disability is significant in its direction in promoting the *personal* rights of people with disability. This contrasts the approach of the UNDRIP that promotes the rights of Indigenous *peoples* as a collective, which is discussed further below.

In terms of its legal effect, the CRPD has the standing of a convention under the international human rights system, and as such imposes legally binding obligations upon its signatory nation-states. The human rights provisions of the CRPD are implemented into national law through 'co-ordination mechanisms' (Article 33). In the Australian public policy setting, the co-ordination mechanism through which the obligations under the CRPD are implemented into national disability policy is principally the *National Disability Strategy* (Coalition of Australian Governments 2010) which sets the overarching public disability policy in Australia. There are special initiatives that are national policy priorities under the *National Disability Strategy*, most notably the National Disability Insurance Scheme that provides personalized support programs to people with severe and profound disability. State jurisdictional governments are bound to the obligations imposed by the CRPD at the national level through a *National Disability Agreement* (Coalition of Australian Governments 2009) between the national government and state jurisdictional governments within Australia. The anti-discrimination provisions of the CRPD are further enacted into Australian law through various legislation including the *Disability Discrimination Act* (Commonwealth of Australia 1992). The CRPD's legal status invokes mechanisms of accountability and reporting on the rights of people with disability. Signatory nations are required to report compliance on their obligations through periodic review processes of the United Nations (Articles 35 and 36). In Australia, the internal monitoring mechanism is conducted through the office of the Disability Discrimination Commissioner, housed at the Australian Human Rights Commission, which as Australia's national human rights institution has the powers to independently investigate complaints of disability discrimination. Furthermore, persons with disabilities and their representative organizations are assigned a right under the CRPD to be involved and participate fully in the monitoring process (Article 33.3).

There are material points of difference between the CRPD and the UNDRIP that go beyond the differing groups of rights-holders that they focus on. As a statement of cultural rights, the UNDRIP describes the collective rights that Indigenous groups are entitled to exercise for their self-determination and cultural preservation. The language in describing Indigenous groups as '*Peoples*' is significant in emphasizing their collective rights to self-determination, which is a point of contrast with the emphasis on personal rights of '*persons*' with disability entailed within the CRPD.

There are also material differences in legal effect of the two instruments under international human rights law. Unlike the CRDP, the UNDRIP is a 'Declaration' and does not enjoy the legal standing of a convention within the international human rights system. It articulates, and even asserts the rights of Indigenous peoples, but does not necessarily secure the rights of Indigenous peoples through a mechanism that is legally binding upon nations. Instead, the rights articulated within the UNDRIP are an aspirational, non-binding set of principles that guide nation-states in recognizing and promoting the rights of Indigenous Peoples for their self-determination and cultural preservation. The Australian Government's current official position is that it supports the UNDRIP, although that was not initially the case as Australia was one of the four countries to vote against it when it came into effect in 2007, only supporting it some two years later in 2009 following a change in government. As a non-binding Declaration, there is no legal compulsion to enact it into domestic law and policy, and there are only occasional references to the UNDRIP in Australian Indigenous policy. This is unlike the CRPD which has a direct implementation mechanism in the *National Disability Strategy*. Nonetheless, there are independent mechanisms to promote Indigenous rights through the office of the Aboriginal and Torres Strait Islander Social Justice Commissioner at the Australian Humans Rights Commission, and progress in promoting the rights of Indigenous Peoples is monitored through the Australia's reporting to the Universal Periodic Review process.

Whilst the CRPD and UNDRIP are predominantly standalone documents on rights of people with disability and Indigenous peoples, respectively, there are touchpoints that acknowledge the intersectional in rights for Indigenous people with disability. In its preamble, the CRPD acknowledges its 'concern' for marginalized sub-groups within the disability community, including Indigenous people with disability amongst other subgroups of the disability community who 'are subject to multiple or aggravated forms of discrimination' (United Nations 2006). The UNDRIP makes direct reference to Indigenous peoples with disability within the body of the Declaration through Article 21 in respect to taking measures to improve the social and economic conditions that they experience:

1. Indigenous peoples have the right, without discrimination, to the improvement of their economic and social conditions, including, inter alia, in the areas of education, employment, vocational training and retraining, housing, sanitation, health and social security.
2. States shall take effective measures and, where appropriate, special measures to ensure continuing improvement of their economic and social conditions. Particular attention shall be paid to the rights and special needs of indigenous elders, women, youth, children and ***persons with disabilities*** (United Nations 2007).[6]

These references acknowledge the unique constitution in the rights of Indigenous people with disability, yet both instruments fall short of being able to make tangible commitments that secure their rights as a uniquely marginalized group within Indigenous and disability populations. The 'concern' in the preamble of the CRPD is not followed through with an article that is dedicated to protection of rights of Indigenous people with disability as a uniquely marginalized group of persons with disability. The absence of a direct reference to Indigenous disability rights within the body of the CRPD dilutes the legal obligation upon signatory nations to implement mechanisms that advance the rights of Indigenous people with disability, and further, the accountability of a nation's record in securing their rights as disclosed through the obligatory reporting mechanisms. The UNDRIP is more explicit than the CRPD in detailing the rights of Indigenous peoples within the body of the instrument, yet as an 'aspirational' document, it lacks the legal gravitas within international human rights legal frameworks to impose accountability upon nations in a meaningful way.

The net effect upon the realization of rights for Indigenous people with disability is that the CRPD and UNDRIP operate independently of each other, and their unidimensional design fails to fully capture the composite rights of people facing inequality and discrimination relatable to two or more of their identities. Traversing both Indigenous peoples and persons with disability, the rights of Indigenous peoples with disability could conceivably be secured through either the CRPD or the UNDRIP,

[6] Article 21. Italics added by the author.

or both. However, the evidence of social equality across multifaceted domains that Australian Indigenous people with disability face compared to other groups presented earlier indicates that the rights of Indigenous peoples with disability are effectively served by neither. Nonetheless, the respective acknowledgement of the Indigenous rights of people with disability in both instruments provides some promise that a more nuanced understanding in intersectional rights of multiply marginalized peoples can be undertaken as the next frontier in the development of international human rights frameworks. Later this chapter will explore how an Indigenous interpretation of 'cultural rights' within the CRPD may be a means for making an intersectional connection.

## Translation of Rights in Domestic Indigenous and Disability Policy

Within the Australian federated system of government, there is a multiplicity of policy initiatives, frameworks and plans that impact upon the lives of Indigenous people with disability. To highlight the degree of fragmentation of public policy affecting Indigenous people with disability, Australia has nine governments at the federal, state and territory level, as well as 547 local governing bodies. Issues affecting Indigenous people with disability transcend numerous policy domains, from Indigenous affairs to disability, health, law and justice, education, employment, transport and housing. The government agencies responsible for an area of social policy default to a thematic or 'sectional' approach, in contrast to an intersectional approach. As a consequence, Indigenous policies consider people with disability within the Indigenous population as incidental beneficiaries in a whole of population approach, and reciprocally disability policy considers Indigenous people within the disability population as incidental beneficiaries in a whole of population approach. Much like the unidimensional structure of the human rights frameworks, the sectional design of domestic public policy is inadequate in capturing the impact of multiple marginalization.

Elevating the deficiencies in sectional policy design to the national level, there are two main social policy initiatives of the Australian Commonwealth Government that affect Indigenous people with disability. One policy is the *National Indigenous Reform Agreement*, more commonly known as the *Closing the Gap Framework* (Coalition of Australian Governments 2007), that aims to reduce the inequality in health and social outcomes of Indigenous people compared to other Australians. Another separate and unconnected policy framework is the *National Disability Strategy* (Coalition of Australian Governments 2010) that, as discussed earlier, is an overarching national policy approach to improving access to support services and social outcomes for people living with disability, their families and carers.

The *Closing the Gap Framework* comprises a set of measurable targets for health and social equality in the areas of life expectancy; child mortality rates; school attendance; literacy and numeracy; educational attainment and employment outcomes. The significance of a policy target under the *Closing the Gap Framework* is that it is underpinned by a partnership agreement between the Commonwealth Government and State and Territory Governments that have a funding commitment towards programs to attain equality in outcomes for that targeted area. There is also a process of reporting of outcomes towards 'closing the gap' in health and social equality between Indigenous people and other Australians, which is delivered annually in an address to the Australian Parliament by the Prime Minister.

Despite the statistical data on the disparities of social inequality between Indigenous people with disability and Indigenous people without disability of the kind presented earlier in this chapter, there has been no meaningful recognition on the impact of disability as a determinant of attaining Indigenous equality within the *Closing the Gap Framework* since its inception in 2008. The First Peoples Disability Network (Australia), an Indigenous Disabled Peoples Organization, has maintained advocacy for a stand-alone target for the equitable inclusion of Indigenous people in the National Disability Insurance Scheme, as well as compartmentalized targets for the inclusion of people with disability within established Indigenous policy areas such as education, employment and access to health care. For example, achieving equality in educational attainment for the entire Indigenous population does not acknowledge the specific access barriers that Indigenous children with disability might face to attaining equality in access to their education, over and above their status as an Indigenous child. Consequently, social equity programs provided through Indigenous education policy may focus upon cultural inclusion but ignore disability inclusion. As another example, the target to attain equality in employment outcomes for Indigenous people does not factor in how disability-related discrimination in employment practices may coincide with race-based discrimination to curtail the prospect of attaining equality in employment outcomes across the entire Indigenous population. Defying the data and sustained human rights advocacy, the concern of Indigenous people with disability has been actively disacknowledged within *Closing the Gap* policy and buried underneath the 'too hard basket'.

Another aspect of an unconnected social policy framework is the *National Disability Strategy* (Coalition of Australian Governments 2010). The *National Disability Strategy* has identified six policy priority areas with distributed responsibilities across various government agencies, including inclusive and accessible communities (including the physical environment, transport, communications, social and cultural life); rights protection, justice and legislation (including anti-discrimination and interaction with justice systems); economic security (including employment and income support); personal and community support (including provision of disability support services); learning and skills (including early childhood and education) and health and well-being (including access to health, interaction between the health and disability services).

The establishment of a National Disability Insurance Scheme (NDIS) is a key policy initiative of Australian disability policy, and amounts to a $28 billion undertaking to provide increased access to disability services by people with severe and profound disability. The NDIS establishes a market-based model for the provision of disability services and focuses on promoting personal agency, paraphrased as 'choice and control'. However, there are gaps in the provision of basic public infrastructure within remote Indigenous communities, such as housing, access to clean water and electricity, food security, roads, footpaths and transport. Many issues that inhibit access by people with disability are structural, whereas the market model design of the NDIS assumes these public infrastructures are in place. In the hierarchy of community need, addressing fundamental issues of survival, such as homelessness and chronic hunger, take precedence over the capacity of the NDIS to make an impact at the personal level. However, the responsibility for addressing the structural issues in Indigenous communities is beyond the remit of the NDIS, and it instead resides in another, unconnected arm of government.

In 2017, the Australian Government took a formative acknowledgement of the unique needs of Aboriginal and Torres Strait Islander people with disability through its *Australian Government Plan to Improve Outcomes for Aboriginal and Torres Strait Islander People with Disability* (Commonwealth of Australia Department of Social Services 2017).

As a subsidiary to the National Disability Strategy, the Government's Plan amounted to a stocktake of existing government activities relating to Indigenous people, but for which people with disability might be benefited as members of a larger Indigenous population. Very few of the government's listed activities could be assessed as targeting the unique social inequality experienced by Indigenous people with disability. Furthermore, many fundamentals were missing from the plan. There were no official estimates on the prevalence of disability nor any considered statistical data on the disability profile amongst Indigenous people, both of which are vital in assessing the need for support and developing services and strategies for a culturally informed disability workforce (Gilroy et al. 2017). Lacking the substance of costed future initiatives, the injection of Indigenous disability into public policy discourse that was generated through the Plan has been short-lived.

An insidious outcome of unconnected Indigenous and disability policy is the mechanism of avoidance that it permits. Avoidance of responsibility happens when one part of the health care system disgorges responsibility for addressing social and health inequalities to another part of the system, which in turn disgorges responsibility onwards. In some cases, a circular reference of avoidance is created. One example is the *National Aboriginal and Torres Strait Islander Health Plan 2013–2023* (Commonwealth Department of Health 2013), which is the overarching plan to improve health outcomes for the Indigenous population as a whole. This plan, administered by one Commonwealth government department, transfers responsibility for the unique health requirements of Indigenous people with disability to the *National Disability Strategy*, which is administered by another Commonwealth government department. Further, the *National Aboriginal and Torres Strait Islander Health Plan* assigns responsibility for 'a strong focus on prevention and early intervention to prevent mental health conditions and illness, chronic health conditions and injuries from occurring, including disability' to the NDIS. The *National Disability Strategy* delegates responsibility for health care for Indigenous people with disability through to its companion document, the *Australian Government Plan to Improve Outcomes for Aboriginal and Torres Strait Islander Peoples with a Disability*, which in turn refers responsibility for monitoring progress on improvements in the health status of people with disability back to the *National Aboriginal and Torres Strait Islander Health Plan 2013–2023* and the *Closing the Gap Framework*, which, as stated, has not acknowledged the impact of disability in health outcomes in its policy framework.

Indigenous people with disability are in need of a sophisticated approach to address the pervasiveness of social and health inequality that they experience, in which all parts of a health care system come together collaboratively in accepting joint responsibility for attaining improvements in their health outcomes. Instead, they are met with a policy merry-go-round in which no one aspect of social policy accepts responsibility. This practice of avoidance starts at the policy level, and cascades into finding and resourcing, and sets the tone for what Indigenous people with disability can expect to encounter in front-line service delivery. The unconnectedness of policies affecting Indigenous people with disability as a multi-marginalized group enables the current generation of policy-makers to place what is a complex problem into the 'too hard basket' for the next generation of policymakers to deal with. But as the evidence of pervasive social inequalities has shown, no generation of policymakers have yet stepped up to take on the challenge, even to place the social health and well-being of Indigenous people with disability on the policy agenda. The policy inertia, and poor social and health outcomes that flow from it, can be expected to continue unless the institutionalized practices of avoidance within the policy processes are disrupted.

## An Indigenous Interpretation of 'Cultural Rights' as a Basis for Intersecting Indigenous Rights with Disability Rights

There is one aspect in the life of Indigenous people with disability that defies the pervasiveness of social inequality that otherwise exists in other aspects of their lives. As a sole categorical exception to the evidence of social inequality, Indigenous people with disability participate in their Indigenous cultural and community events at the same rate as Indigenous people without disability (Avery 2018). The parity in cultural and community participation by Indigenous people with disability extends across a range of activities, including participating in community events, participating in ceremony, engaging with their Elders and learning their native language (Australian Bureau of Statistics 2016). The equality they experience in their cultural and social life points to an Indigenous culture that is inclusive of people with disability within community and social life, a cultural value that has been consistently observed in research amongst Australian Indigenous peoples (Avery 2018; Ariotti 1999; King et al. 2014) as well as other Indigenous peoples worldwide (Te Pou o te Whakaaro Nui 2016; Kapp 2013). Being included within the social and cultural life of their Indigenous community has an affirming quality on the health and well-being of Indigenous with disability, and acts to moderate the ill-effects of the social inequality they encounter outside their Indigenous community.

The qualities of an Indigenous culture of inclusion open the consideration as to whether an affirmative philosophy can be extended to interpretations of disability rights. Article 30 of the CRPD recognizes the right of persons with disabilities to take part on an equal basis with others in cultural life, amongst other things (Article 30 (1)), and support of their specific cultural and linguistic identity (Article (30 (4)). The right to participate in cultural life is contextualized within the existing wording by reference to access to sites of cultural significance such as libraries, museum and monuments; the right to artistic expression; the right to sport and leisure and the right to linguistic identity, with specific mention of sign language and Deaf culture. An Indigenous interpretation of cultural rights is not specifically mentioned within the present wording of Article 30 nor is it precluded by it. The door is open to entertain a possibility that an Indigenous interpretation of cultural rights with the CRPD may be a way to promote the affirming qualities of inclusion within disability rights, disrupting the constant focus on restorative rights in which one hand is fighting systemic racism and the other hand is fighting systemic ableism.

Interpreting cultural rights within the CRPD through an Indigenous lens provides an intersection between Indigenous and disability rights that is wanting, acting as a catalyst to open a dialogue on the effects of multiple marginalization for groups of people within the disability community. As cultural rights are articulated within the substantive body of the Convention, there is a pathway to cascade these human rights principles into domestic disability policy, enabling the mechanisms of accountability that are already embedded within the CRPD.

An Indigenous interpretation of cultural rights does more than provide a pragmatic way to address intersectional inequality for Indigenous groups within the disability community or facilitate Indigenous peoples' cultural expression. There are people with disability who aren't Indigenous who might look at the intrinsic qualities of an Indigenous culture of inclusion and say 'we want that'. The *Uluru Statement from the Heart*, a statement of self-determination from Australian Indigenous people, speaks of Indigenous children who will 'walk in two worlds and their culture will be a gift to their country' (National Constitutional Convention 2017). Invoking this sentiment, a culture of inclusion does not just sit solely with Indigenous people with disability, but is a gift that can be shared with all people with disability.

## References


Ariotti, L. 1999. 'Social construction of Anangu disability'. *Australian Journal of Rural Health*, 7: 216–222.

Australian Bureau of Statistics (ABS). 2016. *National Aboriginal and Torres Strait Islander Social Survey, (NATSISS) 2014–15.* Rel. 4714.0.

Australian Bureau of Statistics (ABS). 2018a. *Estimates of Aboriginal and Torres Strait Islander Australians, June 2016.* Rel. 3238.0.55.001.

Australian Bureau of Statistics (ABS). 2018b. *Life Tables for Aboriginal and Torres Strait Islander Australians, 2015–2017.* Rel. 3302.0.55.003.

Avery, S. 2018. *Culture Is Inclusion: A Narrative of Aboriginal and Torres Strait Islander People with Disability.* First Peoples Disability Network (Australia). Sydney.

Coalition of Australian Governments. 2007. *National Indigenous Reform Agreement (Closing the Gap).*

Coalition of Australian Governments. 2009. *National Disability Agreement.*

Coalition of Australian Governments. 2010. *National Disability Strategy 2010–2020.*

Commonwealth of Australia. 1992. *Disability Discrimination Act.*

Commonwealth of Australia—Attorney General's Department. 2019. *Royal Commission into Violence, Abuse, Neglect and Exploitation of People with Disability. Letters Patent.*

Commonwealth of Australia—Department of Health. 2013. *National Aboriginal and Torres Strait Islander Health Plan 2013–2023.*

Commonwealth of Australia—Department of Social Services. 2017. *Australian Government Plan to Improve Outcomes for Aboriginal and Torres Strait Islander People with Disability.*

Crenshaw, K. 1991. 'Mapping the margins: Intersectionality, identity politics, and violence against women of color'. *Stanford Law Review*, 43(6): 1241–1299.

Ferdinand, A., Paradies, Y., and Kelaher, M. 2012. *Mental health impacts of racial discrimination in Victorian Aboriginal communities: The 'Localities Embracing and Accepting Diversity' (LEAD) experiences of racism survey.* The Lowitja Institute. Melbourne.

Gilroy, J., Dew, A., Lincoln, M., and Hines, M. 2017. 'Need for an Australian Indigenous disability workforce strategy: Review of the literature'. *Disability and Rehabilitation*, 39(16): 1664–1673.

Human Rights and Equal Opportunities Commission. 1997. *Bringing them home: National inquiry into the separation of Aboriginal and Torres Strait Islander children from their families*. Commonwealth of Australia. Sydney.

Hunter, B. 2000. *Social exclusion, social capital, and Indigenous Australians: Measuring the social costs of unemployment*. Australian National University. Canberra.

Johnston, E. 1991. *Report of the Royal Commission into Aboriginal deaths in custody*. Australian Government Publishing Service. Canberra.

Kapp, S.K. 2013. 'Navajo and Autism: The beauty of harmony'. In Moore, M. (Ed.) *Moving beyond boundaries in disability studies: Rights, spaces and innovations* (77–90). Routledge. Abingdon, Oxford

King, J.A., Brough, M., and Knox, M. 2014. 'Negotiating disability and colonisation: The lived experience of Indigenous Australians with a disability'. *Disability and Society*, 25(5): 738–750.

Larson, A., Gillies, M., Howard, P.J., and Coffin J. 2007. 'It's enough to make you sick: The impact of racism on the health of Aboriginal Australians'. *Australian and New Zealand Journal of Public Health*, 31(4): 322–329.

McGlade, H. 2012. *Our greatest challenge: Aboriginal children and human rights*. Aboriginal Studies Press. Canberra.

Moreton-Robinson, A. 2003. 'I still call Australia home: Indigenous belonging and place in a white postcolonising society'. In Ahmed, S. (Ed.) *Uprootings/Regroundings: Questions of home and migration* (23–40). Berg Publishing. New York.

National Constitutional Convention. 2017. *Uluru Statement from the Heart*. Uluru.

Reynolds, H. 2013. *Forgotten war*. New South Books. Sydney.

Smith, A. 1776. *The wealth of nations*. Public Domain.

Sweet, M. 2017. *'Acknowledgement': A social journalism research project relating to the history of lock hospitals, lazarets and other forms of medical incarceration of Aboriginal and Torres Strait Islander people*. PhD thesis, University of Canberra. Canberra.

Te Pou o te Whakaaro Nui. 2016. *Te Reo Hāpai: The language of enrichment*. At: https://www.tepou.co.nz/uploads/files/Te%20Reo%20Hapai/Te%20Reo%20H%C4%81pai%20-%20The%20Language%20of%20Enrichment.pdf.

United Nations. 2006. *Convention on the Rights of Persons with Disabilities* (A/RES/61/106).

United Nations. 2007. *United Nations Declaration on the Rights of Indigenous Peoples* (A/RES/61/295).

CHAPTER 12

# Examining Australia's Performance in Realising CRPD Obligations in Health Through the Lens of COVID-19

*Helen Dickinson, Gwynyyth Llewellyn, and Anne Kavanagh*

## Introduction

Article 25 of the Convention on the Rights of Persons with Disabilities (CRPD) obligates States parties to provide equal access to health care. Australia was one of the first signatories of the CRPD after it opened for

H. Dickinson (✉)
University of New South Wales, Canberra, ACT, Australia
e-mail: h.dickinson@adfa.edu.au

G. Llewellyn
University of Sydney, Sydney, NSW, Australia
e-mail: gwynnyth.llewellyn@sydney.edu.au

A. Kavanagh
University of Melbourne, Melbourne, VIC, Australia
e-mail: a.kavanagh@unimelb.edu.au



F. Felder et al. (eds.), *Disability Law and Human Rights*, Palgrave Studies in Disability and International Development,
https://doi.org/10.1007/978-3-030-86545-0_12

signature on 30 March 2007; Australia ratified the CRPD in July 2008 and the Optional Protocol in August 2009. Yet, despite this support for the CRPD, we still find that there is significant evidence that people with disability face inequities with respect to health outcomes (Kavanagh et al. 2015; Emerson et al. 2011). In this chapter we examine the experience of Australians with disability during the COVID-19 pandemic to explore the degree to which these inequities have been exacerbated during this public health crisis and led to poorer outcomes.

The Australian experience shows that while there has been progress in implementing the provisions of the CRPD, there have also been significant deficiencies, most notably in relation to accessibility of health services and reducing discrimination in health care. The health outcomes of Australians with disability remain far poorer than those of their non-disabled peers. Australians with disability are more likely to have chronic health conditions, poor diets, low incomes and low labour force participation and are less likely to use preventative health care. We argue the COVID-19 pandemic has shone a light on a number of these existing inequities, but this has also provided an opportunity to address some long-standing issues that have often been seen as particularly intransigent. We ultimately argue that the only way for Australia to mitigate the worst health impacts of the current pandemic and any future emergencies is to more effectively implement the CRPD, particularly, but not solely, with respect to the health provisions.

The chapter is structured as follows. Firstly, we provide an overview of the Australian disability context outlining the major features of this system and some of the recent reform trajectories. We then provide an account of the health obligations outlined in the CRPD, noting that health considerations go beyond just the health-specific article. In the following section we explore how well the CRPD has been implemented in relation to health, before exploring Australia's COVID-19 experience to date with respect to people with disability. We conclude by noting where recent progress has been made and where there are priorities for future action.

## The Australian Disability Context

In recent years the Australian service system has undergone significant reform. In part this has been in response to some of the worrying outcomes for people with disability relative to non-disabled peers and in comparison to other OECD countries (as we will explore in more detail below). The most significant of these developments is the introduction of a National Disability Strategy (NDS) and the creation of the National Disability Insurance Scheme (NDIS). In this section we provide a brief overview of these two initiatives.

The NDS was devised in 2010 as a ten-year national plan for improving life for Australians with disability, their families and carers and at the time of writing is under review. The NDS was endorsed by all governments with the aim of achieving "an inclusive Australian society that enables people with disability to fulfil their potential as equal citizens" (Commonwealth of Australia 2011, p. 8). The NDS was established to provide a high-level policy framework to give coherence to government activity across public policy with respect to disability; improve performance of services in delivering outcomes for people with disability; give visibility to disability issues and ensure inclusion of people with disability in the development and implementation of public policy and, provide national leadership in terms of inclusion of people with disability. The strategy adopts the principles set out in Article 3 of the CRPD and covers six policy areas with articulated desired outcomes, agreed policy directions and areas for future action. Although one of the policy areas of the NDS relates specifically to health and well-being, this strategy has not generally been seen to have a significant impact on people with disability (Mellifont and Smith-Merry 2016). The NDS is a complex strategy and the competing needs and interests of government and a full range of stakeholders mean that the implementation process has proved highly problematic.

Traditionally Australian disability services have been the responsibility of state and territory governments, and different models developed across the eight jurisdictions (Fisher et al. 2010). The funding and organising picture for disability services was complex, with splits between state and territory and federal responsibilities. Added to this complexity was the existence of insurance-based funding of injury-related rehabilitation and disability supports, and those funded privately as a result of public liability claims. What this meant was that individuals who acquired a disability through for example a road traffic accident or at work may have been entitled to greater levels of service provision through the relevant insurer than someone born with a disability or acquiring a non-injury-related disability (Dickinson 2017). The creation of the NDIS was intended to provide consistency to disability services across jurisdictions, although in reality injury-related insurance schemes still exist, and public liability claims are also possible meaning there is some complexity within the current system. It is estimated that around 10% of the 4.1 million people with disability in Australia are identified as having a significant and ongoing disability and are eligible for the NDIS.

Federal government has committed $22 billion per year to this scheme to provide individualised funding to approximately 460,000 participants. Given this magnitude, the NDIS has been described as one of the most expansive policy reforms this country has seen in over a decade (Malbon et al. 2019). It is also fair to say that given the scale and costs of the NDIS it has been first and foremost in public and political discourse in the disability space to the detriment of other initiatives such as the NDS.

The 2013 introduction of the NDIS significantly changed the relationship of the Commonwealth and the states and territories with respect to providing support to people with disability. The NDIS was designed to provide a nationally consistent approach to maximise choice and control by people with disability over the support and services they receive. The NDIS does not replace mainstream services such as health and education and there have been issues reported in terms of the interface with these (Dickinson and Carey 2017). Of the one in five Australians with disability, 90% are not eligible for NDIS services and continue to rely on mainstream services, which are organised across a confusing arrangement of state/territory and federal responsibilities. All Australians are entitled to universal health care provided by Medicare funded by the Australian Government (Boxall and Gillespie 2013). While state governments bear responsibility for funding and oversight of hospitals, primary and community care and aged care are under the jurisdiction of the federal government. Such a division creates a number of challenges in practise with respect to continuity of care and effective preventative services.

Although we have seen significant investment and activity in the Australian disability arena in recent years, there still remain a number of critical fault lines that have important implications for the lives of people with disability and their families. In the next section we explore the commitments that the CRPD affords with respect to health.

## Health and the CRPD

Article 25 of the CRPD focuses on health, setting out an obligation for States parties to provide equal access to health care: "the highest attainable standard of health without discrimination on the basis of disability".

Prohibiting discrimination against persons with disability and preventing discriminatory denial of health care or health services are actions required by States parties. The article states that in particular States parties shall:

a. Provide persons with disabilities with the same **range, quality and standard of free or affordable health care and programmes** as provided to other persons, including in the area of sexual and reproductive health and **population-based public health programmes**;
b. Provide those **health services needed by persons with disabilities specifically because of their disabilities**, including early identification and intervention as appropriate, and services designed to minimise and prevent further disabilities, including among children and older persons;
c. Provide these health services as **close as possible to people's own communities**, including in rural areas;
d. **Require health professionals to provide care of the same quality to persons with disabilities as to others**, including on the basis of free and informed consent by, inter alia, raising awareness of the human rights, dignity, autonomy and needs of persons with disabilities through training and the promulgation of ethical standards for public and private health care;
e. Prohibit discrimination against persons with disabilities in the provision of health insurance and life insurance where such insurance is permitted by national law, which shall be provided in a fair and reasonable manner;
f. Prevent discriminatory denial of health care or health services or food and fluids on the basis of disability.

We have added emphasis to the text above to highlight which of these are most relevant to the COVID-19 pandemic and will be covered most substantively in this chapter.

It is important to note that while access to health services is a core feature of this article, they are not the only driver of health outcomes. Rather, it is the social determinants of health (the environments in which people live, play, work, and interact) that are crucial for health outcomes (Marmot 2010). What this means is that although article 25 has a focus on health, this does not mean that other articles do not play a role in influencing health outcomes.

## How Well Has Australia Implemented the CRPD in Relation to Health?

In this section we consider the degree to which Australia has been successful in making progress in the implementation of the CRPD in relation to the health of Australians with disability. We do this firstly by providing some broad observations regarding health and related outcomes for Australians with disability and then reflect on a few key areas. We start by considering the degree to which people with disability are still discriminated against in relation to health services and whether health services are more accessible as a result of the CRPD. We finish this section by exploring issues as they specifically relate to children and young people as a group that face particular challenges in accessing appropriate health services.

Generally speaking, the health of Australians with disability is poorer than non-disabled people across most health outcomes, including those unrelated to their impairment (World Health Organization 2014; Emerson et al. 2018). People with disability are more likely to be overweight or obese, smoke, physically inactive or have poor diets (Australian Institute of Health and Welfare 2019). They also have higher rates of health service use and chronic conditions such as diabetes, heart disease, and are less likely to use preventative health care (Chen et al. 2009; Llewellyn et al. 2011). Australians with disability fare particularly badly in global terms—they have the lowest relative income and one of the lowest levels of labour force participation of all OECD countries (OECD 2009). Australians with disability also have a weekly median income less than half of those without disability (Australian Bureau of Statistics 2016). All of these factors have a significant impact on health outcomes, compounding the issues faced in accessing appropriate health services that we discuss in more detail below. Further, this demonstrates the importance of other articles of the CRPD in the creation and maintenance of good health. Factors such as housing and employment are closely correlated with health status, so to consider health solely in terms of access to health services misses the wider perspective on health outcomes (Green et al. 2020). Yet, Australian disability policy has typically paid little attention to the social determinants of health (Embrett and Randall 2014).

### *Discrimination*

The Australian health system has long discriminated against people with disability. This has led to high numbers of preventable deaths, particularly among people with intellectual disabilities. For example, several studies have uncovered a 27-year life expectancy gap for people with intellectual disability, largely due to deaths from avoidable causes (Trollor et al. 2017; Reppermund et al. 2020). The Australian Government's initial report (United Nations 2012) to the Committee on the Rights of Persons with Disabilities (the Committee) paid little attention to Article 25. Australia relied on evidence in the Disability Discrimination Act 1992 (Cth) s 24, amended in 2009, para. 151 (the DDA) to demonstrate commitment to and progress on Article 25. The DDA makes discrimination unlawful in relation to services except where providing non-discriminatory access would involve unjustifiable hardship for the agency involved. Under this provision, health services cannot discriminate against an individual on the basis of disability by refusing to provide a service, altering the terms and conditions of provision of the service, or providing the service in a different manner. While laudable, this provision only speaks to overt discrimination (with or without intent) by a health service provider on the grounds of disability. There are three foundational errors when relying on the DDA to comprehensively cover the ongoing discrimination experienced by people with disability in Australia accessing health care. There are three forms of covert discrimination not covered by the DDA that exclude people with disability from health care (Australian Human Rights Commission 2019).

The most frequently encountered form of covert discrimination makes health care *inaccessible* for people with disability. This comes from entrenched physical, information and communication and attitudinal barriers (Australian Institute of Health and Welfare 2015). Health care provider attitudes to people with disability are also a source of harmful discrimination. Their attitudes are often outdated or clearly prejudicial without regard to right to life (Australian Human Rights Commission 2020), their knowledge minimal and often plainly wrong (there is no national standard for including teaching about how to provide health care to people with disability in medical and health curricula). For example, the stereotypical assumption that presenting health issues, whatever these might be, are inevitably caused by disability and therefore "untreatable" (Australian Civil Society Shadow Report to the United Nations

Committee on the Rights of Persons with Disabilities 2019). Additionally, underfunding of health services (particularly in rural and regional areas) leaves people with disability in a precarious position. Underfunding results in long waiting lists, people with disability are inevitably given lower priority. Their right to the same range, quality, standard and free or affordable health care as other persons is denied.

The Disability International Council (2012) in its invited submission regarding Australia urged the Committee to strongly encourage the State party to,

> adopt and implement a comprehensive and *global health care strategy and plan for persons with disabilities (comprising the promotion, preventive measures, assistance and rehabilitation)* (our italics) and covering all types of disabilities, ethnic groups and persons with disabilities living in urban and rural areas. (p. 30)

This recommendation has not been actioned. No such plan exists. There is no national plan advanced by the Australian Government Department of Health to protect and advance the health and well-being of Australians with disability (interestingly for the first time and after considerable advocacy, a Management and Operational Plan for People with Disability, now in its third iteration—September 2020, was formulated in late April 2020). In contrast, the National Mental Health and Suicide Prevention Plan is now in its fifth iteration. Health and well-being is the sixth and final area of policy action in the NDS. Yet, governance arrangements for responsibility for the NDS lie with the Community and Disability Services Ministers—"with support from Ministers in other portfolios who may act as champions for disability issues, such as those dealing with education" (Commonwealth Government 2011, p. 66). Projected championship of people with disability has not resulted in a national plan to progressively realise the right to health as required by Article 25. There is no Australian Government central point of reference for health care for people with disability. The task of progressing universally accessible, quality and non-discriminatory health services for people with disability staffed by knowledgeable health care personnel falls to each state and territory government. Their willingness and commitment to do so varies with the quantum of funds allocated for this purpose. For Australians with disability the promise of Article 25 for their right to the highest attainable standard of health without discrimination rings hollow.

### *Accessibility*

As outlined above, provision of health care for all Australians for the most part remains the responsibility of states and territories. Confusion has arisen about what can reasonably be regarded as a disability support service (and therefore NDIS provided) and services that are primarily health care requiring health-trained rather than disability-trained personnel. Confusion is increased by the inclusion of allied health and therapy services in NDIS participant plans. At the same time, allied health and therapy services continue to be provided in hospital and community settings for people with disability typically under the umbrella of early intervention, rehabilitation or health prevention and health promotion. Since the introduction of the NDIS various attempts have been made to clarify this starting in 2013 with the Principles to Determine the Responsibilities of the NDIS and Other Service Systems (Council of Australian Governments 2015) and most recently as guidance on NDIS funding for disability-related health supports in October 2019 (National Disability Insurance Agency 2019). The underlying issue however remains. That is, how to distinguish between support needs that are most appropriately met by disability services and their disability-trained workforce and support needs arising from a health condition (or illness or injury), most appropriately met by health systems and their health care workforce.

Article 9 of the Convention concerns accessibility which is fundamental in all areas of life for people with disability. General Comment No. 2 (United Nations 2014) of the Committee makes it plain that universal accessibility is critical to ensure the rights of people with disability are realised. Cost, inconvenience and objections from others to accessibility are not acceptable reasons for delaying or obstructing progress on accessibility for people with disability. Accessibility for people with disability is a broad-based concept applicable to all. When the accessibility requirements of a particular individual cannot be met by universal accessibility, Article 9 presents recourse to reasonable accommodations; reasonable accommodation is the only instance when the hardship imposed by doing so can be argued as a reason for not proceeding with an accessibility measure. This means that States parties cannot use austerity measures as an excuse for not progressing accessibility for all persons with disability.

Accessibility is too often narrowly thought of as accessible buildings and accessible public transport. Although both are necessary to ensure equitable access to health care, they are not sufficient. Accessibility encompasses information and communication, information and communication technologies and systems, and any facilities and services open to or provided to the public. At issue in health care, for example, is providing population activities such as health promotion campaigns and preventative health services that are accessible, welcoming and of benefit to people with disability.

Public health measures during a health emergency need to consider accessibility to prevent the neglect or exclusion of people with disability. Ensuring the right of people with disability to access health care at the same time as ensuring their safety and well-being requires a carefully considered public health response. Without the framework of a national health care strategy for people with disability and advance planning for health emergencies caused by natural disasters or pandemics, responses are more likely to be reactive, highly resource-intensive and typically not sustainable once the immediate crisis has passed (United Nations Office of the Human Rights Commissioner 2015). An Australian national health care strategy and plan for people with disability could reasonably be expected to identify the existing entrenched accessibility barriers to health care including, but not limited to, transport, cost, geographical location, health provider attitudes and lack of knowledge about disability, and to set time frames with specific deadlines and commitments to the provision of the human and material resources necessary to remove the barriers.

As outlined earlier, Health and Well-being is one of six areas designated for policy outcomes within the NDS. The first policy direction under this outcome area required all health service providers to have the capabilities to meet the needs of people with disability. This requirement put state and territory governments on notice to reform mainstream and specialist health services so that people with disability could access health care and receive services that met their needs. The NDS also put Australia on notice with regard to its performance in progressively implementing the Convention including the right to health.

The first opportunity to report to the Committee following the implementation of the NDS came with Australia's combined second and third periodic reports submitted in late 2018 and distributed by the Committee on 5 February 2019 (United Nations 2019a).[1] In this

[1] National reporting on the NDS had fallen by the wayside following two reports to the Council of Australian Governments primarily describing actions rather than measurable outcomes for people with disability.

combined report, the Australian Government made claims for progress in some areas of health such as telehealth services. However, submissions to the Committee painted a quite different picture. The Australian Human Rights Commission (2019), for example, drew attention to a recent report of the Australian Institute of Health and Welfare (2017) on the health of Australians with disability that found:

- one in six people with disability aged under 65 years experienced discrimination by health staff
- two in five people with disability aged under 65 years had difficulty accessing medical facilities
- one in five people with disability aged under 65 years delayed or did not see a GP because of the cost
- people with disability aged under 65 years living in the community in outer regional and remote areas were less likely than those living in major cities to see a GP, medical specialist or dentist.

Furthermore, the AHRC noted the continuing substantially elevated mortality rates for people with intellectual disability, with twice as high rate of avoidable deaths as the general population. With regard to health care providers, they noted in particular that "health professionals face challenges communicating with people with intellectual disability, distinguishing health problems from the disability, and diagnosing complex health conditions" (AHRC 2019, p. 25).

The Committee distributed its *Concluding observations on the combined second and third periodic reports of Australia* on 15 October 2019 (United Nations 2019b). The Committee reiterated the requirement for Australia to adhere to Article 25, recommending to the Australian Government that "all persons with disabilities ... have access to information on an equal basis with others and to affordable, accessible, quality and culturally sensitive medical equipment and health services, including sexual, reproductive and mental health services" (United Nations 2019b, p. 12). The Committee further recommended all health care services be based on a non-discriminatory human-rights model of disability and that all health care practitioners receive training on this model of disability.

Individually and together the Concluding Observations, the AHRC submission, the AIHW (2017) report findings (and many others, for example, Australian Institute of Health and Welfare 2019) demonstrate significant inequality in the provision of health services to Australians with disability. The policy actions to reform mainstream and specialist services announced via the NDS almost ten years previously have not succeeded. Mainstream and specialist services remained largely inaccessible due to information, communication, cost, transport and geographical barriers and people with disability remain subject to discriminatory practises. Australia's health care system is still falling short of providing accessible, readily available health care capable of meeting the health care needs of people with disability.

### *Children and Young People with Disability*

Article 7 of the CRPD speaks to the particular situation of children and young people with disability. This Article was included by the drafters of the CRPD based on evidence that including children only as a sub-population of persons with disability, although necessary, would not be sufficient to ensure recognition of children's rights as "persons". Of immediate relevance are the serious deficiencies in implementing the following parts of Article 7 which specify (in part) that "the best interests of the child shall be a primary consideration" and "children with disabilities have the right to express their views freely on all matters affecting them" (United Nations Department of Economic and Social Affairs 2006, p. 8).

The *National Framework for Protecting Australia's Children 2009–2020* (National Framework), a landmark achievement, has paid scant attention to children with disability, and when it does so, frames disability through a lens of risk (Department of Social Affairs 2009). Overall, legislation, policies, service standards and compliance frameworks that apply to children and young people in Australia do not incorporate the rights of children and young people with disability as articulated in the Convention and in the Convention on the Rights of the Child (CRC) (United Nations Office of the Human Rights Comissioner 1989). This means there is no national framework, standard or requirement to meet the obligation under Article 7, point 2 that the "best interests of the child shall be a primary consideration".

There is no national children's data framework in Australia. There are a few purpose-built datasets for example in child protection, out-of-home care and education (Australian Institute of Health and Welfare 2014). This means the number of children and young people with disability is unknown. The available datasets cannot be reliably disaggregated by disability as state and territory jurisdictions use different definitions or are unable or not willing to use nationally agreed disability identifiers (Australian Institute of Health and Welfare 2020). This leaves children and young people with disability "hidden" in the broader population of Australian children and young people. Tracing their life choices and outcomes in health care and listening to their experiences with health personnel and their views on the health care system is not easily achieved.

There is urgent action required to incorporate the rights of the CRPD and specifically Article 7 into legislation, policies and programmes that apply to Australian children and young people. The development of the next iteration of the National Framework for Protecting Australia's Children, due for implementation in 2021, provides one opportunity to do this. Furthermore, action is required as recommended by the Australian civil society report to the Committee, November 2019 which stated a need to: "Develop comprehensive strategies and mechanisms to ensure that children and young people with disability can participate in consultations, decision-making processes and policy development that affect their lives" (Australian Civil Society Shadow Report to the United Nations Committee on the Rights of Persons with Disabilities 2019, p. 18).

### *Summarising Key Lessons*

As this section has demonstrated, while the provisions set out in Article 25 of the CRPD are well-intentioned and have the potential to deliver on a number of the health-related issues that people with disability face, the implementation of this to date has been rather limited. We have highlighted where there are particular challenges and the evidence relating to health and health outcomes for people with disability indicate patchy realisation of human rights. While initiatives such as the National Disability Strategy offer potential, they remain unfulfilled and as we demonstrate in the following section this has real implications in the context of a crisis pandemic situation.

## COVID-19 and the Australian Experience

Having provided a broad account of the degree to which Australia has been successful in implementing the CRPD in relation to right to health, we now move on to consider what COVID-19 has illustrated about the status and position of people with disability. Some people with disability may be more "at risk" in the context of a health emergency such as a pandemic, because of underlying health conditions. Evidence from previous pandemics shows that health inequities worsen during epidemics as more marginalised communities have fewer resources (financial and social) and struggle to access necessary supplies and services (Quinn and Kumar 2014). Any inequities that already exist within a society are further illuminated in emergency situations such as pandemics. We argue that although Australia has largely been "lucky" in the COVID-19 pandemic in comparison to other countries, we have seen a number of issues emerge that continue to demonstrate inequities for people with disability. However, there are also some positives we can take from this experience, with action around some areas that have traditionally been neglected.

### *Challenges for People with Disability*

Australia started to mobilise a COVID-19 response for aged care and Indigenous people relatively early on within the pandemic. The need to develop a national plan for people with disability was recognised somewhat later in early April 2020 (a global pandemic was declared by the World Health Organisation on the 11 March 2020). The plan covers prevention, testing, access and use of personal protective equipment (PPE) for people with disability and disability support workers. States and Territories also released their own plans. A website was launched with tailored, accessible information and resources for people with disability, families, health care providers and disability services (Commonwealth Department of Health 2020).

The Australian Government relied initially on the National Disability Insurance Agency and its sister agency, the NDIS Quality and Safeguards Commission, to deliver advice and responses for people with disability, their families and carers and service providers. Research suggests that people with disability and their families have experienced a significant lack in relevant information and that, particularly early on in the pandemic, information was often contradictory across different agencies and levels of government (Dickinson and Yates 2020). Further, particularly early on in the pandemic there were significant challenges in being able to find accessible information, where adjustments have been made for people with disability.

The disability service sector response has varied, with providers deciding on their own pandemic responses, resulting in inconsistent decisions where some have ceased services, while others remained open (Kavanagh 2020). The quasi-market of the NDIS can partly explain this with providers' financial viability at risk if they close (Dickinson et al. 2020). The Australian Government took too long to realise the disability service sector lacked the necessary preparation, training, resources and capacity to address the health vulnerabilities of people with disability and to effectively implement the required public health measures. Disturbingly, infection rates among people with disability and support workers are not routinely reported. Australia as a country has seen relatively low numbers of infections (26,652 by 14 September) and deaths (810 by 14 September) although the state of Victoria has seen a second wave of infection through late July, August and September. Given this, adaptations to health and disability services have not really been tested in much of the country and the poor outcomes seen elsewhere have not materialised. As such, concerns that disabled people might be deprioritised in health care (e.g. triaged out of ventilator access) have not been realised so far.

Australia began opening up after its first lockdown over May and June with testing and tracing regimes in place. However, an outbreak in Melbourne has seen the highest levels of community transmission since the pandemic began. Strict restrictions were re-introduced in late June in specific suburbs and extended to all of Metropolitan Melbourne on 8 July. Schools closed, although some special schools remained open for children with disability. Despite repeated concerns about inability to physically distance on school buses, and the known challenges with personal hygiene for some students with disability, special school buses have continued to operate and now there is the very real prospect of outbreaks in special schools. These challenges reflect some of the difficult issues of balancing health and education and working across sectors. Oversight and quality assurance of disability services needs to be stepped up, and a system to comprehensively track infection rates and deaths among disabled people is required.

### *Positives to Emerge Out of the Pandemic*

Particular modifications to health and allied services were made during the pandemic to the benefit of some people with disability and these were often issues that had previously remained stubborn to reform. One such action is an extension of telehealth medical and allied health consultations. Although Australia had introduced Medicare benefits for these services for people with disability in July 2011 (and reported this as progress on Article 25 in the Initial Report), these were limited by the type of service and only for those in eligible rural and remote locations. The pandemic made apparent the need to quickly extend Medicare-rebated telehealth services to all in the community, a much appreciated change in policy as a number of people self-isolated in an attempt to avoid catching the virus (People with Disability Australia 2020). Telehealth overcomes some accessibility barriers such as transport and inaccessible service points; however, it can also create additional ones including non-existent or poor telephone or internet access. It is not a one-stop solution to the entrenched barriers to health care that exist for Australians with disability. Telehealth is not an option for people within the DeafBlind community, for people with disability who require examinations or for some people with different means of communication. Not all in the community will want or need to use telehealth services in "normal" times; choice in this matter for people with disability ought to reside with the individual to ensure their right to equal (and achievable) access to health care. As yet, the Australian Government has made no commitment as to whether they will continue Medicare-rebated telehealth services in the future, although some people with disability could benefit from such access.

Another area we have seen positive activity is in relation to greater coordination between health and disability sectors. Overall, state and territory governments were more agile than in non-pandemic times in realising that, as a health emergency, the COVID-19 pandemic required a coordinated public health response including for people with disability. While traditionally there have been challenges in coordination between the Commonwealth and state and territory departments of health, during the pandemic we have seen discussions to ensure the health needs of people with disability in a broad sense were considered and not simply left to the disability sector.

Closer working relationships between the Commonwealth and the state and territory departments of health facilitated urgent discussions to ensure the health needs of people with disability were considered by health authorities and not left to an unprepared disability service sector and their disability-not-health-trained workforce. Disability Liaison Officers were introduced to public hospitals in some States. Disability not for profit organisations and advocates have worked with health departments, health care professionals and academics to develop and disseminate templates for individualised emergency preparedness COVID-19 plans (Collaborating4Inclusion 2020), hospital passports (Admission2Discharge Together 2020) and return to school plans for children with disability. All of which are activities that help people with disability transition through different services in a way that non-disabled people often take for granted.

Another positive of the COVID-19 pandemic has been that some state governments have worked hard to discharge people with disability from hospitals into the community, when some of these people have been in hospital for significant time periods. Community supports were arranged for these individuals, where it was previously seen as too difficult, as plans were made to free up hospital beds in preparation for those diagnosed with COVID-19. Regardless of this, we have still seen people with disability report difficulties in accessing care including health care providers' unwillingness to listen to them about their needs (e.g. need for direct support to continue if hospitalised). When people with disability reported that health care providers did not listen to them about their need for direct support to continue if they were hospitalised, the Victorian government listened, issuing a directive that people with disability who needed support workers or carers in hospital were able to do so, regardless of hospital visitor restrictions.

Australia has thus far been "lucky" that we have not seen clusters associated with congregate settings, like other countries have. Although in late July, early August we did start to see outbreaks in group homes. In the main because we have been successful in curbing the pandemic we have avoided the disastrous consequences for people with disability in congregate environments observed in the UK and US, for example. However, as restrictions ease people with disability become more vulnerable to outbreaks and so oversight and regulation (critical to managing public health emergencies) remains important. What the COVID-19 pandemic demonstrates is that people with disability in Australia still face a series of inequities in terms of gaining access to health services. People with disability have not been a priority for government, despite the very real risks that many in this group face. But this experience has also shown that some of the issues that have challenged the full implementation of the CRPD are not intractable. In an emergency context, government agencies have demonstrated that they are capable of working together and overcoming some of the issues that have dogged the system for some time.

## Conclusion

As outlined through this chapter, Australia is not meeting all of its obligations under Article 25 of the CRPD and the COVID-19 pandemic has shone a spotlight on a number of the inequities that people with disability face as a result. While this emergency situation has forced action around a few areas that are important in terms of realising the CRPD, it is clear there is much work yet to do. Here we reflect on the parts of Article 25 that are most urgently in need of attention in dealing with issues relating to the ongoing pandemic.

Article 25(a) refers to providing people with disability with access to the same range, quality and standard of health care and programmes as provided to other persons. Australia's COVID-19 response to people with disability was developed later than some other key groups (e.g. Indigenous, aged care) and inappropriate adjustments were made, compounding the range of existing limitations in accessing health services. However, COVID-19 may have improved access for some people with disability through changes to telehealth services. It is important to note that these changes will not have had a positive impact for all people with disability, but there is much we can learn from this experience and it may be a viable option in reducing some of the health care accessibility challenges that some people with disability face on a day to day basis (provided current arrangements are continued).

Article 25(b) refers to the provision of health services needed by persons with disability specifically because of their impairment. In this respect we saw a slow response in recognising these issues and the health vulnerabilities of some people with disability. For example, in-home testing only became available in August of 2020 in Victoria, but is not available in other parts of the country despite strong advocacy. It is not possible for some people with disability to attend traditional testing services, for example, where there are sensory and behavioural issues for some people with autism or where those who are immunocompromised do not want to risk leaving their home for a test for fear of infection.

Article 25(c) refers to health services being delivered as close as possible to people's own communities, including in rural areas. In a number of areas testing services were difficult to access for individuals as they were a significant distance from their home. For example, in the mid-North Coast of New South Wales residents had to travel from Taree at least one hour by car to testing services, despite this being a centre with a high proportion of people with disability (Centre of Research Excellence in Disability and Health 2018). Eventually this issue was addressed and there are now two testing sites in Taree, but it is likely that such proximity issues are repeated throughout the country.

Article 25(d) refers to providing care of the same quality to people with disability as to others. A number of disability advocates expressed fear that people with disability might be deprioritised should health resources become pressed (Kavanagh 2020). As Australia has not had the same number of cases and therefore pressure on health resources as some other countries we have yet to see this eventuate. However, advocates are still concerned that should an emergency situation emerge that people with disability may be deprioritised.

While no doubt some gains have been made in realising the ambitions of the CRPD it is clear that Australia still has some way to go. These issues have been highlighted through the COVID-19 pandemic and realising the full aspirations of the CRPD is necessary if we are to truly realise equitable health outcomes for people with disability.

## References

Admission2Discharge Together. 2020. Find out how the A2D folder can help improve your health experience. Available from http://a2d.healthcare/. Accessed 27 August 2020.

Australian Bureau of Statistics. 2016. Disability, ageing and carers, Australia: Summary of findings, 2015. Canberra: ABS.

Australian Civil Society Shadow Report to the United Nations Committee on the Rights of Persons with Disabilities. 2019. In response to the list of issues prior to the submission of the combined second and third periodic reports of Australia [CRPD/C/AUS/QPR/2-3]. Canberra: Compiled by the Commonwealth of Australia. 2011. National Disability Strategy 2011–2020.

Australian Human Rights Commission. 2019. Information concerning Australia's compliance with the Convention on the Rights of Persons with Disabilities. Sydney: AHRC.

———. 2020. Guidelines on the rights of people with disability in health and disability care during COVID-19. Sydney: AHRC.

Australian Institute of Health and Welfare. 2014. A new approach to child protection data: Implemention of the Child Protection National Minimum Data Set. Available at https://www.aihw.gov.au/reports/child-protection/a-new-approach-to-national-child-protection-data/contents/table-of-contents. Accessed 17 July 2020: AIHW.

———. 2015. Access to health services by Australians with disability 2012. Canberra: AIHW, Bulletin 129.

———. 2017. Access to health services by Australians with disability. Available at https://www.aihw.gov.au/reports/disability/access-health-services-disability/contents/content. Accessed 17 July 2020.

———. 2019. People with disability in Australia. Canberra: AIHW.

———. 2020. Child protection data 2018–19. Available at https://www.aihw.gov.au/reports/child-protection/child-protection-australia-2018-19/contents/table-of-contents. Accessed 17 July 2020: AIHW.

Boxall, A. & J. A. Gillespie. 2013. *Making medicare: The politics of universal health care in Australia*. Sydney: UNSW Press.

Centre of Research Excellence in Disability and Health. 2018. Spatial distribution of adults with disabilities in Australia: A small are analysis of the 2016 Census. Melbourne CREDH.

Chen, L., Y. Chou, J. Tsay, C. Lee, P. Chou & N. Huang. 2009. Variation in the cervical cancer screening compliance among women with disability. *Journal of Medical Screening*, 16, 85–90.

Collaborating4Inclusion. 2020. Person-Centred emergency preparedness. Available from https://collaborating4inclusion.org/pcep/. Accessed 27 August 2020.

Commonwealth Department of Health. 2020. Coronavirus (COVID-19) advice for people with disability. Available from https://www.health.gov.au/news/health-alerts/novel-coronavirus-2019-ncov-health-alert/advice-for220people-at-risk-of-coronavirus-covid-19/coronavirus-covid-19-advice-for-people-with-disability. Accessed 23 June 2020: Australian Government Department of Health.

Commonwealth of Australia. 2011. 2010–2020 National Disability Strategy: An initiative of the Council of Australian Governments Canberra: Commonwealth of Australia

Council of Australian Governments. 2015. Principles to determine responsibilities NDIS and other services. Canberra. Available from https://www.coag.

gov.au/sites/default/files/communique/NDIS-Principles-to-Determine-Responsibilities-NDIS-and-Other-Service.pdf. Accessed 17 July 2020: COAG.

Department of Social Affairs. 2009. National Framework for Protecting Australia's Children. Available at https://www.dss.gov.au/our-responsibilities/families-and-children/publications-articles/protecting-children-is-everyones-business. Accessed 17 July 2020.

Dickinson, H. 2017. Individual funding systems: What works? *Evidence Base*, 1–18.

Dickinson, H. & G. Carey. 2017. Managing care integration during the implementation of large-scale reforms: The case of the Australian Disability Insurance Scheme. *Journal of Integrated Care*, 25, 6–16.

Dickinson, H., G. Carey & A. M. Kavanagh. 2020. Personlisation and pandemic: An unforseen collision course? *Disability & Society*.

Dickinson, H. & S. Yates. 2020. More than isolated: The experience of children and young people with disability and their families during the COVID-19 pandemic. Melbourne: Report prepared for Children and Young People with Disability Australia.

Disability International Council. 2012. DisabCouncil's independent review Australia. Geneva. Available from http://disabilitycouncilinternational.org/Resources.php. Accessed 17 July 2020: DisabCouncil.

Embrett, M. G. & G. E. Randall. 2014. Social determinants of health and health equity policy research: Exploring the use, misuse, and nonuse of policy analysis theory. *Social Science & Medicine*, 108, 147–155.

Emerson, E., Baines, S., Allerton, L. and Welch, V. 2011. Health inequalities and people with learning disabilities in the UK: 2011. *Improving health and lives: Learning disabilities observatory*. Durham.

Emerson, E., G. Llewellyn, R. Stancliffe, H. Badland, A. M. Kavanagh, G. Disney & Q. Zhou. 2018. A fair go? Measuring Australia's progress in reducing the disadvantage for adults with disabilities 2001–2016. Melbourne: Centre of Research Excellence in Disabiilty and Health.

Fisher, K. R., R. Gleeson, R. Edwards, C. Purcal, T. Sitek, B. Dinning, C. Laragy, L. D'Aegher & D. Thompson. 2010. Effectiveness of individual funding approaches for disability support. Occasional Paper 29, Canberra: Australian Government Department of Families, Housing, Community Services and Indigenous Affairs.

Green, C., H. Dickinson, G. Carey & A. Joyce. 2020. Barriers to policy action on social determinants of health for people with disability in Australia. *Disability & Society*.

Kavanagh, A. M. 2020. Protecting people with disability during the pandemic. *Pursuit by the University of Melbourne*. Available from: https://pursuit.unimelb.edu.au/articles/protecting-people-with-disability-during-the-pandemic. Accessed 19 June.

Kavanagh, A. M., Krnjacki, L., Aitken, Z., LaMontagne, A. D., Beer, A., Baker, E. and Bentley, R. 2015. Intersections between disability, type of impairment, gender and socio-economic disadvantage in a nationally representative sample of 33,101 working-aged Australians. *Disability and Health Journal*, 8(2), 191–199. https://doi.org/10.1016/j.dhjo.2014.08.008

Llewellyn, G., S. Balandin, A. Poulos & L. McCarthy. 2011. Disability and mammography screening: Intangible barriers to participation. *Disability and Rehabilitation*, 33, 1755–67.

Malbon, E., Alexander, D., Carey, G., Reeders, D., Green, C., Dickinson, H. and Kavanagh, A. 2019. Adapting to a marketised system: Network analysis of a personalization scheme in early implementation. *Health and Social Care in the Community*, 27(1), 191–198.

Marmot, M. 2010. *Fair society, healthy lives: The Marmot review. Strategic review of health inequalitites in England post-2010*. London: Institute for Health Equity.

Mellifont, D. & J. Smith-Merry. 2016. Laying or delaying the groundwork? A critical framing analysis of Australia's National Disability Strategy from an implementation planning perspective. *Disability & Society*, 31, 929–947.

National Disability Insurance Agency. 2019. National Disability Insurance Scheme Funding for disability-related health supports Available at https://www.ndis.gov.au/news/3688-funding-disability-related-health-sup ports Accessed 17 July 2020: NDIA.

OECD. 2009. Sickness, disability and work: Keeping on track in the economic downturn. Paris: OECD.

People with Disability Australia. 2020. People with disability and COVID-19. Canberra: PWDA.

Quinn, S. & S. Kumar (2014) Health inequalities and infectious disease epidemics: A challenge for global health security. *Biosecurity and Bioterrorism: Biodefence Strategy, Practice and Science*, 12, 263–273.

Reppermund, S., P. Srasuebkul, K. Dean & J. Trollor. 2020. Factors associated with death in people with intellectual disability. *Journal of Applied Research Intellectual Disabilities*, 33, 4209.

Trollor, J., P. Srasuebkul, H. Xu & S. Howlett. 2017. Cause of death and potentially avoidable deaths in Australian adults with intellectual disability using retrospective linked data. *BMJ Open*, 7, 13489.

United Nations. 2012. Implementation of the Convention on the Rights of Persons with Disabilities. Initial reports submitted by States parties under article 35 of the Convention. Australia. Distributed 7 June 2012. https://tbinternet.ohchr.org/_layouts/15/treatybodyexternal/Download.aspx?sym bolno=CRPD%2fC%2fAUS%2f1&Lang=en: Committee on the Rights of Persons with Disabilities.

———. 2014. Committee on the Rights of Persons with Disabilities. General Comment No.2 (2014) Article 9: Accessibility Available at https://digitallibrary.un.org/record/812025?ln=en Accessed 17 July 2020.
———. 2019a. Combined second and third periodic reports submitted by Australia under article 35 of the Convention, due in 2018 Available from https://tbinternet.ohchr.org/_layouts/15/treatybodyexternal/Download.aspx?symbolno=CRPD%2fC%2fAUS%2f2-3&Lang=en Committee on the Rights of Persons with Disabilities.
———. 2019b. Concluding observations on the combined second and third periodic reports of Australia In. Available at https://digitallibrary.un.org/record/3848618?ln=en Accessed 17 July 2020: Committee on the Rights of Persons with Disabilities.
United Nations Department of Economic and Social Affairs. 2006. Convention on the Rights of Persons with Disabilities. Available at https://www.un.org/development/desa/disabilities/convention-on-the-rights-of-persons-with-disabilities.html. Accessed 17 July 2020.
United Nations Office of the Human Rights Comissioner. 1989. Convention on the rights of the child. Available at https://www.ohchr.org/en/professionalinterest/pages/crc.aspx. Accessed 17 July 2020.
United Nations Office of the Human Rights Commissioner. 2015. Thematic study on the rights of persons with disabilities under article 11 (relating to situations of risk and humanitarian emergencies) of the Convention on the Rights of Persons with Disabilities. Available at https://www.ohchr.org/EN/Issues/Disability/Pages/Article11.aspx. Accessed 17 July 2020.
World Health Organization. 2014. Better health for people with disabilities. The WHO Global Action Plan. Geneva: WHO.

# Index





F. Felder et al. (eds.), *Disability Law and Human Rights*, Palgrave Studies in Disability and International Development,
https://doi.org/10.1007/978-3-030-86545-0

D



E

The manufacturer's authorised representative in the EU is Springer Nature Customer Service Centre GmbH, Europaplatz 3, 69115 Heidelberg, Germany. If you have any concerns regarding our products, please contact ProductSafety@springernature.com

Printed and bound by CPI Group (UK) Ltd, Croydon, CR0 4YY
30/09/2026
02225704-0004